# Employment in Crisis

WORLD BANK LATIN AMERICAN AND CARIBBEAN STUDIES

# Employment in Crisis
## The Path to Better Jobs in a Post-COVID-19 Latin America

**Joana Silva, Liliana D. Sousa,
Truman G. Packard, and Raymond Robertson**

# Contents

*Foreword*                    *ix*
*About the Authors*           *xi*
*Acknowledgments*             *xiii*
*Executive Summary*           *xv*
*Abbreviations*               *xxi*

1   Overview ...................................................................................................................1
    Rationale for this report ...........................................................................................1
    Road map .................................................................................................................4
    Key insights ..............................................................................................................5
    Three dimensions of the policy response.................................................................10
    Implications for the COVID-19 crisis .....................................................................16
    Notes........................................................................................................................17
    References ................................................................................................................18
    Annex 1A: Background papers written for this report .............................................20

2   The Dynamics of Labor Market Adjustment ........................................................23
    Introduction ............................................................................................................23
    Labor market flows: Unemployment versus informality ..........................................26
    Job destruction and job creation in times of crisis ..................................................33
    A changing employment structure and the disappearance of good jobs ...................41
    Conclusion ...............................................................................................................44
    Notes........................................................................................................................45
    References ................................................................................................................46
    Annex 2A: Additional analysis of employment transitions.......................................48

3    The impact on workers, firms, and places ......................................................................... 51
     Introduction .................................................................................................................... 51
     Workers: A bigger toll on the unskilled.............................................................................. 53
     Firms: The cost of limited market competition .................................................................. 63
     Places: The role of local opportunities and informality ...................................................... 68
     Conclusion ...................................................................................................................... 70
     Notes.............................................................................................................................. 71
     References ....................................................................................................................... 72

4    Toward an integrated policy response ............................................................................... 77
     Introduction .................................................................................................................... 77
     Three key policy dimensions............................................................................................. 80
     Aggregate: Stronger macroeconomic stabilizers ................................................................. 82
     Social protection and labor systems: Cushioning the impact on workers and
     preparing for change .........................................................................................................87
     Structural: Greater competition and place-based policies..................................................... 109
     Conclusion ...................................................................................................................... 123
     Notes.............................................................................................................................. 125
     References ....................................................................................................................... 127

Boxes
4.1   Family allowances as de facto unemployment insurance ............................................... 99
4.2   Brazil's social protection response to the COVID-19 (coronavirus) pandemic ......................... 101
4.3   Latin America and the Caribbean's social protection and labor responses to the
      COVID-19 (coronavirus) contraction of 2020.................................................................... 104
4.4   Permanent, systemic shocks: Responses to job dislocation caused by structural changes .......... 108
4.5   How well have regional policies performed at strengthening economic opportunities? ............ 120
4.6   Evidence on the effects of place-based policies on mobility and labor market outcomes.......... 121

Figures
1.1   Persistent employment loss following crises: The myth of economic recovery ................................ 2
1.2   How adjustment works and the policies that can smooth it ........................................................ 10
1.3   Stabilizers and macroeconomic frameworks: Policy reforms ....................................................... 12
1.4   Addressing crises' impacts and preparing workers for change: Policy reforms ............................. 15
1.5   Tackling structural issues that worsen the impacts of crises on workers........................................ 16
2.1   Quarterly fluctuations in unemployment and GDP growth, 2005–17 .......................................... 27
2.2   Quarterly net flows into formal and informal employment, 2005–17 .......................................... 30
2.3   Part-time work as a margin of adjustment in Argentina, 2005–15 ............................................... 33
2.4   Quarterly job loss, formal and informal sectors, 2005–17......................................................... 35
2.5   Quarterly net job finding rates, formal and informal sectors, 2005–17 ....................................... 37
2.6   Gross job flows in Brazil and Ecuador, formal sector.................................................................. 38
2.7   Gross job flows and differential rates in large and small firms in the
      formal sector.................................................................................................................... 39

2.8    Net job creation rates in Brazil and Ecuador's formal sectors..........................................40

2.9    Quarterly share of workers entering unemployment per wage decile, formal and informal sectors, 2005–17.......................................................................................42

2.10   Impulse response functions, by type of employment, during the 30 months after the beginning of the recession ...........................................................................43

2.11   Estimates of Okun's Law for countries in the LAC region, 1991–2018........................45

2A.1  Quarterly net flows into part-time work, formal and informal sectors, 2005–17 ........48

3.1    Effect on wages of displacement caused by plant closings in Mexico ..........................55

3.2    Unemployment rates by cohort, Argentina and Colombia............................................56

3.3    Employment and wage effects of higher local unemployment at labor market entry in Mexico .......................................................................................57

3.4    Dynamic effects of the global financial crisis on workers.............................................59

3.5    Heterogeneity in effects of the global financial crisis across workers ...........................61

3.6    Dynamic effects of the global financial crisis on workers by skill .................................62

3.7    Dynamic effects of the global financial crisis on firms .................................................65

3.8    Effects of the global financial crisis on Brazilian workers depending on sectoral concentration and state ownership ..........................................................67

3.9    Effects of the global financial crisis on Brazilian workers depending on local labor market informality .........................................................................................70

4.1    How adjustment works and a triple entry of policies to smooth it ...............................81

4.2    Wage and unemployment responses during crises in the 2000s versus crises in the 1990s, Brazil and Mexico .................................................................................84

4.3    Sensitivity of unemployment and wages to output fluctuations ...................................85

4.4    Stabilizers and macroeconomic frameworks: Policy reforms ......................................87

4.5    Effective coverage of unemployment benefits, selected countries, latest available year ...............90

4.6    Economic cycle, unemployment, and spending on labor policies and programs .........................92

4.7    Level and composition of government spending on social assistance transfer programs, selected LAC countries....................................................................................97

4.8    Insufficient support, with many left behind ................................................................98

4.9    Coverage of social registries and support received through social assistance programs during the COVID-19 pandemic ........................................................100

4.10   Expansion of cash transfer programs in response to crises .........................................100

B4.2.1 Brazil's COVID-19 social protection and labor response strategy for two major vulnerable groups ...........................................................................................101

4.11   Positive effects of welfare transfers on local formal employment..............................102

B4.3.1 Stylized social protection and labor policy responses to the COVID-19 pandemic...................104

4.12   Employment and reemployment policies, by the nature of the shock causing displacement ......106

4.13   Addressing crises' impacts and preparing for change: Policy reforms .......................109

4.14   Employment protection legislation in OECD member countries and selected Latin American countries, 2014 or most recent data......................................................111

4.15   Regulation of employment in the LAC countries, circa 2019 ....................................112

4.16   Flexibility of labor regulation and spending on human capital and labor programs in selected countries in LAC compared to other regions ...............................114

4.17   Labor market regulation instruments and the duration of unemployment .................115

4.18   Tackling structural issues that worsen the impacts of crises on workers.....................122

**Map**

4.1   Unemployment insurance throughout the world .......................................................... 89

**Tables**

1A.1   Background papers written for this report ............................................................... 20

2.1   Cyclical components of GDP growth, the unemployment rate, and net flows out of the
labor force ................................................................................................................ 28

2.2   Cyclicality of net flows across sectors and out of employment, 2005–17 ................... 31

2.3   Correlation of job loss across sectors .................................................................... 36

2A.1   Cyclicality of employment transitions, by gender and skill level ............................... 49

3.1   Presence of negative effects on employment and wage scarring, by gender and education .......... 63

4.1   Landscape of formal unemployment income support in the LAC region .................... 88

# Foreword

In a region as volatile as Latin America and the Caribbean (LAC), the recurrence of crises should teach lessons that can be translated into better public policy responses. Looking back and learning from past crises is particularly relevant at a time when the devastating effects of the COVID-19 (coronavirus) pandemic shatter years of progress on many fronts, including job creation and new opportunities, the formalization of employment, and poverty reduction. Latin America and the Caribbean must give a different answer to the usual problems.

That is precisely what this report is about. Drawing on decades of data on economic shocks and labor market responses in the LAC region, it analyzes the effects of crises on workers and firms to help regional leaders direct policies and scarce resources in ways that bolster long-term, inclusive economic growth.

*Employment in Crisis: The Path to Better Jobs in a Post-COVID-19 Latin America* has three core messages. First, large crises in the LAC region have led to persistent employment loss. The evidence shows that crises are often turning points in employment, marking the beginning of strong negative deviations that only worsen as time passes. This effect happens because the short-run impact of a crisis on the labor market is felt more strongly through unemployment than through shifts to informality.

At the same time, long-running structural changes are shifting the nature of work across the LAC region and globally. Crises accelerate these changes and thus the reduction of opportunities in what are traditionally considered "good jobs"—the stable, protected employment associated with the formal sector. In this way, a crisis does not just temporarily shape worker flows—it also has significant, long-lasting effects on the structure of employment. The result is that traditional formal sector opportunities are slowly shrinking in the LAC region.

Second, crises in the LAC region have very different impacts across workers, sectors, and locations. Low-skilled workers suffer from longer-term scarring, while higher-skilled workers rebound fast, exacerbating the region's high level of wage inequality.

The characteristics of employers and places affect the severity and duration of crises' scars on workers. Formal workers suffer smaller employment and wage losses in localities with higher informality. And reduced job flows can decrease individual welfare, but workers in localities with more job opportunities, including informal jobs, bounce back better.

Third, crises can have positive effects that increase an economy's efficiency and productivity. However, these effects are dampened in the LAC region because of its less competitive market structure. Rather than becoming more agile and productive during economic downturns—allowing the "creative-destruction" process—protected sectors and firms gain more market share and crowd out others, trapping valuable resources.

It doesn't have to be like this. As the LAC region faces the biggest synchronized downturn in its modern history as a consequence of the COVID-19 pandemic, the region has placed a strong emphasis on managing the short-run effects of the crisis and has succeeded in cushioning some of its initial economic effects. However, this report's results show that job losses caused by crises can be particularly painful in the LAC region because of the region's sluggish recoveries. Thus, more is needed than what has been done in the past.

What can be done? *Employment in Crisis* proposes a mix of policies capable of contributing to improving labor market conditions and laying the foundations for equitable development. The key initial step is to put strong, prudent macroeconomic frameworks and automatic stabilizers in place to shield labor markets from potential crises. Sound fiscal and monetary policies can preserve macroeconomic stability and avert system-wide financial strain in the face of a shock. Fiscal reforms, including less distortive taxation, more efficient public spending, financially sustainable pension programs, and clear fiscal rules, are the first line of defense against crises. The report also proposes countercyclical income support programs, such as unemployment insurance and other timely transfers to households during downturns, as well as social protection and labor policies.

Stronger macroeconomic stabilizers and reforms to social protection and labor systems are not enough, however. Jump-starting job recovery by supporting vigorous job creation is also needed. In this context, competition policies, region-specific policies, and labor regulations are a third key policy dimension. Without addressing these fundamental issues, recoveries in the LAC region will remain characterized by sluggish job creation.

**Carlos Felipe Jaramillo**
*World Bank Vice President,*
*Latin America and Caribbean*

# About the Authors

Truman G. Packard is a lead economist in the Social Protection and Jobs Global Practice of the World Bank Group, currently serving as human development practice leader for Mexico. Truman was the lead author of the Social Protection and Jobs report *Protecting All: Risk Sharing for a Diverse and Diversifying World of Work*. He also led the World Bank team that delivered the regional report *East Asia Pacific at Work: Employment, Enterprise, and Well-Being* in 2014. He served on the teams that produced *Golden Growth: Restoring the Lustre of the European Economic Model*, published in 2012, and the World Development Report for 2009, *Reshaping Economic Geography*. Truman led the World Bank's Human Development program in the Pacific Islands, Papua New Guinea, and Timor-Leste, and he has been part of teams delivering financial and knowledge-transfer services to governments in Europe and Central Asia, East Asia and the Pacific, and Latin America and the Caribbean. Trained as a labor economist, Truman's work has focused primarily on the impact of social insurance—including pensions, unemployment insurance, and health coverage—on households' labor supply decisions, saving behavior, and risk management. Truman holds a Ph.D. in economics from the University of Oxford in the United Kingdom.

Raymond Robertson is a professor and holder of the Helen and Roy Ryu Chair in Economics and Government in the Department of International Affairs at the Bush School of Government and Public Service as well as the director of the Mosbacher Institute for Trade, Economics, and Public Policy. He is a research fellow at the Institute for the Study of Labor in Bonn, Germany, and a senior research fellow at the Mission Foods Texas-Mexico Center. He was named a 2018 Presidential Impact Fellow by Texas A&M University.

Joana Silva is a senior economist in the Office of the Chief Economist for Latin America and the Caribbean of the World Bank. She has expertise in labor economics, international trade, poverty and inequality, firm productivity, and policy evaluation. Her research has been published in leading academic journals, including the *American Economic Review* and the *Journal of International Economics*. She has authored four books, including two

World Bank regional flagship reports: *Wage Inequality in Latin America: Understanding the Past to Prepare for the Future* and *Inclusion and Resilience: The Way Forward for Social Safety Nets in the Middle East and North Africa*. She has led several World Bank lending operations and has extensive experience advising governments, in particular on the design and implementation of economic reforms, social programs, and monitoring and evaluation systems. She holds a Ph.D. in economics from the University of Nottingham.

Liliana D. Sousa is a senior economist in the Poverty and Equity Global Practice of the World Bank. Her research focuses on questions related to the labor market, including employment shocks, decisions around immigration and remittances, and women's economic inclusion. She has led and contributed to several studies and books, and her research has been published in *Labour* and the *Review of Development Economics*. She is currently the World Bank's poverty economist for Angola and São Tomé and Príncipe and was previously the poverty economist for Brazil and, before that, Honduras. Prior to joining the World Bank in 2013, she was an economist in the Center for Economic Studies at the US Census Bureau. She received her Ph.D. in economics from Cornell University.

# Acknowledgments

This book would have been impossible without the support of a generous team of colleagues and collaborators. Special thanks are due to Martin Rama, chief economist for the Latin America and the Caribbean Region, World Bank. He provided valuable comments and suggestions at various stages during the production of this report. Sebastian Melo provided outstanding research assistance.

This report greatly benefited from the comments and suggestions of our peer reviewers at the World Bank Concept Note and Decision Meetings, including Rafael Dix-Carneiro, professor of economics, Duke University; Roberta Gatti, chief economist for the Middle East and North Africa region, World Bank; Denis Medvedev, practice manager for Firms, Entrepreneurship, and Innovation, World Bank; Julian Messina, lead economist, Inter-American Development Bank; and the meetings' chair, Carlos Felipe Jaramillo, regional vice president for the Latin America and the Caribbean Region, World Bank. The report was developed under the guidance of Martin Rama. It was also discussed in dedicated authors' workshops held December 10, 2018, and March 2, 2020. The authors are very grateful for insightful comments from Kathleen Beegle (World Bank), Andres Cesar, Marcio Cruz (World Bank), Augusto de la Torre (Columbia University), Ximena Del Carpio (World Bank), Guillermo Falcone, Maria Marta Ferreyra (World Bank), Alvaro Gonzales (World Bank), Henry Hyatt (US Census Bureau), Tatjana Karina Kleineberg (World Bank), Maurice Kugler (George Mason University), Daniel Lederman (World Bank), Daniel Mateo (University of Southern California), Samuel Pienknagura (International Monetary Fund), Daniel Riehra, Bob Rijkers (World Bank), Dena Ringold (World Bank), Sergio Schmukler (World Bank), Erwin Tiongson (Georgetown University), Carlos Végh (John Hopkins University), Lucila Venturi (Harvard Kennedy School), and Guillermo Vuletin (World Bank).

This report builds on a series of background papers (further described in annex 1A to chapter 1). The team is grateful to all the authors of those papers.

Design, editing, and production were superbly coordinated by Amy Lynn Grossman, who made the process simple and smooth. Laura Handley, of Publications Professionals LLC, and Sandra Gain skillfully edited the English version. Leonardo Padovani translated the volume into Portuguese, and Sara Horcas translated it into Spanish. The team would also like to thank Jacqueline Larrabure: this report would not have been possible without her unfailing administrative support.

# Executive Summary

A better policy framework for preventing, managing, and helping people recover from crises is crucial to lifting long-term growth and improving livelihoods in Latin America and the Caribbean (LAC). The need for this policy framework has never been more urgent as the region faces the monumental task of recovery from the worldwide COVID-19 (coronavirus) pandemic. Whether specific policy responses will deliver the expected growth dividends is an open question. The answer will depend on the underlying understanding of how labor markets adjust to crises and on the quality of the policies enacted.

This report studies how crises change labor market flows in the LAC region, assesses how these changes affect workers and the economy, and identifies key policy responses to the needs of working people in the wake of crises. It does so using two distinct but complementary lenses: the macroeconomic perspective, focused on the effects of cyclical fluctuations and crises on aggregate labor market flows, and the microeconomic perspective, focused on crises' uneven effects across different workers, firms, and regions. The report brings together the main findings of a large research project involving ten background papers focused on the

dynamics of labor adjustments in the LAC region in the wake of shocks, the long-term implications of short-term shocks and their driving mechanisms, and the effects of policies on labor market adjustments. It uses household and labor force surveys (cross-sectional and panel), longitudinal employer-employee matched data, and analysis of national accounts to assess labor market dynamics. It also exploits firm shocks stemming from crises in order to quantify their impacts on labor markets, disentangling their effects from those of concomitant secular forces that also affect employment and productivity over long horizons. Finally, it develops structural models and explores rare quasinatural experiments to assess the welfare implications of crises and to derive better policy responses to them.

The report's key findings are threefold. **First, crises lead to significant losses of employment and earnings, but their impacts vary across countries, sectors, and workers.** Different labor market dynamics hide behind similar reductions in employment. Even with the LAC countries' large informal economies, which serve as buffers by absorbing some excess labor, outright unemployment remains a significant margin of labor market adjustment to economic shocks in the short run. In Mexico, for example, a decrease of 1 percentage point in GDP growth is associated with an increase in the unemployment rate of 7.9 percent. These large gross flows to unemployment lead to significant reductions in household income, increasing vulnerability as well as expanding and deepening poverty. Among households not living in poverty, a job loss by the household's main earner would push 55 percent of them into poverty.

The LAC region's high informality and formal sector job protections suggest a hierarchy in adjustment costs, wherein informal workers, who have fewer protections, face the highest likelihood of job loss regardless of skill. Indeed, workers in lower-income quintiles are more likely in general to experience negative labor transitions than are workers in higher-income quintiles. However, this study's results suggest that formal employment is overall more responsive to growth shocks than informal employment. Although job loss was part of the equation, the key driver of increases in unemployment during the 2008–09 global financial crisis was a sharp drop in net job finding rates in the formal economy.

Crises do not just temporarily shape worker flows—they also have significant, long-lasting after-crisis effects on the structure of employment. These effects are such that traditional formal employment opportunities are gradually shrinking in the economies of the LAC region. It takes LAC economies many years to recover from the contraction in formal employment induced by a crisis—20 months after the start of a recession, overall employment remains lower, and formal employment remains lower for more than 30 months afterward. Significant macroeconomic aftereffects of crises persist for multiple years, and formal employment indices remain substantially depressed. This effect happens throughout the region, despite differences in labor markets across countries. Although longer-running structural shifts are changing the nature of work globally, crises further contribute to reducing employment opportunities in what were traditionally considered "good jobs"—the standard, stable, protected employment associated with the formal sector.

**Second, this report finds that some workers recover from displacement and other livelihood shocks, while others are left scarred by them.** In the LAC region, scarring is more prominent for lower-skilled workers, particularly those with no college education. For example, in Brazil and Ecuador, workers with higher education suffer minimal impacts from crises on their wages and only short-lived impacts on their employment, but the effects on the average worker's employment and wages are still present nine years after the beginning of a crisis. Those who enter the labor market during a crisis face a worse start to their careers, from which it is difficult to recover.

Although the specific mechanisms for scarring and its duration vary between men and women, the overall story across countries in the LAC region is similar—among both men and women, scarring is more likely for those with lower levels of schooling and unlikely for those who are college-educated. It is also far more likely to occur through higher unemployment and informality rates years down the road than through lower wages.

Importantly, the conditions in local labor markets affect the severity of crisis-induced employment and earnings losses for workers. Persistent earnings losses may reflect a lack of opportunities in the economic rebound, not just scarring caused by the loss of human capital associated with a period of unemployment or lower-quality employment. In the wake of a crisis, employment losses last longer for formal workers in localities with larger primary sectors, smaller service sectors and fewer large firms.

At the same time, the presence of a large informal economy may protect some workers from shocks. Employment and wage losses in response to a crisis are smaller for formal workers in the private sector who live in localities with higher rates of informality. This finding suggests that informality, including self-employment, can be an important employment buffer in the medium to long run as workers transition from unemployment to formality.

This report shows that the reduction in job flows caused by a crisis decreases welfare but that workers in localities with more job opportunities, either formal or informal, bounce back better. Where employment is scarce, there is less worker churning, which in turn results in lower-quality job matches. These low-quality matches reduce firms' productivity growth and workers' lifetime earnings and welfare. After a severe crisis, employment may not recover to what it had been before; the crisis may push the labor market into a new, depressed equilibrium.

**Third, this report argues that crises can have positive cleansing effects that increase efficiency and productivity. However, the LAC region's less competitive market structures may dampen this effect, hampering productivity growth.** Job losses spurred by an economic crisis can reduce productivity by destroying employer-employee matches and the job-specific human capital arising from them. That said, large economic disruptions can also free workers and other inputs of production from low-productivity firms, allowing them to move to more-productive firms as the economy recovers. Similarly, crises can spur reallocation of firms out of sectors with very low productivity.

However, this study shows that sectors and firms sheltered from market competition adjust less during a crisis, suggesting they are less likely to experience this cleansing effect. In sectors where a few firms hold a large percentage of the market share, a shock does not lead to downward adjustments of real wages or employment. Although the workers in these sectors are better insulated from crises, the costs of this protection are borne by the economy as a whole. Rather than becoming more agile and productive during economic downturns, protected firms gain more market share and further crowd out competition, trapping resources that could be used more efficiently elsewhere. This phenomenon is particularly concerning in the LAC region,

which exhibits little market contestability, high inequality, and low productivity growth.

These three findings have important policy implications, which are all the more relevant in the context of the COVID-19 crisis, the biggest coincident downturn faced by the LAC region in decades. Because crises have a negative effect on the region's welfare in the short-run, as well as on its potential for economic growth in the medium run, policy makers should aim not just to cushion the economic effect of crises but also to mitigate their adverse impacts on workers, firms, and locations. Policies should pay just as much attention to building efficiency and resilience—the ability to bounce back when exposed to an adverse shock—as to managing the short-run effects of crises.

This report proposes a three-pronged policy response to crises. First, *strong, prudent macroeconomic frameworks and automatic stabilizers* should be the first line of defense protecting labor markets against potential crises, whether these crises are caused by external or internal forces. Sound fiscal and monetary policies can protect macroeconomic stability and avert system-wide financial strain in the face of a shock.[1] The LAC region's monetary policy has improved significantly since the 1990s, reducing the incidence of downturns and, with a few exceptions, averting large financial crises. However, fiscal policy is key to macroeconomic policy, and the region's recent track record in this area is weaker. LAC countries' fiscal policies have tended to be procyclical rather than countercyclical. Economic upturns often lead to rapid growth in public spending that proves difficult to sustain, while downturns see dramatic drops in government revenue, forcing painful cuts in government budgets and the vital services they finance. Fiscal reforms, including less-distortive taxation, more-efficient public spending, financially sustainable pension programs, and clear fiscal rules, are crucial to protect against crises.

Countercyclical income support programs, such as unemployment insurance and other transfers to households in bad times, limit the damage from contractions and help economic recovery. However, these instruments are currently missing in most LAC countries and are only weakly responsive to shocks in the countries where they are present. Two-thirds of countries in the region do not offer national-level, countercyclical income support plans for displaced workers. Where these programs do exist, as in Argentina, Brazil, and Uruguay, there is only a weak correlation between unemployment insurance claims and economic activity.

Moreover, one challenge faced by the LAC region is that large segments of its workforce earn their living informally and cannot be reached through traditional unemployment insurance. Nonetheless, this report shows that the expansion of transfer programs targeted on the basis of household need rather than whether a lost job was formal or informal can perform a key complementary stabilizing function by supporting local demand, thus generating aggregate benefits for the local economy in addition to individual-level benefits.

To address their lack of automatic stabilizers, LAC countries could consider creating or reforming their unemployment insurance programs, making short-term compensation programs permanent and enabling these programs to adapt to changing conditions more swiftly. By building on the region's already-extensive social safety nets and making some of these programs state-contingent and automatically activated when, for example, unemployment rises above a determined threshold, welfare losses and labor market adjustment costs could be lowered in the wake of future shocks.[2] This change should be accompanied by clear rules about the duration of benefits, strategies for scaling down benefits as crises resolve, and the programs' fiscal costs.

However, some crises will still occur, even in the presence of a robust macroeconomic policy shield, and how to cushion their long-term impacts on workers is a key question. The scarring effects documented in the LAC region imply that higher long-term growth could be achieved in the region

if crisis-induced, worker-level human capital decay were reduced. Strengthening recoveries will also require going beyond short-term income support to protecting human capital and promoting faster, higher-quality transitions for displaced workers into new jobs.

To achieve this objective, a second key reform is needed. It consists of *increasing the capacity of LAC countries' social protection and labor policies and coalescing them into systems that provide income support as well as preparation for new jobs* through reskilling and reemployment assistance (known as active labor market programs, or ALMPs).

More effort is needed to move away from fragmented and rigid social protection and labor programs toward integrated, adaptable programs that build on comprehensive and dynamic social registries and operate as coherent, concerted *systems*. This change will entail providing policy packages that are able to cushion the short-term impacts of crises, prevent lasting human capital losses, and facilitate the redeployment of working people with reskilling and reemployment support.

However, the need to increase the coherence of the LAC countries' social protection and labor systems and the coordination among their interventions is long-standing, and the region is now living through the consequences of not having all the tools it needs to respond to the current COVID-19 crisis. Recent evidence suggests that the global pandemic and governments' quick actions to expand some assistance programs can lead to progress in a crucial step: building better social registries that are linked and interoperable with other administrative information management databases. This step can be undertaken in the short run, and it can reduce poverty and inequality by informing the targeting of resources to those most affected by crises.

Reemployment will remain crucial to avoiding scarring, but the evidence available on the effectiveness of the LAC countries' ALMPs to date can be discouraging. On the basis of that evidence, the region should renew its policy emphasis on reemployment support services and incorporate four elements rarely associated with traditional ALMPs: (a) specificity to the particular needs of job-seekers; (b) coherence and coordination with other parts of the social protection and labor system (most obviously unemployment income support plans); (c) monitoring of the programs' implementation and evaluation of their impact; and (d) adequate resources from national budgets.

Importantly, although social protection and labor policies are typically the first instruments deployed to mitigate the impact of crises, they also play a crucial continuous role in enabling access to opportunities by building human capital (such as education), which, as shown in this report, increases workers' resilience and ability to rebound from crises.

However, stronger macroeconomic stabilizers and reforms to social protection and labor systems are not enough to change the outcomes of crises in the LAC region. More vigorous job creation is needed in order to generate better recoveries, and this change will require removing structural constraints. The sectoral and spatial dimensions behind the region's poor labor market adjustments must be addressed, or else recoveries in the LAC region will remain characterized by sluggish job creation.

In this context, *competition policies, regional policies, and labor regulations* are a third key policy dimension. For example, this report highlights the dichotomy between firms in the LAC region: some are exposed to competition, and others are protected and hence less prone to restructuring, which is an important source of productivity gains. The report also highlights the low geographical mobility of the region's working people, which magnifies the welfare effects of crises, and pockets of labor rigidity that hinder necessary transitions and adjustments in the labor market.

The findings in this report, together with a growing related literature, suggest that place-based policies could address the LAC region's lack of geographic mobility and maximize the gains to workers from relocation. Reducing pockets of labor rigidity—especially those caused by restrictions on human resource decisions by firms and individuals—could speed up labor market adjustments and shorten transitions. Similarly, addressing protectionism and unfair market conditions through better competition laws, lower subsidies, less state participation, and better public procurement practices could promote stronger recoveries. Policy responses to crises need to tackle those issues, with varying weights depending on the country, the period, and other circumstances.

As the LAC region faces significant economic and social fallout from the COVID-19 pandemic, integrated approaches will pave the way to lower vulnerability and greater preparedness for crises. Over the past year, the region has focused on its initial response to the emergency. Drawing upon lessons from past crises, the findings of this report offer new insights into policy responses focused on workers, sectors, and places. Together, these responses will support a faster and more inclusive recovery from the current crisis, laying the foundation for future economic growth.

## Notes

1. Monetary and fiscal stabilization policies are powerful tools to respond to crises; they include the management of a country's capital account, exchange rate policy, fiscal rules, and sovereign welfare funds as well as interest rate adjustment. Although these policies are crucial, they are not the main focus of this study.
2. During the COVID-19 crisis, many LAC countries took some of these steps: they expanded cash transfer programs and introduced short-term compensation programs to mitigate unnecessary job losses, including work-time banking, furloughs, and job retention subsidies.

# Abbreviations

| | |
|---|---|
| ALMP | active labor market program |
| AUH | Asignación Universal por Hijo |
| CCT | conditional cash transfer |
| COVID-19 | coronavirus |
| EPL | employment protection legislation |
| EU | European Union |
| GDP | gross domestic product |
| hh | household survey |
| HR | human resource |
| IADB | Inter-American Development Bank |
| I2D2 | International Income Distribution Database |
| LABLAC | Labor Database for Latin America and the Caribbean |
| LAC | Latin America and the Caribbean |
| LMP | labor market programs |
| OECD | Organisation for Economic Co-operation and Development |
| OLS | ordinary least squares |
| PATH | Program for Advancement through Health and Education |
| PCA | principal component analysis |
| PREGRIPS | Registro Integrado de Programas Sociales del Estado Plurinacional de Bolivia |
| RS | Registro Social |
| RSH | Registro Social de Hogar |
| SA | social assistance |
| SEDLAC | Socio-Economic Database for Latin America and the Caribbean |
| SIFODE | Sistema de Focalización de Desarollo |
| SIMAST | Information System of the Ministry of Social Affairs and Labour |
| SIMS | Database of Labor Markets and Social Security Information Systems |
| SISBEN | Sistema de Selección de Beneficiarios de Programas Sociales |
| SIUBEN | Sistema Único de Beneficiarios |

| | |
|---|---|
| SP | social protection |
| STC | short-time compensation |
| TFP | total factor productivity |
| UCT | unconditional cash transfer |
| UI | unemployment insurance |

For a list of the 3-letter country codes used by the World Bank, please go to https://datahelpdesk .worldbank.org/knowledgebase/articles/906519-world-bank-country-and-lending-groups.

# Overview | 1

Economic crises result in significant hardships for millions of people around the globe, especially the poorest, who, with few assets and little savings, are more vulnerable to income shocks. A better policy framework to prevent, manage, and help people recover from crises is crucial for countries in Latin America and the Caribbean (LAC) to accelerate long-term growth and improve the livelihoods of their people. The need for this policy framework has never been more urgent as the region faces the monumental task of recovering from the worldwide COVID-19 (coronavirus) pandemic. However, whether such a framework will deliver the expected growth dividends is an open question. The answer will depend on the underlying understanding of how labor markets adjust to crises and on the quality of the policies enacted.

## Rationale for this report

The LAC countries experience macroeconomic fluctuations more frequently and often more severely than most other regions of the world. And *crises*, not a single crisis, characterize the recent history of most countries in the region. One-third of the fiscal quarters between 1980 and 2018 were periods of crisis

in one or more countries in the region.[1] The LAC countries have rebounded from some of these crises, but others have altered their economic trajectories. This phenomenon is illustrated in figure 1.1, which shows the severity and persistence of employment losses following Brazil's debt crisis in the early 1980s, the Asian financial crisis of the 1990s in Chile, and the 2008–09 global financial crisis in Mexico. In addition to weak rebounds from crises, countries in the region have also experienced generalized economic stagnation since 2013.

Although much has been written about the frequency and severity of economic crises in the LAC region, less is known about how these episodes affect workers, in both the short run and the long run, and about how to respond to these effects with policies. Focusing on workers is important, because the long-run impacts of crises on labor markets may drive deeper losses in income than has been previously understood. Moreover, if crises destroy human capital, they can have long-run effects on aggregate economic growth.

Several open questions are impeding progress in this field. First, how large is the impact of crises on workers? The effects of

**FIGURE 1.1  Persistent employment loss following crises: The myth of economic recovery**

*Source:* Regis and Silva 2021.
*Note:* The vertical bars indicate recessions. Series are seasonally adjusted. Data are from the first quarter of each year.

crises in the LAC region are superimposed on a slowing trend of slowing employment and productivity (Fernald et al. 2017). Disentangling their impact on this slowdown from that of other factors is difficult because concomitant secular forces, such as technological progress and globalization, also affect employment and productivity over long horizons (Ramey 2012). Second, research thus far has focused separately on crises' short- and long-run effects, but how are these effects linked? In the missing medium term, defined as the 8–12 years after the start of a crisis, crises appear to result in microeconomic transformation with persistent but poorly understood effects. And third, how can policy makers improve the outcomes of crises? Because of the emergency mode of crises, robust evidence is lacking on the effectiveness of the main policy instruments used to intervene in them. However, newly available, granular data and advances in empirical approaches have opened the door to a much deeper understanding of this issue.

The need for this analysis and policy framework has never been more urgent as the LAC region faces the monumental task of recovering from the worldwide COVID-19 pandemic. This flagship research project examines how labor market flows in the region adjust in face of economic shocks, assesses how the employment adjustments in response to these shocks affect workers in the short, medium, and long runs, and discusses key policy responses to mitigate these shocks' negative consequences. Its findings provide a new understanding of the medium- and long-term implications of crises for labor markets and suggest policy responses to the 2020 COVID-19 crisis.

This study draws on existing data on economic shocks in Latin America. These shocks include permanent shocks, such as technological change and the trade liberalizations of the 1990s,[2] and transient shocks, such as exchange rate fluctuations. Some transient shocks are sector- or location-specific or are idiosyncratic to a particular set of households, while others are systemic, affecting the region's whole economy. Although each type of crisis has implications for productivity and welfare, this study focuses on economic crises: large, negative economic shocks (rather than small fluctuations in gross domestic product [GDP]) that are systemic rather than idiosyncratic and transient rather than permanent. Through novel identification strategies and the use of new data, this study aims to tease out the effects of shocks from those of concomitant secular forces that also affect employment and productivity. Finally, although crises also have important noneconomic consequences, this study focuses only on their economic implications.

Although this study was prepared within the context of the COVID-19 crisis and includes some analysis of this crisis's immediate impacts, such as the evolution of the economy in 2020, the study's goal is more general than this crisis. First, given the LAC region's pattern of frequent crises, the study aims to understand the effects of crises in general, not just of the COVID-19 crisis, on labor markets in the region. Second, in order to understand how labor markets in the region adjust to crises and to unpack the underlying mechanisms driving these adjustments, the analysis necessarily draws upon the medium- and long-term effects of earlier crises. Although the COVID-19 crisis, projected to be the most severe labor market recession in some countries' histories, differs from any previous crisis and comes along with supply disruptions and prolonged uncertainty, it also shares some features with previous crises.[3] These features include a global recession, a sharp fall in demand for many months, and financial stress or impending financial crises in some countries. Indeed, the available information on unemployment in 2020 suggests that the COVID-19 crisis induced a pattern of unemployment similar to that observed in previous crises, for example, with lower-skilled workers more directly affected than higher-skilled workers. Although the source of the shock is different, the COVID-19 crisis's similarities to previous crises suggest that these events can offer relevant lessons for the present and, importantly, for future crises.

This study proposes a new understanding of how the LAC region's labor markets adjust to crises, triangulating effects on workers, sectors and firms, and localities. This approach follows from the study's finding that job losses caused by crises are particularly painful in the LAC region because of the region's sluggish recovery processes. The pace of job creation depends on demand-side factors, like firms and locations, not just

on workers. How do sectors and firms adjust employment and wages? What other margins of adjustment are used, beyond shedding jobs, and what are their medium- to long-run effects on efficiency? How do the characteristics of localities (such as their economic structure) matter? This study will examine each of these questions.

The effects of a crisis also depend on a second crucial dimension, one being discussed globally during the COVID-19 crisis: the policy response to the crisis and whether it successfully connects welfare considerations with the country's growth agenda. Few doubt that avoiding crises in the first place is a priority. A more stable macroeconomic environment decreases the incidence of growth shocks, while automatic stabilizers such as countercyclical income support for job seekers serve to smooth the impacts of shocks on the national economy. These measures are a crucial first shield against economic crises, but they are largely lacking in the LAC region. Correcting this deficiency will require adjusting not only fiscal and monetary policies but also social protection and labor policies.

However, even in the presence of a robust macroeconomic policy shield, some crises will still occur, and what to do to cushion their impact on workers is a key question. This study argues that there is scope, when increasing the capacity of the LAC region's social protection and labor policies, to coalesce these policies into *systems* that provide income support as well as prepare workers for new jobs through reskilling and reemployment assistance. But will these measures be enough to spur job creation and generate better recoveries? Considering the evidence presented in this report, there is an urgent need for LAC countries to also tackle structural problems, including low product market competition in some sectors, contestability issues, and the spatial dimensions behind poor labor market adjustment. Without addressing these fundamental issues, economic recoveries in the LAC region will continue to be characterized by sluggish job creation.

## Road map

This study brings together the macroeconomics of the effects of cyclical fluctuations and crises on GDP and the microeconomics of these crises' uneven effects across workers, sectors, and regions. It builds on the main findings of a large research project that produced 10 background papers focused on the dynamics of labor adjustments to shocks in the LAC region, the long-term implications of short-term shocks, the mechanisms driving these shocks, and the effects of policies on labor market adjustment (see annex 1A for additional details).

This study is organized around three analytical themes that are key to understanding how labor markets adjust to crises and the consequences of these adjustments on workers in the short and long terms:

- **Chapter 2: The Dynamics of Labor Market Adjustment** studies how crises have affected labor market flows in the LAC region over the past 20 years and assesses the extent to which they shape its employment structure. Rather than focusing on one number (for example, the unemployment rate or the elasticity of unemployment to output changes), it considers the mechanisms of labor market adjustment, the cyclicality of job flows, the extent to which these flows are heterogenous across firms and workers, and whether employment adjustments lead to changes in employment structure.
- **Chapter 3: The Impact on Workers, Firms, and Places** evaluates the medium- to long-term effects of shocks on labor market outcomes at the worker, firm, and locality levels, extending beyond welfare to include broader efficiency issues. It (a) evaluates the magnitude and duration of the medium- to long-term costs of crises for affected workers in terms of earnings and employment and identifies the types of workers most at risk for long-term welfare losses; (b) offers causal

explanations and empirical evidence on *how* crises affect sectors and firms and how they affect efficiency in the medium to long run; and (c) explains *why* these microeconomic processes play out so differently for workers and firms in different localities.

- **Chapter 4: Toward an Integrated Policy Response** assesses the suitability of the current policy framework to address the long-term nature of labor market adjustments and discusses potential reforms to macroeconomic, social-protection and labor, and competition and place-based policies that could help cushion the short- and long-term impacts of crises and address their sources at the sector-and-firm and location levels, bridging welfare and growth agendas.

This study builds on the key findings of the background papers and includes a richer treatment of the literature and a summary of recent policy interventions in order to provide new insights into current policy debates. The background papers and complementary analysis developed by this study use rich and varied data sources and analytical approaches, including new evidence from harmonized household and labor force surveys (cross sectional and panel) for 17 LAC countries; longitudinal employer-employee matched data for Brazil and Ecuador (following all formal workers and firms for more than 15 years); and national accounts, which were analyzed to assess labor market dynamics. To examine the causal effects of crises, the study also exploits firm shocks stemming from foreign demand shocks. These exogenous shocks allow crisis effects to be disentangled from those of other forces that affect employment and productivity over long horizons. This evidence is complemented with findings from a structural model developed using detailed data from Brazil to assess the welfare implications of labor market adjustments.

## Key insights

This study offers new insights into each of its three analytical themes: the dynamics of labor market adjustment; the impact of crises on workers, firms, and places; and policy responses to crises.

### Crises have significant impacts on the structure and dynamics of employment in Latin America

How do crises change labor market flows? A macroeconomic shock results in microeconomic reallocation at the worker and firm levels. At these defining moments, workers' and firms' fates are linked. Firms can adjust their number of employees, hours of work, and wages paid, and workers can choose to accept these offers or search for other options. From these interactions, a new short-run equilibrium is formed.

#### Negative shocks result in unemployment more than informality in the short run

According to new research for this report, the short-term adjustment to crises occurs primarily through unemployment (Sousa 2021). Although exits from the labor force and shifts to part-time work do not appear to be significant margins of adjustment, Sousa (2021) finds a strong negative correlation between formal and informal job flows in five of the six countries analyzed (reductions in formality are often accompanied by increases in informality, and vice versa), where the countries' large informal economies serve as de facto safety nets by absorbing excess labor. But even with this buffering function, outright unemployment remains a significant margin of labor market adjustment to economic shocks in the LAC region.

The large gross labor flows to unemployment, in turn, represent significant reductions in household income, increasing vulnerability as well as expanding and deepening poverty. Labor income represents 60 percent of household income among the poorest 40 percent of households in LAC countries. Among households not living in poverty, a job loss by the main earner would push 55 percent into poverty. And job loss imposes costs on workers that go far beyond the immediate loss of income.[4] Economic adjustment through unemployment is also especially costly because jobs are more quickly lost than gained; in other words, employment losses can persist for a substantial period following a crisis.

#### Net loss of formal employment is driven by reduced job creation

This report reveals that most of the reduction in employment in response to a crisis occurs in the formal sector. This result is important, because the potential for good worker-job matches, firm-specific earnings premiums, and match-specific human capital is highest among people who are employed in the formal economy. Fluctuations in unemployment are determined by the rates of transitions into and out of unemployment—job loss and job finding rates, respectively. During economic downturns, these rates are driven by increased job destruction (existing positions are eliminated), reduced job creation (new positions are not created), and lower levels of job reallocation, or churning, as fewer workers voluntarily leave their positions to look for better matches.[5] Addressing each of these transitions will take different policy tools. The relative contribution to unemployment of each type of transition varies across labor markets; some studies of high-income economies find that cyclical unemployment is driven by reduced job finding rates, while others find that it is driven by increased job separation rates.[6]

Sousa (2021) finds low cyclicality of job losses across formal and informal employment. Instead, in most countries analyzed, adjustment in employment during the global financial crisis of 2008–09 was driven by a drop in net job finding rates that was larger in the formal economy than in the informal economy. Zooming in on the formal economy, Silva and Sousa (2021), using worker-firm linked administrative data from Brazil and Ecuador, find that a reduction in job creation, rather than an increase in job destruction, drives lower formal employment during crises—net formal job losses are driven by a reduction in new formal employment. They also find that although larger firms tend to be more productive and more resilient to crises, they also exhibit higher cyclical fluctuations in labor demand. That is, although the firms themselves are resilient, employment in them may not be the most resilient to economic shocks. Once the higher "death rates" of small firms are taken into account, the patterns of employment fluctuation look very similar for small and large firms.

Are labor flows for lower-skilled or informally employed workers more cyclical than those for formally employed or higher-skilled workers? The LAC region's combination of large informal economies and workers of widely varying skill levels suggests a hierarchy in adjustment costs, wherein informal workers, who have fewer job protections, face the highest likelihood of job (and livelihood) loss regardless of skill. Workers in the lower income quintiles are more likely in general to experience negative labor transitions than workers in the higher income quintiles—but overall, this study's results suggest that high-skilled employment is more responsive to growth shocks than low-skilled employment. This finding is consistent with the aforementioned greater cyclicality of employment in large firms and higher cyclical job losses among formally employed workers, because such workers are more likely to be skilled.

*Stable and protected job opportunities are gradually shrinking in the LAC region*
Changes in labor market dynamics can lead to changes in the composition of an economy's workforce. The potential macroeconomic aftereffects of a crisis on the structure of employment can shape the crisis's medium- to long-term effects on employment and wages. As this study reveals, crises

in the LAC region have significant effects on the structure of employment that last for several years (Regis and Silva 2021). In Brazil, Chile, Ecuador, and Mexico, the shrinkage of standard formal employment has been strong and long-lasting. It takes LAC economies multiple years to recover from the contraction in formal employment induced by a crisis. For 20 months after the start of a recession, overall employment tends to remain lower, and formal employment remains lower for more than 30 months. Significant macroeconomic aftereffects of crises persist for multiple years, leaving formal employment indices substantially depressed. This effect happens throughout the region despite differences in labor markets across countries.

Although long-running structural shifts are changing the nature of work, crises further contribute to reducing employment opportunities in what were traditionally considered "good jobs"— the standard, stable, protected employment associated with the formal sector. Moreover, although informal work seems to be a long-term buffer of crises in some countries, including Brazil and Chile, in others, such as Ecuador and Mexico, informal employment is stagnant or falls in response to crises. These results suggest that a crisis has the potential to push the labor market into a new equilibrium between formal and informal employment, with long-term implications for welfare and productivity.

### Crises scar workers, but the characteristics of firms and places affect the severity and duration of these scars

Although the evidence presented thus far suggests that economic crises have detrimental impacts at the aggregate level, how severe are their impacts on individual workers and the economy? What do they mean for welfare and efficiency when the three main dimensions of labor market adjustment (workers, sectors, and localities) are considered? The impacts of a crisis leave scars on workers and firms. Many workers do not fully recover even in the long run;

their earnings do not bounce back and their careers follow a different, worse track. The biggest losers lose a lot. Firms adjust to crises in ways that affect their efficiency and resilience down the road. Overall, crises scar workers, but the structure of product markets and the conditions within local labor markets affect the severity of these scars.

### Low-skilled workers suffer most from scarring, while high-skilled workers suffer small and brief impacts

How extensive is scarring from economic crises in Latin America, and what forms does it take? This flagship research project analyzes scarring across three dimensions—that caused by job loss, by initial conditions at entry, and by the effects of crises on firms. In the case of scarring caused by job loss, this study finds large and long-lasting wage effects from displacement because of firm closure. For example, two years after the closure of a plant, wages were 11 percent lower for displaced workers than for nondisplaced workers. Four years later, the wage gap was 6 percent. Wages did not fully recover until nine years after the closure (Arias-Vázquez, Lederman, and Venturi 2019).

Next, this project examines scarring in the LAC region caused by the labor market conditions when new workers first enter the labor force (Moreno and Sousa 2021). Are there long-term employment and wage consequences of entering the labor market during a downturn, generating what the popular press calls "a lost generation"? This question is particularly salient for the LAC region, given its high rates of youth unemployment and its investments in increasing and improving educational outcomes at the secondary and tertiary levels. Are these investments in the region's human capital stock undermined by frequent crises?

Using detailed data for four LAC countries, the project's findings confirm that entering the labor market during a crisis can have long-term consequences. However, this scarring is found in employment outcomes (lower participation rates, higher unemployment rates, and higher likelihood of working informally) rather than in long-term effects on earnings. And it is more prominent among lower-skilled workers (those with no college education) than among higher-skilled workers. For example, in Brazil and Ecuador, effects on workers' employment and wages persist for an average of 9 years after the beginning of a crisis. Workers with higher education tend to suffer small impacts from the crisis on their wages and very short-lived impacts on their employment (Moreno and Sousa 2021). Similarly, Fernandes and Silva (2021) find stronger scarring effects from the 2008–09 global financial crisis in employment and wage outcomes for lower-skilled workers than for higher-skilled workers in the formal sector in Brazil and Ecuador. One explanation for this effect is that competition is lower for skilled jobs because of the relative scarcity of college graduates in the LAC region. In other words, scarring likely exacerbates the region's high level of wage inequality across skills.

Switching gears to consider how economic shocks pass from firms to their employees, Fernandes and Silva 2021 find that among workers with similar initial observable characteristics, it is more difficult for workers of the firms that are most affected by a crisis to recover from the shock. However, the effects on workers vary according to their employers' or firms' characteristics; for example, the effects are smaller for workers in large firms. Evidence in this report also shows that workers who lose their jobs, even if they regain employment later, experience a lasting decline in their earnings. Furthermore, unskilled workers suffer the most from this decline, which has implications from an equity and poverty-reduction perspective.

### Reduced job flows can decrease individual welfare, but workers in localities with more job opportunities, including informal jobs, bounce back better

Negative aggregate demand shocks and crises reduce welfare in part by reducing job flows (Artuc, Bastos, and Lee 2021). Because of this effect, during slowdowns and crises, job match quality falls. The estimated utility from job match quality also decreases, because workers become less mobile during crises. A structural model for Brazil, developed in a background paper for this project, shows that an adverse external shock to a local labor market lowers welfare significantly within the market and that low mobility across regions magnifies this impact (Artuc, Bastos, and Lee 2021).

This report finds larger and longer-lasting losses in employment (and sometimes in wages) in the wake of a crisis for formal workers in localities with larger primary sectors, smaller service sectors, and fewer large firms (Fernandes and Silva 2021). In such cases, these workers' persistent losses in earnings may reflect their lack of opportunities in the rebounding economy, not just scarring in the traditional sense of a persistent loss of human capital associated with a period of unemployment or lower-quality employment.

On the other hand, the presence of a large informal economy may protect some workers against shocks. This study finds smaller employment and wage losses in response to crises for formal workers in the private sector who live in localities with higher rates of informality (Fernandes and Silva 2021). This finding suggests that informality can be an important employment buffer in the medium- to long-run, when workers may transition from unemployment to informal employment. Such an effect was shown by Dix-Carneiro and Kovak (2019) in the case of adjustment to trade liberalization. Indeed, transitions from unemployment to informal employment were twice as common in the Brazilian data as transitions from unemployment to formal employment.

## Crises can have positive cleansing effects that increase efficiency and productivity, but less competitive market structures mitigate these effects

As an economy transitions to a new equilibrium, many workers lose their jobs or see their earnings fall, some firms go out of business, and new entrants into the

labor market struggle to start their careers. Efficiency changes permanently, and positive employment effects depend on the economy's ability to create jobs. Because firms are a key transmission channel of crisis effects to individual workers, the speed of workers' adjustment and the outcomes of the new equilibrium also depend on the initial structure of the economy's product markets, rents, and rent-sharing mechanisms.

### Crises can increase productivity and efficiency

During a crisis, employer-employee matches and the job-specific human capital arising from them, which often take a long time to build and would regain viability when the economy goes back to normal, may be permanently dissolved only because of the severity of the temporary shock. These job losses may slow the ramping up of production later, and they imply losses in productivity; however, they can also have an important cleansing effect and lead to increased productivity at both the firm and market levels.

A crisis can also have persistent effects on technology, which can be a margin of adjustment firms use to cope. Firms adjust to crises through changes in productivity, changes in demand for various skills, markups, and changes in their products to make them more appealing to consumers (Mion, Proenca, and Silva 2020). Negative demand shocks cause more-affected firms to reduce their capital-to-worker ratios in some countries, such as Ecuador, whereas in other countries, such as Brazil, firms simply adjust their employment and wages (Fernandes and Silva 2021). Firms also, in the presence of a negative external demand shock, increase the skill content of their production (the share of skilled labor in their total employment) in countries such as Argentina (Brambilla, Lederman, and Porto 2012), Brazil (Mion, Proenca, and Silva 2020), and Colombia (Fieler, Eslava, and Xu 2018).

Moreover, crises can affect the structure of a country's economy. They induce firm exit—not on impact, but around two years after the shock, as shown in Brazil and Ecuador (Fernandes and Silva 2021). Debt overhang problems may also occur and have the potential to scar firms. Crises destroy less-resilient firms and increase the market share of more-resilient ones. In addition to their effects on existing firms, crises can have persistent effects on firms that are created in bad times. Demand is a key driver of firm capabilities, and if firms start at a time when demand is low, they will have more difficulty developing their network of clients and learning how to work well with them. New evidence from the United States indicates that firms that are born in times of crisis end up stunted—that is, they grow slowly throughout their life cycles, even when times improve (Moreira 2018). These crisis effects can have persistent implications for the economy, and firms may find it difficult to revert them.

By inducing firm exit, bad economic times can have a cleansing effect and increase productivity. Suppose that a labor market is subject to large friction, so that very-low-productivity firms can survive by hiring workers for very low wages. Given the labor market's friction, workers who receive these low-wage offers take them—the opportunity cost of continuing their job search is high because job matching rates are low. Therefore, these low-productivity firms can essentially trap resources that could be more efficiently used elsewhere. In this context, large economic disruptions can have a cleansing effect by freeing workers from such firms and allowing those workers to reallocate themselves to more-productive firms as the economy recovers. Similarly, crises could allow reallocation out of sectors that have been living in very low productivity at the margin of survival. This effect is good as long as the economy sees job creation after the crisis is over. However, the effects of crises on productivity have gone in the other direction in Brazil: crises there have led to persistent reductions (not increases) in firm productivity. In Ecuador, on the other hand, crises have caused a positive, but small, increase in productivity (Fernandes and Silva 2021).

*Protected sectors and firms adjust less during a crisis, suggesting less opportunity for cleansing effects in these sectors*

There is a complex interplay between labor markets, product markets, and local conditions—and understanding it is essential to crafting sound economic policies. Going beyond the firm and considering the role of market structure, this project's data from Brazil show that employment in more-protected firms, defined as those facing less competition, is less affected by crises compared with employment in less-protected firms (Fernandes and Silva 2021). In sectors in which a few firms hold a large percentage of the market share, a bad shock does not lead to any downward real wage adjustments. Instead, it can lead to an increase in employment: the opposite of what normal economic mechanisms would bring about. Similarly, employment responds less to a negative export shock if the firm in question is state-owned.

Although workers in protected firms are better insulated from crises than those in other firms, the costs of this protection are borne by the economy, which ends up with lower overall productivity. Importantly, this result suggests that the presence of protected firms and sectors in the LAC region may contribute to its low level of productivity by reducing the potential gains in efficiency and productivity caused by crises. Rather than becoming more agile and more productive during economic downturns, protected firms can increase their market share and further crowd out competition. As noted above, they may also trap resources that could be used more efficiently elsewhere.

Although this study focuses on Latin America and the Caribbean, its findings have implications for understanding the upgrading process in other regions as well. In particular, the study's results reinforce the idea that crises affect employment and productivity in the long run, not just in the short run. The study's particular setting, the LAC region, has the advantage of allowing the clean identification of a causal relationship between crises and a broad range of welfare and efficiency effects, but the study's basic findings seem likely to apply more broadly.

## Three dimensions of the policy response

Considering the importance of demand to an economy's well-being and the triangle of workers, firms, and locations, how can policies mitigate the impacts of crises on workers and promote better recovery from crises? This study shows that crises have a meaningful negative effect on welfare in the LAC region. The labor market scarring effects it documents are likely to hamper the region's economic growth potential. To mitigate them, policies should try to cushion the effects on workers in the short run: shock impacts spread in unequal ways across workers and firms, and many of them will not regain their lost jobs, wages, or clients. But policies should pay just as much attention to efficiency and resilience, promoting the

ability to bounce back when exposed to an adverse shock, which can be aided by healthy economic growth.

Figure 1.2 presents a framework for thinking about the relevant areas of policy. Strong, prudent macroeconomic frameworks and automatic stabilizers (the shield in figure 1.2) are the first line of defense to shield labor markets from crises. Prudent fiscal and monetary policies are also powerful instruments, preventing many types of crises and ensuring the fiscal space needed to provide support and avert system-wide financial strain when crises do occur.[7]

In addition to macroeconomic policies, the typical automatic stabilizer used in Organisation for Economic Co-operation and Development (OECD) countries is unemployment insurance, which many LAC countries lack. This type of social protection and labor program is key to cushioning the impact of crises on formal workers. However, many workers in the LAC region are informal, and

FIGURE 1.2    **How adjustment works and the policies that can smooth it**

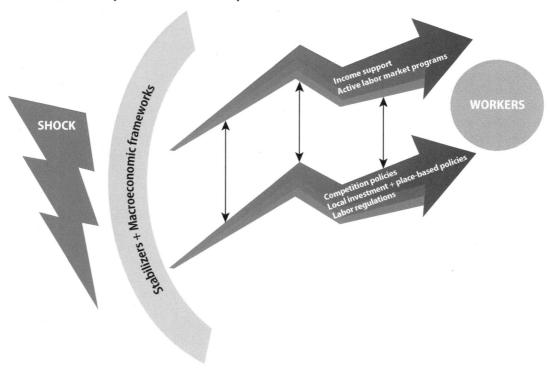

*Source:* World Bank.

the best way to protect their incomes and consumption is through cash and noncash transfers. Targeted on the basis of household need rather than whether a lost job was formal or informal, these programs soften the extent to which labor market adjustments translate into short-term and long-term impacts on the poor and vulnerable. Because reemployment is crucial to avoid scarring, reskilling and reemployment services (known as active labor market programs) are a third crucial type of social protection and labor program. The key role of a country's social protection and labor system in determining the size and persistence of a crisis's impacts is illustrated by the upper arrow in figure 1.2.

Although social protection and labor systems can cushion the impacts of crises on workers, they do not address the structural issues that help determine the magnitude of these impacts. For example, this study highlights a dichotomy between protected (because of their market power and lack of competition) and unprotected firms in the LAC region and the region's low geographic mobility among workers, both of which magnify the welfare effects of shocks. The study also highlights pockets of labor rigidity that are slowing transitions across jobs. Hence, competition policies, regional policies, and labor regulations (illustrated by the lower arrow in figure 1.2) are a third key dimension in policy responses to crises. This dimension touches on important structural issues that may explain poor adjustment, that might require interventions at the sector and locality levels (in addition to worker-level and economywide interventions), and that interact with the aforementioned social protection and labor needs and incentives (as illustrated by the vertical arrows in figure 1.2). The policy response to a crisis must squarely tackle the relevant structural issues, which will have different importance in each country or setting.

Given the complexity of labor market adjustments to economic crises in the LAC region, this report argues that countries can improve their responses by advancing on three fronts.

## Automatic stabilizers and macroeconomic frameworks as shields

The LAC region has significantly improved its macroeconomic framework over the past few decades. Because of these efforts, the region has fewer domestic crises than it used to. With few exceptions, large monetary crises have not occurred in the region since the 1990s; instead, factors exogenous to the region now drive most of its crises. One important development is that most countries in the region have lowered their inflation. In the 1980s and 1990s, when the region had high inflation, crisis adjustment through lower real wages was often mechanical: as inflation spiked during a crisis, real wages fell. Now, adjustment to crises is mostly done by changing employment, which is associated with long-lasting scarring effects, as mentioned earlier in this chapter (Robertson 2021).

Obviously, it is better to avoid crises whenever possible. A prudent macroeconomic framework is key to reducing the frequency of crises. But some crises are unavoidable. Monetary and fiscal stabilization policies are a powerful tool to respond to such crises. These policies include the management of the country's capital account, interest rates, exchange rate policy, sovereign welfare funds, and fiscal rules. Importantly, having fiscal space to provide a demand stimulus may be key to resolving a crisis, but the space available depends on current as well as past decisions. Fiscal reforms with a long-term perspective are key; these reforms may involve tackling difficult issues, including tax policy, energy subsidies, the efficiency of social spending, and the financial stability of old-age pension systems as populations age.

To protect a country from external shocks, a strong set of automatic stabilizers is key. Among these stabilizers are nationally administered income protection arrangements, such as unemployment insurance, and other forms of countercyclical income support that expand in bad times to help affected individuals. These programs stimulate consumption, providing a demand stimulus that limits damage and helps speed recovery.

Automatic stabilizers help households smooth their consumption, reducing the immediate impact of the shock on aggregate demand and employment and therefore mitigating the magnitude and composition of its effects on labor markets. In other words, these policies can reduce the severity of a crisis.

The LAC region still needs stronger automatic stabilizers in order to ensure effective fiscal responses to crises. Missing or poorly functioning aggregate stabilizers limit governments' ability to offer dynamic, countercyclical spending, which makes crises harder to manage and amplifies the effects of shocks.

Beyond large-scale unemployment insurance programs, other policies can also serve as automatic stabilizers. During the COVID-19 crisis, for example, strategies like work-time banking, furloughs, job retention subsidies, and short-term compensation programs[8] have made up an important share of the spending meant to help limit the short- and long-term harm of layoffs. Social assistance cash transfer programs have also been expanded, and evidence in this project shows that their expansion has increased employment at the aggregated local economy level, in addition to causing positive effects on poverty and inequality (Gerard, Naritomi, and Silva 2021). Installing some of these instruments as permanent parts of their respective countries' automatic stabilizers could lower losses and adjustment costs in the wake of future shocks. Some of these programs could be made state-contingent and automatically activated when, for example, unemployment rises above a determined threshold. These microeconomic policies have macroeconomic consequences.

A more complete characterization of the policy areas that can be focused on in order to achieve stronger macroeconomic frameworks and create automatic stabilizers (policy dimension 1) is given in figure 1.3.

**FIGURE 1.3**   **Stabilizers and macroeconomic frameworks: Policy reforms**

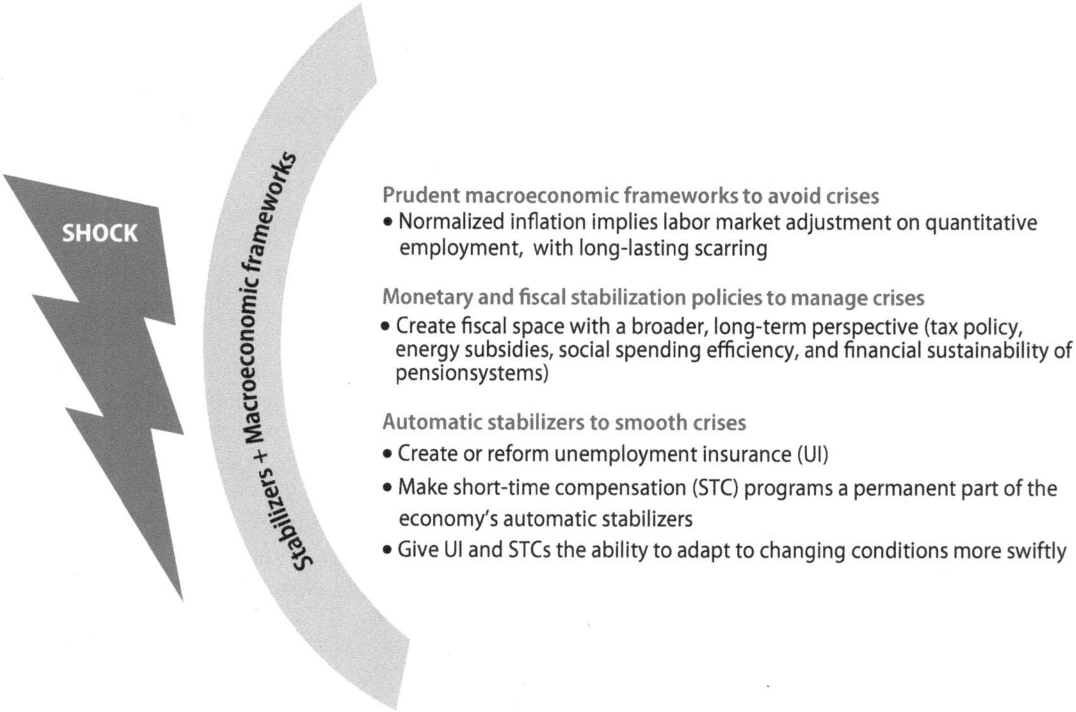

SHOCK

Stabilizers + Macroeconomic frameworks

Prudent macroeconomic frameworks to avoid crises
- Normalized inflation implies labor market adjustment on quantitative employment, with long-lasting scarring

Monetary and fiscal stabilization policies to manage crises
- Create fiscal space with a broader, long-term perspective (tax policy, energy subsidies, social spending efficiency, and financial sustainability of pension systems)

Automatic stabilizers to smooth crises
- Create or reform unemployment insurance (UI)
- Make short-time compensation (STC) programs a permanent part of the economy's automatic stabilizers
- Give UI and STCs the ability to adapt to changing conditions more swiftly

*Source:* World Bank.

## Workers: A policy package for cushioning crises' impacts and preparing for change

The labor scarring documented in this study and its adverse impact on countries' productivity potential imply that greater long-term growth could be achieved in the LAC region if crisis-induced, worker-level human capital decay was reduced. This change would require cushioning the short-term impact of job loss through income support to protect welfare. However, displaced workers need more than just income support to recover from crises; they also need social protection and labor systems that help build human capital and promote faster, higher-quality transitions into new jobs. Social protection and labor systems should help people to renew and redeploy their human capital. In this broader sense, reforms to the LAC region's existing social protection and labor policies and systems are needed. These reforms will, in turn, affect labor market flows and provide a responsive system that contributes to countries' automatic stabilizers.

Although some workers can benefit from expansionary macroeconomic policies, this study shows that others are scarred more permanently by crises and are unlikely to respond to such policies. Social protection and labor systems would be the second line of response to avoid or mitigate the aforementioned scarring effects. However, in general, and despite tremendous advances in the past thirty years, countries in the LAC region still lack reliable and robust income protection paired with effective job-search support services. The need for such programs is intensified by the fact that the margin of adjustment to crises has shifted toward the quantity of employment, resulting in more cuts in hours, more dismissals, and, as shown by research for this study, much slower creation of new formal employment relationships. Most people who lose their jobs or whose livelihoods are otherwise adversely impacted in a downturn are largely unprotected.

Governments around the world have learned the importance of strong social protection and labor systems to limit scarring and other human capital losses caused by crises. Despite advances in this area, formal assistance in the case of labor income loss—or other losses of livelihood associated with economywide transitory shocks—is still beyond the reach of most people in the LAC region. Two-thirds of LAC countries do not yet offer nationally administered income support plans for people who lose their jobs. These countries rely instead on severance pay mandates, which perform poorly in the context of systemic shocks. In terms of job search support, most LAC countries spend very little on active labor measures, and even those that spend more have poor track records for their programs.

At the same time, countries' social protection and labor systems are oriented principally toward providing cash transfers to chronically poor households. Although these programs offer vital "last-resort" support and in some countries are able to quickly scale up during crises, they still fall short of meeting the needs of most displaced workers. In the COVID-19 crisis, countries have relied heavily on cash transfer programs to get money into the hands of vulnerable people quickly. Some of these programs have been more effective than others: for example, the success of these efforts in the LAC region is largely determined by the coverage of the population by social registries, which allow programs to be quickly expanded to include previously uncovered and newly vulnerable groups. Countries that entered the COVID-19 crisis with low-coverage social registries and weaker social assistance programs were less able to provide robust income protection.

How can LAC countries do better for workers and communities in terms of social protection and labor responses to crises? Policy actions to buffer the effects of crises on workers can be organized into the following categories:

1. *Augmenting unemployment income support through the creation or redesigning of unemployment insurance.* A history of frequent systemic shocks combined with the emergence of a significant middle class has created more demand for robust unemployment insurance mechanisms in LAC countries than exists in other regions (De Ferranti et al. 2000). Past crises and the 2020 pandemic shock have dramatically demonstrated the usefulness of unemployment income support systems with deep and extensive risk pools that provide a channel for additional, extraordinary support measures when needed. In Latin America, several countries have implemented changes to their social insurance plans that loosen eligibility requirements and increase benefits. For example, Brazil and Chile, in addition to paying benefits to displaced workers, used their unemployment insurance systems to implement subsidized furlough measures and other employee-retention programs. These systems make all the difference in how well labor markets adjust to crises.

2. *Improving the capacity of social assistance transfer programs to be robust and responsive.* There are three main policy priorities when improving the dynamism of social assistance cash transfers. First is improving the "adaptability" of these programs, that is, their capacity to respond to shocks (such as economic or natural disasters), including by establishing comprehensive and dynamic social registries that are usable across social programs. On the basis of a rare quasi-natural experiment, Gerard, Naritomi, and Silva (2021) show that expanding welfare programs has aggregate benefits for the entire local economy in addition to individual-level benefits. Second is moving from budgeted programs to protection guarantees, thus transforming these programs into safety nets that can expand to catch all those vulnerable to impoverishment before they become poor (Packard et al. 2019). Third is preventing

the emergence of assistance "ghettos" by structuring benefits to incentivize the return to work (with support from augmented reemployment services).

3. *Building robust and coordinated employment services to get people back to work quickly.* Several lessons from international experience can be used to guide the reform of reemployment support services. First, it is important to move away from single interventions and toward providing an *integrated package of services* (such as combinations of coaching, training, information, and intermediation, all informed by market demand). Even individuals who are affected by the same type of shock seldom face identical constraints to accessing new jobs. Hence, the success of a reemployment program depends on its ability to adapt its services to different profiles and needs. Second, to make this change, public employment assistance services need strong registration and statistical profiling systems. Finally, modern monitoring and evaluation practices are key to assessing the results of programs and to introducing course corrections when needed. Making larger, more effective programs fiscally sustainable will require diverse sources of financing: when governments make risk-pooling structures more widely available to cover shocks with uncertain and catastrophic losses, it is reasonable to expect resources contributed by people and firms to meet the needs of more-foreseeable and less-costly shocks. Today, most active labor measures are financed from general budget expenditures, spreading already small allocations too thin.

4. *Supporting working people through periods of change by enhancing their skills.* This effort involves strengthening technical education and vocational training, expanding short-cycle higher education programs to reach low-income students, and conditioning the funding for such programs upon participants' employability.

A more complete characterization of the policy areas that can be focused on in order to achieve stronger social protection and labor responses to crises (policy dimension 2) is given in figure 1.4. Evidence from multiple contexts shows that each of these priority areas can make a real difference in labor market adjustment.

## Sectors and places: Tackling structural issues

This study shows how factors beyond the labor market affect the magnitude of the impacts of crises on workers. Structural challenges in the LAC region act to slow and even to prevent necessary labor market adjustment, hence weakening economic recoveries and causing lasting effects on efficiency as described above. These structural issues can change the nature—and the impact on people—of a systemic shock from transitory to long-term.

The policy implication of this study's findings and the related literature is that even if macroeconomic and social protection and labor policies are pristine and flawlessly implemented, better outcomes could still be achieved for workers in crises by complementing these policies with sectoral and place-based policies to deal with any structural issues impeding strong recoveries from crises.

Such policies would address inefficiencies in labor market adjustment resulting from labor market legislation, product markets' structures, insufficient geographic mobility, and localized economic depression. Addressing these structural challenges will require changes in legal frameworks and regulations as well as targeted public investment. A more

**FIGURE 1.4    Addressing crises' impacts and preparing workers for change: Policy reforms**

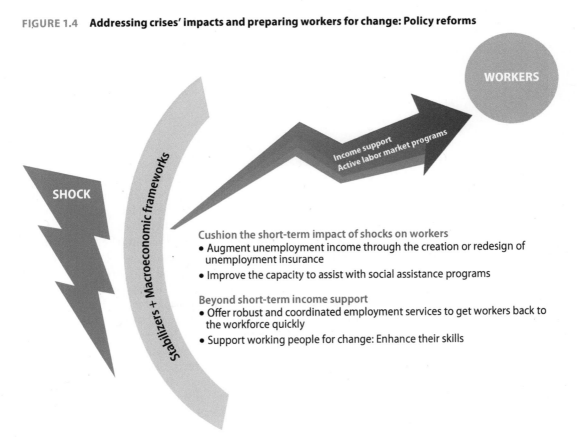

*Source:* World Bank.

FIGURE 1.5 **Tackling structural issues that worsen the impacts of crises on workers**

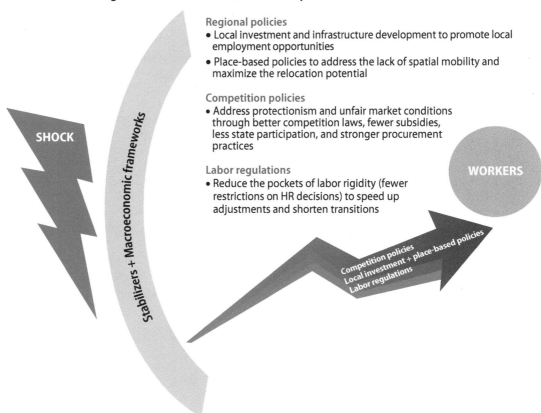

**Regional policies**
• Local investment and infrastructure development to promote local employment opportunities
• Place-based policies to address the lack of spatial mobility and maximize the relocation potential

**Competition policies**
• Address protectionism and unfair market conditions through better competition laws, fewer subsidies, less state participation, and stronger procurement practices

**Labor regulations**
• Reduce the pockets of labor rigidity (fewer restrictions on HR decisions) to speed up adjustments and shorten transitions

*Source:* World Bank.
*Note:* HR = human resource.

complete characterization of the policy areas to focus on in order to tackle the structural issues that worsen the impacts of crises on workers (policy dimension 3) is given in figure 1.5.

## Implications for the COVID-19 crisis

The COVID-19 pandemic is a convulsive, catastrophic crisis that is exacting a savage toll on labor markets in the LAC region. The region is experiencing an extraordinary rate of employment destruction and massive negative income shocks. While the predictions for 2020 were dire due to the widespread job loss experienced across the region, the significant increase in social spending across the region—and especially in Brazil—greatly mitigated the impact and, in fact, is believed to have marginally reduced overall levels of poverty and inequality. (Diaz-Bonilla, Moreno Hererra, and Sanchez Castro 2020). In this crisis, projected to be the most severe labor market recession in some countries' history, millions of workers in Latin America and the Caribbean have lost their jobs, and millions more have seen significant reductions in their earnings. And this loss is not expected to be evenly shared across the income distribution, with some workers (such as those who cannot work remotely) impacted more than others. (Diaz-Bonilla, Moreno Hererra, and Sanchez Castro 2020).

Although this crisis—which was triggered by the public health imperatives of mitigating a global pandemic—is exceptional, it is also one more in a long series of aggregate demand shocks that have hit the countries of the LAC region. On one hand, the COVID-19 crisis has several distinctive features. First, the lockdown has been bad for many workers and worse for those for whom home-based work (or access to high-quality internet) is not an option. Second, prolonged uncertainty about the crisis's duration and outcome, particularly with regard to how employment will rebound, has delayed investment. And third, some countries have made stronger policy responses to this crisis than ever before.

On the other hand, this crisis is not so different from previous ones. A large part of its effects on the LAC region derives from the global recession it has caused, a sharp fall in demand for many months, and impending financial crises in some countries. The LAC region has a history of frequent and often severe economic slowdowns. What happens to workers during these slowdowns is determined largely by aggregate demand fluctuations (plus some self-inflicted domestic crises or mismanagement).

This deep crisis arrived just as many governments in the LAC region were grappling with known structural challenges. It has accelerated some long-run structural shifts that have been changing the nature of work, magnifying their potential to reduce employment opportunities in what were traditionally considered "good jobs"— the standard, stable, protected employment associated with the formal sector (Beylis et al. 2020).

The aforementioned employment dynamics observed in many LAC countries will lead to sizable labor scarring effects stemming from the COVID-19 crisis. Sector and location characteristics are likely to further magnify these effects for some workers. However, the three-dimensional policy framework proposed in this study provides a roadmap that could lead to a more resilient recovery. How public and business policies address the current challenges will shape the progress of the economies of the LAC region and the well-being of the region's workers and citizens for decades. The challenge is immense, but now is the defining time to take it on.

## Notes

1. Following Vegh and Vuletin (2014), this paper defines a crisis as beginning in the quarter in which real gross domestic product (GDP) falls below the preceding four-quarter moving average and as ending in the quarter in which real GDP returns to the precrisis level. This statistic was calculated using quarterly GDP series from International Financial Statistics and Haver Analytics. Although the specific number of crises that took place over this time period is sensitive to the definition of crisis used, independently of that definition, this result shows that unlike in developed countries, where output evolution is characterized by smooth cycles, Latin America experiences frequent and pronounced crises.

2. There is an extensive literature on the dynamics of labor market adjustment to technological change and international trade. See, for example, Acemoglu and Restrepo (2017); Autor et al. (2014); Autor, Dorn, and Hanson (2015); Dauth, Findeisen, and Suedekum (2017); Dix-Carneiro and Kovak (2017, 2019); and Utar (2018).

3. Unique features of the COVID-19 crisis include lockdowns and the health risks associated with personal contact, which had detrimental effects on many jobs, particularly informal jobs, and led to worse job losses in industries for which home-based work is not an option. Another key feature of this crisis is the prolonged uncertainty it has generated, which has delayed investment and hiring, casting additional doubt on how employment is going to rebound.

4. These statistics were estimated by the authors on the basis of Socio-Economic Database for Latin America and the Caribbean data (World Bank and Center for Distributive, Labor and Social Studies).

5. Although it is not a focus of this study, migration is an additional margin of quantitative adjustment in employment. This factor is relevant across the LAC region—for example, in the large flows of migrants from the República Bolivariana de Venezuela to neighboring countries, mainly Colombia. The Caribbean in particular is known for high unemployment and high migrant outflows; displaced workers often leave Caribbean countries in response to employment loss when there is slack in those countries' labor markets.

6. Such studies include Elsby, Hobijn, and Sahin (2013) and Shimer (2005).

7. Monetary and fiscal stabilization policies are powerful tools to respond to crises. Although these policies are crucial to crisis mitigation, they are not the main focus of this study.

8. In contrast to the United States' experience during the COVID-19 crisis, job retention programs in several European countries have served millions of workers. The magnitude of the human capital destruction (scarring effects) averted by these programs depends on: (a) the estimated losses in human capital that would have been caused by the period of unemployment or nonemployment; (b) the unemployment permanently averted—that is, the workers in these programs who would otherwise have been fired (directly or indirectly via firm bankruptcy or closure for lack of liquidity); and (c) the unemployment temporarily averted—that is, the workers who are supported now but will be fired after the end of the support period, or even before then, because of their firms' bankruptcy. In terms of costs per worker, such programs make sense from the governments' perspectives, because without these programs, unemployment insurance would have to be paid in full to each laid-off worker. Three key choices when implementing such programs are their size, their duration, and their coordination with existing unemployment insurance and social assistance. They are adequate for temporary, short-lived shocks but not for extended crises. As a crisis continues, key trade-offs arise: should the program continue to support all workers or only some? If the program is targeted, how should it choose who to support and for how long? In case of longer spells of nonemployment, should the program continue to support jobs or shift to supporting workers in case their jobs have been eliminated? These decisions are difficult, and a combination of instruments might be needed to avoid large increases in poverty and unemployment when job retention programs are abruptly terminated.

## References

Acemoglu, D., and P. Restrepo. 2017. "Secular Stagnation? The Effect of Aging on Economic Growth in the Age of Automation." *American Economic Review* 107 (5): 174–79.

Arias-Vázquez, A., D. Lederman, and L. Venturi. 2019. "Transitions of Workers Displaced Due to Firm Closure." Unpublished paper.

Artuc, E., P. Bastos, and E. Lee. 2021. "Trade Shocks, Labor Mobility, and Welfare: Evidence from Brazil." Background paper written for this report. World Bank, Washington, DC. (See also annex 1A for additional details on this background paper.)

Autor, D. H., D. Dorn, and G. H. Hanson. 2015. "Untangling Trade and Technology: Evidence from Local Labour Markets." *Economic Journal* 125 (584): 621–46.

Autor, D. H., D. Dorn, G. H. Hanson, and J. Song. 2014. "Trade Adjustment: Worker-Level Evidence." *Quarterly Journal of Economics* 129 (4): 1799–1860.

Beylis, G., R. Fattal-Jaef, R. Sinha, M. Morris, and A. Sebastian. 2020. *Going Viral: COVID-19 and the Accelerated Transformation of Jobs in Latin America and the Caribbean.* World Bank Latin American and Caribbean Studies. Washington, DC: World Bank.

Brambilla, I., D. Lederman, and G. Porto. 2012. "Exports, Export Destinations, and Skills." *American Economic Review* 102 (7): 3406–38.

Dauth, W., S. Findeisen, and J. Suedekum. 2017. "Trade and Manufacturing Jobs in Germany." *American Economic Review* 107 (5): 337–42.

De Ferranti, D., G. Perry, I. S. Gill, and L. Servén. 2000. *Securing Our Future in a Global Economy.* World Bank Latin American and Caribbean Studies. Washington, DC: World Bank.

Diaz-Bonilla, C., L. Moreno Herrera, D. Sanchez Castro. 2020. *Projected 2020 Poverty Impacts of the COVID-19 Global Crisis in Latin America and the Caribbean.* Washington, DC: World Bank.

Dix-Carneiro, R., and B. K. Kovak. 2017. "Trade Liberalization and Regional Dynamics." *American Economic Review* 107 (10): 2908–46.

Dix-Carneiro, R., and B. K. Kovak. 2019. "Margins of Labor Market Adjustment to Trade." *Journal of International Economics* 117: 125–42.

Elsby, M. W., B. Hobijn, and A. Sahin. 2013. "Unemployment Dynamics in the OECD." *Review of Economics and Statistics* 95 (2): 530–48.

Fernald, J. G., R. E. Hall, J. H. Stock, and M. W. Watson. 2017. "The Disappointing Recovery of Output after 2009." Working Paper 23543, National Bureau of Economic Research, Cambridge, MA.

Fernandes, A., and J. Silva. 2021. "Labor Market Adjustment to External Shocks: Evidence for Workers and Firms in Brazil and Ecuador." Background paper written for this report. World Bank, Washington, DC. (See also annex 1A for additional details on this background paper.)

Fieler, A. C., M. Eslava, and D. Y. Xu. 2018. "Trade, Quality Upgrading, and Input Linkages: Theory and Evidence from Colombia." *American Economic Review* 108 (1): 109–46.

Gerard, F., J. Naritomi, and J. Silva. 2021. "The Effects of Cash Transfers on Formal Labor Markets: Evidence from Brazil." Background paper written for this report. World Bank, Washington, DC. (See also annex 1A for additional details on this background paper.)

Mion, G., R. Proenca, and J. Silva. 2020. "Trade, Skills, and Productivity." Unpublished paper.

Moreira, S. 2018. "Firm Dynamics, Persistent Effects of Entry Conditions, and Business Cycles." Unpublished paper.

Moreno, L., and L. Sousa. 2021. "Early Employment Conditions and Labor Scarring in Latin America." Background paper written for this report. World Bank, Washington, DC. (See also annex 1A for additional details on this background paper.)

Packard, T., U. Gentilini, M. Grosh, P. O'Keefe, R. Palacios, D. Robalino, and I. Santos. 2019. *Protecting All: Risk Sharing for a Diverse and Diversifying World of Work*. Washington, DC: World Bank.

Packard, T., and J. Onishi. 2021. "Social Insurance and Labor Market Policies in Latin America and the Margins of Adjustment to Shocks." Background paper written for this report. World Bank, Washington, DC. (See also annex 1A for additional details on this background paper.)

Ramey, V. 2012. "Comment on Fiscal Policy in a Depressed Economy." *Brookings Papers on Economic Activity* 2012 (1): 279–90.

Regis, P., and J. Silva. 2021. "Employment Dynamics: Timeline and Myths of Economic Recovery." Background paper written for this report. World Bank, Washington, DC. (See also annex 1A for additional details on this background paper.)

Robertson, R. 2021. "The Change in Nature of Labor Market Adjustment in Latin America and the Caribbean." Background paper written for this report. World Bank, Washington, DC. (See also annex 1A for additional details on this background paper.)

Shimer, R. 2005. "The Cyclical Behavior of Equilibrium Unemployment and Vacancies." *American Economic Review* 95 (1): 25–49.

Silva, J., and L. Sousa. 2021. "Job Creation and Destruction in Small and Large Firms in Brazil and Ecuador." Background paper written for this report. World Bank, Washington, DC. (See also annex 1A for additional details on this background paper.)

Sousa, L. 2021. "Economic Shocks and Employment Adjustments in Latin America." Background paper written for this report. World Bank, Washington, DC. (See also annex 1A for additional details on this background paper.)

Utar, H. 2018. "Workers beneath the Floodgates: Low-Wage Import Competition and Workers' Adjustment." *Review of Economics and Statistics* 100 (4): 631–47.

Vijil, M., V. Amorin, M. Dutz, and P. Olinto. 2021. "The Distributional Effects of Trade Policy in Brazil." Background paper written for this report. World Bank, Washington, DC. (See also annex 1A for additional details on this background paper.)

Vegh, C. A., and G. Vuletin. 2014. "The Road to Redemption: Policy Response to Crises in Latin America." *IMF Economic Review* 62 (4): 526–68.

## Annex 1A: Background papers written for this report

**TABLE 1A.1  Background papers written for this report**

| Author and title | Key research questions | Country coverage, data, and time frame |
|---|---|---|
| *Dynamics of labor market adjustment* | | |
| Regis, P., and J. Silva. "Employment Dynamics: Timeline and Myths of Economic Recovery." | How large and long-lasting is the destruction of formal jobs? What is the timeline of the observed contraction in jobs after a crisis? Do both formal and informal jobs shrink? | • Brazil, Chile, Ecuador, and Mexico<br>• Longitudinal administrative employer-employee data complemented by cross-sectional national accounts and household survey data<br>• Since 1986 for Brazil, since 2006 for Chile and Ecuador, and since 2020 for Mexico |
| Silva, J., and L. Sousa. "Job Creation and Destruction in Small and Large Firms in Brazil and Ecuador." | How do job creation and job destruction vary across small and large employers in the formal sectors of Brazil and Ecuador? What are the relative contributions of large and small firms to overall unemployment flows? Do the adjustment mechanisms vary across small and large firms and across the two countries? | • Brazil and Ecuador<br>• Longitudinal administrative employer-employee data complemented by cross-sectional national accounts and household survey data<br>• Since 1986 for Brazil and since 2006 for Ecuador |
| Sousa, L. "Economic Shocks and Employment Adjustments in Latin America." | How do worker flows in Latin American economies differ across the wage and household income distributions? How do these flows respond to economic shocks, including the global financial crisis of 2008–09? What types of labor transitions are more and less cyclical? How do labor market adjustments differ when responding to cyclical shocks versus changes in growth trends? How does cyclicality vary across the income distribution? | • Argentina, Brazil, Chile, Ecuador, Mexico, Paraguay, and Peru<br>• Labor force survey (panel data)<br>• 2005 Q1–2017 Q4 |
| *Impact of crises on workers, firms, and places* | | |
| Fernandes, A., and J. Silva. "Labor Market Adjustment to External Shocks: Evidence for Workers and Firms in Brazil and Ecuador." | How does exposure to foreign demand shocks affect workers' employment and wages? What are these shocks' short-, medium-, and long-run effects on labor market outcomes at the individual level? How were workers able to adjust to these negative shocks according to the characteristics of their sectors and local labor markets? | • Brazil and Ecuador<br>• Longitudinal matched employer-employee data<br>• 2004–17 |
| Moreno, L., and L. Sousa. "Early Employment Conditions and Labor Scarring in Latin America." | What is the impact of initial labor market conditions on the earnings and career trajectories of worker cohorts in Latin America? | • LAC 17 countries<br>• Labor force and household surveys (cross-sectional)<br>• Since 1980 |

*(Continued on next page)*

**TABLE 1A.1**   **Background papers written for this report** *(Continued)*

| Author and title | Key research questions | Country coverage and type of data |
|---|---|---|
| *Policy responses to crises* | | |
| Artuc, E., P. Bastos, and E. Lee. "Trade Shocks, Labor Mobility, and Welfare: Evidence from Brazil." | What are the effects of trade shocks on labor mobility and welfare in Brazil? To what extent are workers mobile across sectors, places, and occupations? Beyond their effect on wages, how do trade shocks affect the quality of job matching? | • Brazil<br>• Longitudinal social security records<br>• 1994–2015 |
| Gerard, F., J. Naritomi, and J. Silva. "The Effects of Cash Transfers on Formal Labor Markets: Evidence from Brazil." | What are the effects of the expansion of welfare programs on formal labor markets? What are the expansion's spillover effects to nonbeneficiaries? What is the multiplier effect of Bolsa Familia benefits? | • Brazil<br>• Administrative records on Bolsa Familia recipients and formal workers |
| Packard, T., and J. Onishi. "Social Insurance and Labor Market Policies in Latin America and the Margins of Adjustment to Shocks." | How do social protection systems in Latin America affect the margins of adjustment to shocks? | • All Latin American countries<br>• Administrative data |
| Robertson, R. "The Change in Nature of Labor Market Adjustment in Latin America and the Caribbean." | How has real wage flexibility evolved in the LAC region since the 1980s? Is the documented margin of adjustment to slowdowns and crises in the 2000s different from that of the 1980s and 1990s? Do the two margins differ in relative importance? | • Brazil, Chile, Colombia, and Mexico<br>• Quarterly manufacturing data (cross-section)<br>• 1980–2017 |
| Vijil, M., V. Amorin, M. Dutz, and P. Olinto. "The Distributional Effects of Trade Policy in Brazil." | What is the within-country distributive impact of competition policies? What was the distribution of the welfare gains caused by Brazil's tariff liberalization in the 1990s? | • Brazil<br>• Household expenditure surveys, labor market surveys, and local consumption price data<br>• 1991–99 |

*Note:* The LAC 17 countries = Argentina, Bolivia, Brazil, Chile, Colombia, Costa Rica, Dominican Republic, Ecuador, El Salvador, Guatemala, Honduras, Mexico, Nicaragua, Panama, Peru, Paraguay and Uruguay.

# The Dynamics of Labor Market Adjustment | 2

## Introduction

Crises in Latin America and the Caribbean (LAC) depress labor demand. However, different labor market dynamics may hide behind similar reductions in labor demand. In the months after the COVID-19 (coronavirus) pandemic reached the LAC region, unemployment grew by about 9.8 percentage points in Colombia, 7.6 percentage points in Costa Rica, 2.7 percentage points in Brazil, 1.5 percentage points in Mexico, and 1.3 percentage points in Paraguay. More than 65,000 formal jobs were lost in El Salvador between March and May 2020, and more than 350,000 workers lost their jobs in the Dominican Republic between March and June 2020.[1] Do these statistics mean that Colombia has been more affected by the COVID-19 crisis than the other countries? Not necessarily. The unemployment rate on its own does not fully characterize the impact of a crisis on labor markets.

By complementing key research with new results, this chapter seeks to further the understanding of how labor markets in the LAC region adjust to economic crises. Rather than focusing on one statistic (such as the unemployment rate), it considers the mechanisms of adjustment and their cyclicality and heterogeneity across firms and workers. The chapter answers three questions: (a) What are the principal margins of adjustment of labor markets in Latin America? (b) What are the key mechanisms driving these adjustments? and (c) Do crises affect the employment structure beyond their effects on job flows?

Important to these questions is how firms adjust their wage bill (wages times employment) in response to crises. There are three key dimensions of adjustment. First, firms can try to adjust wages. Second, firms can adjust the hours worked by existing employees (the intensive margin). And third, firms can adjust their number of employees (the extensive margin). Several studies show that in the face of adverse shocks, firms rarely adjust wages. Kaur (2019) finds significant downward rigidity of wages in India. Significant downward rigidity of real wages has also been documented in Mexico (Castellanos, Garcia-Verdu, and Kaplan 2004), South Africa (Erten, Leight, and Tregenna 2019), and many other countries. Downward real wage adjustment is most likely to occur through inflation, which has been relatively low in Latin America over the past two decades.

The existing literature provides little consensus about whether, a priori, firms can be expected to react to a shock by adjusting along the intensive margin or the extensive margin. Empirically, both margins have been shown to be important. Van Rens (2012) argues that in the presence of negative shocks, the intensive margin (hours) is just as affected as the extensive margin (employment) in Organisation for Economic Co-operation and Development (OECD) countries. Taskin (2013) finds a similar result for Turkey and the United States, which is surprising because Turkey has a much larger informal sector than the United States. In India, the lack of downward real wage flexibility induces firms to reduce employment (Kaur 2019).

Institutions also affect firms' adjustment strategies. Regulations around firing are associated with slower adjustment to crises in some Latin American countries (David, Pienknagura, and Roldos 2020) and in Italy (Belloc and D'Antoni 2020), Japan (Liu 2018), and other countries. This slow employment adjustment often comes at the cost of future hiring. Enforcement of these regulations helps make the formal sector more attractive to workers than the informal sector (Abras et al. 2018), and this difference remains a critical component of Latin American labor markets.

The level and composition of informality in the labor market is key to how crises impact workers in Latin American economies. Informality may function as a buffer for employment during bad times, because the costs of entering the informal sector are lower than the costs of entering formal employment (Arias et al. 2018). However, this buffer functions in a nuanced way, because the informal sector is highly heterogenous. Informal workers range from the subsistence self-employed, for whom unemployment is not an option, to informal dependent workers, who may well lose their jobs in response to negative shocks, to relatively skilled workers more typical of the formal sector, who use

informal employment, including in the gig economy, as a temporary stopgap between formal jobs.

What does the heterogeneity of the informal sector mean for unemployment rates during a crisis? Economies with higher levels of subsistence self-employment or of gig workers could expect to see lower levels of unemployment in response to crises. If jobs are lost in a formal sector with low or inadequate unemployment insurance, the informal sector might end up absorbing workers who would otherwise become unemployed (who would perhaps join Uber or start selling refreshments on the street). In this way, an economy that might at first glance appear to be more sheltered from crises or to have smoother adjustment mechanisms could simply have lower reservation wages because of higher (and countercyclical) informality or the limited availability of unemployment benefits.

This chapter begins by considering the role of key potential margins of labor market adjustment across six countries in the LAC region through an analysis of labor flows and transitions in the region. The estimates produced by Sousa (2021) consider four adjustment mechanisms: unemployment, exiting the labor force, shifting to informality, and shifting to part-time work. The paper's results indicate that exits from the labor force and shifts to part-time work do not appear to be significant margins of adjustment, but formal and informal job flows have a strong negative correlation in five of the six countries analyzed. That is, reductions in formality are often accompanied by increases in informality, and vice versa. However, even in economies with large informal sectors that absorb some excess labor, unemployment remains a significant margin of adjustment to economic shocks in the LAC region. Large gross flows to unemployment, in turn, represent significant reductions in household income, increasing vulnerability and poverty. Labor income represents 60 percent of household income among the poorest 40 percent of households in the LAC countries, and among households not living in poverty, a job loss by the main earner would push 55 percent into poverty.[2]

This chapter then digs into the mechanisms underlying the cyclicality of unemployment. Fluctuations in unemployment are determined by changes in transitions into and out of unemployment—job loss and job finding rates, respectively. During economic downturns, these changes are driven by increased job destruction (as existing positions are eliminated), reduced job creation (as new positions are not created), and lower levels of job reallocation, or churning, as fewer workers voluntarily leave their positions to look for better matches. Each of these factors will require different policy tools to address. The relative contribution of each varies across labor markets, with some research in high-income economies finding that cyclical unemployment is driven by reductions in job finding rates and other studies (such as Shimer [2005] and Elsby, Hobijn, and Sahin [2013]) finding that it is driven instead by increased job separation rates.

New evidence produced in the context of this research project shows that the cyclicality of job loss across formal and informal employment is low. Instead, in most countries analyzed, adjustment in employment during the 2008–09 global financial crisis was driven by a drop in net job finding rates, which was larger for formal workers than for informal workers (Sousa 2021). Zooming in on the formal sector through the use of worker-firm linked administrative data from Brazil and Ecuador, another study showed that a reduction in job creation, rather than an increase in job destruction, is what drives lower employment in the formal sector during downturns (Silva and Sousa 2021). Moreover, although larger firms tend to be more productive and more resilient than smaller firms, they also exhibit greater cyclical fluctuations in labor demand. That is, although large firms themselves are resilient, employment at large firms may not be the most resilient to economic shocks. Once the higher death rates of small firms during crises are taken into account, employment

fluctuations look very similar for small and large firms.

Are worker flows more cyclical for low-skilled or informal workers than for formal or high-skilled workers? In LAC economies, which feature a combination of large informal sectors and varying skill levels among workers, there appears to be a hierarchy in adjustment costs, in which informal workers, who have fewer job protections, face a greater likelihood of job loss regardless of skill. Workers in the lower income quintiles are more likely in general to experience negative labor transitions than workers in the higher income quintiles, but overall, this project's results suggest that high-skilled employment is more responsive to growth shocks than low-skilled employment. This finding is consistent with the greater cyclicality of job loss for formal sector workers and employees of large firms, because these workers are more likely to be skilled.

The final section of this chapter considers how the margins of employment adjustment affect the structure of the labor market. Various labor market dynamics can lead to changes in the composition of the workforce, and the macroeconomic aftereffects of a crisis on the employment structure can shape its medium- to long-term effects on employment and wages. Do such effects occur in Latin America? New research produced in the context of this project shows that crises do indeed have significant effects on the employment structure and that these effects can last for several years (Regis and Silva 2021). In the three countries analyzed (Brazil, Chile, and Mexico), the shrinkage of formal employment caused by crises was strong and long-lasting. In two of these countries, informality seems to have been a long-term buffer for employment; in the other one, employment stagnated or fell. At the same time, Artuc, Bastos, and Lee (2021), considering the effects of crises on labor mobility and welfare, find that because of reduced job flows, job match quality falls during slowdowns and crises, reducing estimated utility. These results suggest that a crisis has the potential to push the labor market into a new equilibrium between formal and informal employment, with long-term implications for welfare and productivity.

## Labor market flows: Unemployment versus informality

Economic crises are significant and frequent in the LAC region, and they represent a major obstacle to the region's economic development and poverty reduction. These economic shocks reduce overall demand, reducing demand for labor and eventually leading to quantitative adjustments in employment. In this section, evidence is presented regarding four margins of this quantitative adjustment: unemployment, exit from the labor force, shifting to informality, and shifting to part-time work.

The goal of this section, which is based on Sousa (2021), is to characterize the short-term impacts of cyclical growth fluctuations on the labor market by analyzing how labor market flows vary with the business cycle. Sousa estimates worker flows using data on more than six million labor market transitions constructed from labor force survey panels from the Labor Database for Latin America and the Caribbean (LABLAC) project (a joint project of the Center for Distributive, Labor and Social Studies and the World Bank). The chapter's analysis focuses on urban workers, limiting the extent to which the results are affected by differences across countries in levels of subsistence or low-productivity primary sector activities. The countries considered, those for which sufficient data were available, are Argentina, Brazil, Chile, Ecuador, Mexico, and Peru. The quarterly panels for each country were constructed by linking data from consecutive surveys between the first quarter of 2005 and the fourth quarter of 2017 across individuals between the ages of 15 and 64. These quarterly survey panels were used to calculate quarterly labor flows and transition rates from the individual-level data.

This section discusses both job flows and employment transitions. While job flows measure the *number* of workers that switch between two labor market states in a given period, employment transitions measure the *rates* at which workers switch between these states. Microdata are used to compute the cyclicality of labor transitions (in other words, the deviations from their natural rates or trends). The states of employment considered are formal private wage employment, formal public employment, informal wage employment, self-employment, unemployment, not working, and working part-time. Following Moscarini and Postel-Vinay (2012), cyclicality is measured by constructing growth series (for which growth is measured as quarterly year-to-year GDP growth) and quarterly labor transition series. Economic growth and transitions are detrended by applying seasonal adjustments and a Hodrik-Prescott filter to obtain the cyclical component of these figures. A transition is procyclical when the correlation between the growth cycle and the respective transition series is positive and countercyclical when the correlation is negative.

### Unemployment

In the LAC region, despite differences among countries' labor markets, unemployment is strongly countercyclical in all countries—a not-so-obvious result, given the region's level of informality. Figure 2.1 plots quarterly fluctuations in GDP growth and unemployment rates since 2005 in six of the largest Latin American economies. In each of these economies, unemployment clearly spikes during significant downturns (including the 2008–09 global financial crisis). In more recent years, Brazil and Ecuador have experienced significant downturns, both of which triggered large upticks in unemployment. For example, between the fourth quarters of 2014 and 2016, Brazil shed 2.6 million jobs, and the country's unemployment rate increased from 6.5 percent to 12.0 percent. Although

**FIGURE 2.1    Quarterly fluctuations in unemployment and GDP growth, 2005–17**

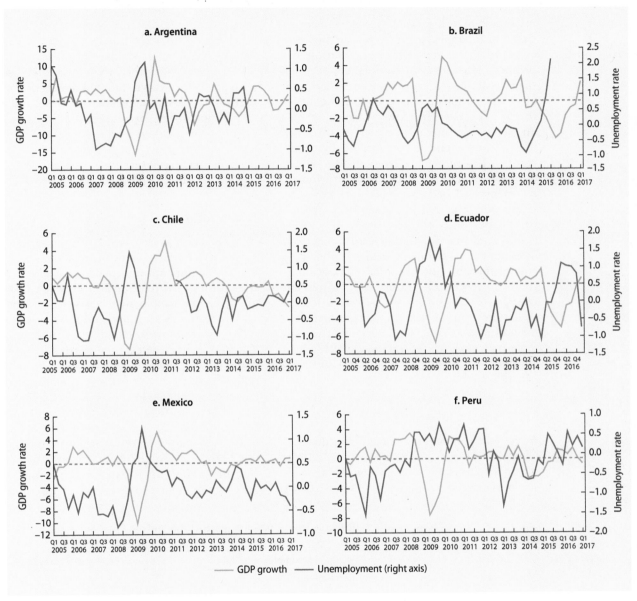

Source: Sousa 2021.
Note: This figure shows the cyclical components of unemployment and GDP growth. These calculations are based on unemployment rates and gross domestic product estimates from national authorities, seasonally adjusted and detrended using a Hodrik-Prescott filter. There is a break in the comparability of the Chilean unemployment series between 2009 and 2011. Because of a change in methodology, the Brazilian unemployment data series ends in 2015. GDP = gross domestic product.

these spikes in unemployment quickly follow economic downturns, employment recovers more gradually than the overall economies. Mexico's employment recovery following the 2008–09 global financial crisis was particularly slow: growth reentered positive territory in the first quarter of 2010 and remained above trend until the end of 2012, but unemployment continued above trend until the end of 2011.

The spikes in unemployment during significant downturns are obvious upon visual inspection of figure 2.1. To measure the cyclicality of unemployment across the business cycle, table 2.1 reports the correlation and ordinary least squares coefficients between the two detrended series (Sousa 2021).[3] Negative correlations reflect countercyclicality—that is, a decrease in growth associated with an increase in unemployment, or vice versa. This countercyclicality is statistically significant in five of the six countries for which data are available. For example, in Mexico, a decrease of 1 percentage point in detrended GDP growth is associated with an increase in the detrended unemployment rate of 7.9 percent. In Peru, however, unemployment does not have a strong cyclical component. A rule of thumb known as Okun's Law states that in the United States, each 1 percent change in real output is associated with a deviation from the natural rate of unemployment of about 0.5 percent, although this estimate may vary by the frequency with which changes are measured (Aguiar-Conraria, Martins, and Soares 2020).

### Exit from the labor force

A secondary indicator of slack labor demand is increased exit from the labor force, reflecting an increase in discouraged workers. Analysis of the cyclical component of net outflows from the labor force shows that these outflows are not countercyclical in the six countries analyzed (table 2.2). Net outflows from the labor force are cyclical in Mexico and Peru, but in both cases they are procyclical: net outflows from the labor force increase with economic growth and fall during downturns. This result suggests that labor force exit is not driven by workers' discouragement; rather, workers tend to hold on to their employment when jobs are harder to find, perhaps to compensate for family members' weaker job-finding prospects.

### Informality

Not all labor market flows emerging from crises are job losses. In Latin America in particular, the significant informal sector dampens the Okun's Law relationship between GDP growth and unemployment (David, Lambert, and Toscani 2019). Fully characterizing the quantitative margin of adjustment during slowdowns in these economies thus requires going beyond unemployment dynamics. The region's low access to unemployment insurance benefits likely lowers reservation wages and shortens job searches. Although these factors lower unemployment in the short term, they may also result in lower-quality job matches.[4] In the LAC region, where the majority of jobs are informal—self-employment (23 percent) or informal

**TABLE 2.1**   **Cyclical components of GDP growth, the unemployment rate, and net flows out of the labor force**

| Countries | Unemployment rate | | Flows out of labor force |
|---|---|---|---|
| | Correlation | OLS | OLS |
| Argentina | −0.557 | −0.061 *** | −1391.3 |
| Brazil | −0.444 | −0.098 ** | −291.5 |
| Chile | −0.489 | −0.110 ** | −1403.9 |
| Ecuador | −0.520 | −0.159 *** | −687.3 |
| Mexico | −0.533 | −0.079 *** | 12980.1 ** |
| Peru | −0.143 | −0.035 | 2519.0 ** |

*Source:* Sousa 2021.
*Note:* This table reports the correlation coefficients and the coefficients from simple OLS regressions of the detrended unemployment rates and detrended GDP growth rates, lagged by one quarter, of the six countries studied. GDP = gross domestic product; OLS = ordinary least squares.
Significance level: * = 90 percent, ** = 95 percent, *** = 99 percent.

dependent wage work (35 percent)[5]—a reduction in positions in the formal sector may lead to more workers entering the informal sector.[6] Is informality doing the dirty work of maintaining employment in Latin American economies?

Earlier research has shown that although informal employment is not always inferior to formal employment in the LAC region, it likely absorbs displaced formal sector workers during downturns. Using Mexican data, Maloney (1999) presents one of the earliest analyses of employment transitions between formal and informal jobs. He concludes that "the labor market for relatively unskilled workers may be well integrated with both formal and informal sectors, offering desirable jobs with distinct characteristics." Bosch and Maloney (2008) find that the sectoral composition of employment is itself cyclical: informal employment is generally countercyclical, while the reverse is true for formal employment. Additionally, Bosch and Maloney (2010), using survey panel data for Argentina, Brazil, and Mexico and continuous time Markov transition processes, find evidence supporting voluntary entry into informal employment, especially self-employment. Even so, when considering transition rates across the business cycle, they find increased likelihood of transitioning from formal to informal wage employment during downturns, especially for young workers.

Indeed, net worker flows across the six countries studied suggest that informal and independent work act like a buffer for employment during economic downturns in the LAC region. Figure 2.2 shows net flows, the difference between the number of new workers entering and exiting a sector in each quarter, for formal private sector jobs and informal or independent jobs. There is a strong negative correlation between formal and informal job flows in five of the six countries analyzed. That is, in these countries, reduced net flows into formality are often accompanied by increased net flows into informality and independent work, and vice versa.

Figure 2.2 shows clear patterns across several of the countries analyzed in net flows into formality and informality during economic downturns. In 2008–09, as the effects of the global financial crisis reverberated across these countries, each experienced a steep loss of formal employment. This loss was accompanied by an increase, although smaller in magnitude, in informal and independent work. The same pattern is seen during later downturns in Argentina, Brazil, Chile, and Ecuador. During the recovery period after these downturns, the trends reverse: informal and independent work declines as net flows into formality increase.

Despite the clear reversal in net flows between formality and informality during crises and recovery periods, these flows are only weakly countercyclical in general— that is, there is only a weak correlation over the full business cycle between workers transitioning into formal and informal work and fluctuations in lagged GDP growth (table 2.2). However, this finding has some exceptions. The net flows suggest that in Argentina and Mexico, independent work (self-employment) may be an inferior employment option used as a buffer during low-growth periods. This observation is supported by procyclical net flows from self-employment into unemployment in both countries, suggesting that formerly self-employed workers increasingly search for dependent employment during periods of higher growth. A similar pattern is found among informal wage workers in Ecuador.

In the relationship between growth and formality, Peru stands apart: the analysis in figure 2.2 suggests that the country experiences higher flows into formality during downturns. The results in table 2.2 further support this observation. Peru's net flows into formality and independent work are both cyclical; the country's flows into formality are countercyclical (flows into formality fall as growth increases) and its flows into independent work are procyclical (flows into independent work increase as growth increases). Net flows from Peru's formal sector to informal

**FIGURE 2.2 Quarterly net flows into formal and informal employment, 2005–17**

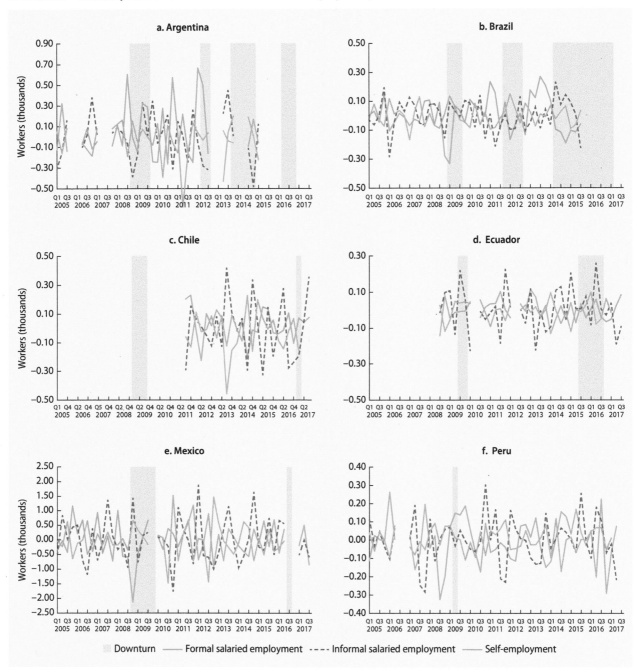

*Source:* Sousa 2021.
*Note:* This figure's calculations are based on the cyclical components of net flows of full-time jobs (new hires minus job losses) in the formal private sector and the informal dependent and independent (self-employed and employers) sectors. These flows are estimated on the basis of the number of workers experiencing employment changes between two consecutive quarters of observation. The cyclical component is estimated with seasonal adjustments and a Hodrik-Prescott filter. The shaded areas in the figures labeled "downturn" represent quarters of negative gross domestic product growth according to estimates from national authorities.

**TABLE 2.2   Cyclicality of net flows across sectors and out of employment, 2005–17**

*OLS coefficients of the cyclical components of net flows and lagged growth*

| Net flows into | Argentina | Brazil | Chile | Ecuador | Mexico | Peru | Note |
|---|---|---|---|---|---|---|---|
| Formality | 474.0 | 1153.3 | 160.5 | 30.4 | 888.7 | −2639.7 | *** |
| Informality | −382.3 | −177.8 | −697.4 | −121.9 | −2879.4 | 465.1 | |
| Informality (wages) | −571.8 | −435.9 | −506.7 | 15.6 | −5439.9 | 165.9 | |
| Independent work | 163.7 | −413.9 | −943.4 | −702.0 ** | −2629.9 | 705.5 | * |

*OLS coefficients of the cyclical components of net flows between employment sectors and lagged growth*

| Quarter 1 | Quarter 2 | Argentina | Brazil | Chile | Ecuador | Mexico | Peru | Note |
|---|---|---|---|---|---|---|---|---|
| Formal (private sector) | Informal | −443.5 | −102.0 | −851.4 | −46.9 | −2660.1 | 1812.1 | *** |
| | Unemployment | 5.7 | −305.7 | 415.4 | 44.7 | 277.6 | 55.3 | |
| | Out of labor force | −101.9 | −555.4 | −12.5 | −123.1 | 393.3 | 299.0 | |
| Informal (wage) | Formal (private sector) | 506.8 | −95.4 | −243.7 | 110.2 | 1759.8 | −997. 3 | ** |
| | Unemployment | 175.6 | 298.8 | 304.5 | 681.6 ** | 776.6 | 971.6 | ** |
| | Out of labor force | −252.22 | 373.3 | 448.2 | −117.0 | 4413.8 | −293.9 | |
| Independent work | Formal (private sector) | −63.3 | 197.4 | 1095.1 | −63.2 | 900.3 | −814.8 | ** |
| | Unemployment | 421.5 * | 33.7 | −595.9 | −39.4 | 2158.3 | 267.8 | |
| | Out of labor force | −756.6 ** | −100.9 | −101.6 | −94.3 | 6580.4 | 860.0 | |

*Source:* Sousa 2021.
*Note:* These calculations are based on the cyclical components of net flows (formal to informal work minus informal to formal work, and so forth) of full-time jobs. The sample analyzed is limited to workers who were in the formal private sector, in the informal wage sector, or independent (self-employed and employers) in the first quarter of observation. Flows are estimated as the number of workers who changed their employment status between two consecutive quarters of observation. The cyclical component of each flow is estimated with seasonal adjustments and a Hodrik-Prescott filter. OLS = ordinary least squares.
Significance level: * = 90 percent, ** = 95 percent, *** = 99 percent.

work are also procyclical, while the country's flows from informality (both dependent and independent work) to formality are counter-cyclical. The question of why this might be the case for Peru (and not the other countries studied) may be worth exploring further in future research. A key distinctive feature of Peru compared with the other countries studied is Peru's high share of self-employed workers and low number of formal salaried employees (Jaramillo and Nopo 2020).

## Adjusting hours worked

A temporary reduction in hours could be an effective alternative to layoffs when a firm faces a temporary decrease in demand. By reducing the hours of employees rather than letting them go, the firm can maintain the employment links it has previously established, reducing firm adjustment costs (current firing costs and future hiring costs), while preserving valuable firm-specific human capital. However, employees whose hours are reduced will see their incomes fall but not be able to tap into unemployment insurance (in the countries where this mechanism exists). Labor regulations restrict the extent to which this option is feasible in the LAC region's formal sector.[7] (These labor regulations are discussed in more detail in chapter 3.) Even so, the option may be an additional margin of adjustment available to the informal sector and independent workers. For example, rather than becoming fully unemployed, self-employed workers may instead reduce their work hours in response to lower demand for their services.

Analysis of net flows into part-time work in the LAC region suggests that this option is not a significant margin of adjustment in the labor market, either in general or in the formal or informal sectors. Figure 2A.1 in annex 2A shows the net flows into part-time work among workers who remain in the same sector (formal or informal), thus isolating the adjustment of existing employment. In Argentina, Brazil, Mexico, and perhaps Peru's formal sector, net flows into part-time work seem to spike in the early part of the 2008–09 global financial crisis, but these flows show similar spikes outside crisis periods. Of the net and gross flows into part-time and full-time work across the six countries and two sectors, only flows into part-time work in the informal sector of Ecuador are correlated with the cyclical component of growth.

Despite the differences in regulations between the formal and informal sectors, in four of the six countries analyzed, net flows into part-time work in the two sectors are positively correlated: they move together, suggesting similar patterns of fluctuations in job finding and churning rates. This correlation is particularly strong in Mexico (with a correlation coefficient of 0.59) and less strong in Argentina (0.24). With a correlation coefficient of –0.23, Chile has the strongest negative correlation between net flows into part-time work in the two sectors.[8]

There is evidence that Argentina's informal sector makes some adjustments through the reduction of hours (panel a of figure 2.3). At the beginning of the global financial crisis, the number of part-time workers flowing into full-time work in Argentina fell below trend, while the number of full-time workers flowing into part-time work greatly surpassed the trend. At the end of the crisis, the data reflected a short but large reversal: flows into full-time work grew significantly above trend. As shown in panel b of figure 2.3, adjustment to part-time status in the formal sector is not strongly correlated with growth. However, transitions across full- and part-time status are highly cyclical for independent workers. Transitions into full-time work are strongly procyclical (increasing during good times and decreasing during bad times), while transitions to part-time work are strongly countercyclical (increasing during bad times and decreasing during good times).

## What are the main margins of adjustment in Latin America?

The analysis above, which measures the cyclicality of labor transitions across job types, shows that despite the evidence of informal employment serving as a buffer for employment in the LAC region, unemployment in the region is strongly countercyclical (despite large differences in labor markets among countries). In contrast, exits from the labor force or shifts to part-time work do not appear to play a big role in Latin American labor markets' adjustment to crises. Importantly, the results presented in this section until now reflect only the short-run adjustments to crises: unemployment is the main margin of adjustment during that period, but in the medium to long run, workers may transition from unemployment to informality, as has been shown by Dix-Carneiro and Kovak (2019).

This section's findings reflect significant changes in Latin America's flows to unemployment during the global financial crisis, despite the relatively low estimates for these shifts given by Okun's Law for Latin America.[9] According to that rule of thumb, the acceleration of GDP growth in the region by 1 percentage point is associated with a contemporaneous (or 1-year lagged) 0.2 percentage point reduction in the unemployment rate. Existing data on the LAC region as a whole do not allow for a precise estimate of this elasticity when restricting the sample to crisis years. However, this estimate can be made for Brazil and Mexico, where we find an elasticity of about 0.5 during crises in the 2000s. In line with this estimate, the latest projections of the impact of the COVID-19 pandemic on the region predict a 9.1 percent drop in regional GDP and a rise of 4 to 5 percentage points in the unemployment rate, which would correspond to a record 44 million workers unemployed.

The important role of the informal sector reflected in this section's findings helps explain why, at the aggregate level, the unemployment rate seems to be less

**FIGURE 2.3    Part-time work as a margin of adjustment in Argentina, 2005–15**

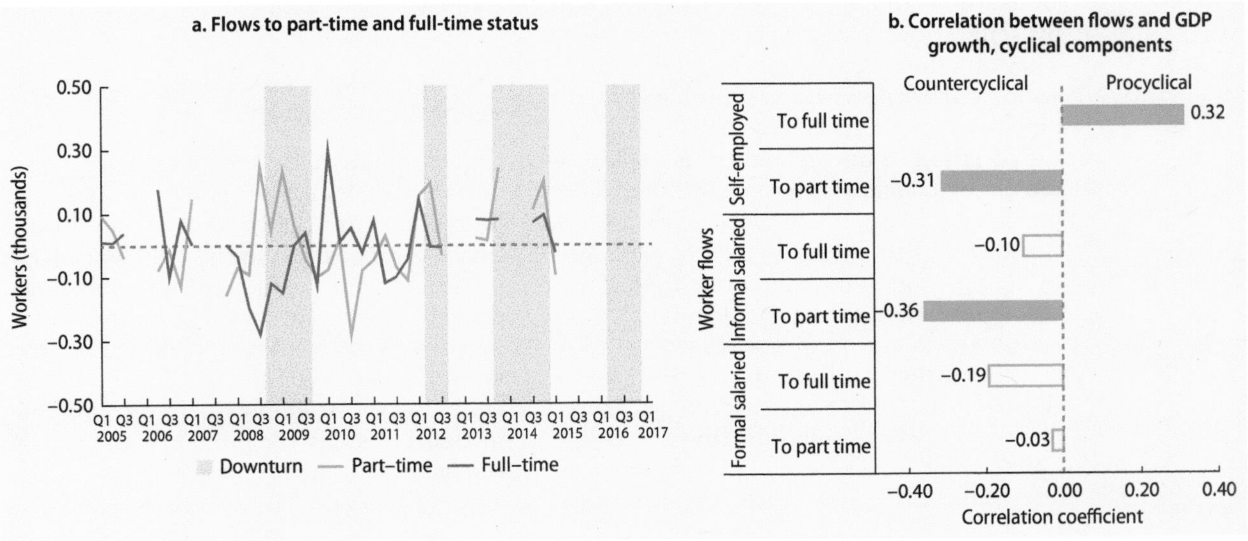

*Source:* Sousa 2021.

*Note:* Panel a reports the cyclical component of flows from full-time to part-time jobs (labeled "Part-time") and from part-time to full-time jobs (labeled "Full-time") in the informal and independent (self-employed and employers) sector. Part-time work is defined as working fewer than 30 hours per week. The flows are estimated as the number of workers who change employment statuses between two consecutive quarters of observation. The cyclical components of these flows are estimated with seasonal adjustments and a Hodrik-Prescott filter. The shaded areas in the figures labeled "downturn" represent quarters of negative gross domestic product (GDP) growth according to estimates from national authorities. Panel b reports the correlation between each of the cyclical components of the quarterly labor flows and GDP growth lagged by one quarter. The correlations represented by colored bars are statistically significant, with confidence levels of 90 percent or higher.

elastic to changes in output in Latin America than in advanced economies and why this elasticity is highly heterogeneous in the region. Although flows into unemployment are an important margin of adjustment in the LAC region, flows into informality complement them as part of the adjustment mechanism. This channel, informal employment, is significantly more limited in advanced economies.

This section's results are in line with recent findings in the international trade literature. Dix-Carneiro and Kovak (2019) document that the regions most exposed to foreign competition following Brazil's trade liberalization (in which the country suffered a negative trade shock) faced medium-run increases in unemployment above the national average but lower than they would have faced if informality did not absorb some workers displaced by trade.

## Job destruction and job creation in times of crisis

As seen in the previous section, unemployment is a primary margin of labor market adjustment in the LAC region. The region's high informality rates and strong protections in the formal sector imply large differences between the two types of jobs in employers' adjustment costs. Eliminating jobs in the formal sector can be expensive because of the contractual and legal obligations of the employer, while job destruction in the informal sector is relatively cost-free for employers, especially for jobs that require low levels of firm- or industry-specific human capital.

This observation suggests that the destruction of informal jobs and the creation of formal jobs would be the margins of adjustment most responsive to slowdowns. Indeed, Bosch and Maloney (2008) find that countercyclical unemployment during recessions in Brazil and Mexico is driven more by job separations among informal workers than by separations from formal employment. They also find decreased hiring in the formal sector during downturns. Similarly, Bosch and Esteban-Pretel (2012) find that cyclical variation in unemployment is explained mostly by changes in the separation rate of informal workers, while cyclical variation in the share of formal employment is explained by changes in the transition rate from informal to formal jobs.

Job flows can be decomposed into job creation flows and job destruction flows (Davis and Haltiwanger 1992). Measurements of gross and net job flows in developing countries are relatively rare (Ochieng and Park [2017] is a recent exception), so the measurements presented in this section are especially valuable. For each firm analyzed, the net change in jobs is calculated per quarter. Firms that lost more employees than they gained are net job destroyers and contribute to job destruction flows. Conversely, firms that end the quarter with more employees than they began with are net job creators and contribute to gross job creation flows. Because these flows are measured at the establishment level, they are limited to formal sector firm employment. For a wider view of employment dynamics, this section also includes worker survey–based concepts of job finding flows and job loss flows. This alternative metric is particularly relevant in the LAC region because it is the only way to measure the informal sector.

Job separation rates are not necessarily the critical adjustment mechanism for labor markets in Latin America: many workers who would otherwise voluntarily quit their jobs postpone that decision during downturns, while other employment opportunities are scarce. This section addresses the following questions: Which jobs are at greater risk during crises: those in the formal sector or those in the informal sector? And within the formal sector, are jobs more at risk in large or small firms? The section focuses on the underlying dynamics that determine

unemployment and on how these dynamics differ across types of jobs and employers.

## Job loss and job finding rates during economic downturns

As noted earlier in this chapter, the worker-based analogues for job creation and job destruction are the concepts of job finding and job loss, respectively, which are based on worker data rather than establishment data. This alternate perspective allows for the inclusion of flows into and out of the informal sector. Rates of job loss for full-time workers by sector of employment are presented in figure 2.4. As the global financial crisis rippled across the LAC countries, job losses notably increased in most sectors of most countries. As one might expect, the sector least affected was independent workers, who are largely low-skilled and self-employed. Table 2.3 reports the correlation coefficients between the cyclical components of each of these trends, showing strong correlations in job loss between the two informal sectors (informal wage work and independent work). The table also reveals a strong positive correlation between formal and informal salaried work in four of the countries analyzed—showing that job losses by dependent workers exhibit similar responses during the business cycle in both sectors.

Significantly, in most countries analyzed, adjustment in employment during the 2008–09 global financial crisis appears to have been driven by a drop in net job finding rates, which was larger for formal workers than for informal workers. This trend was particularly pronounced in Mexico and Peru. The net job finding rate of a sector—the worker side of net job creation—is calculated as the number of new workers joining the sector in excess of the number of workers leaving the sector in a particular quarter, as a share of the sector's employment. Table 2.2, in the previous section, revealed the low cyclicality of job loss across the three sectors—formal private sector dependent work, informal dependent work, and independent work.

**FIGURE 2.4**    **Quarterly job loss, formal and informal sectors, 2005–17**

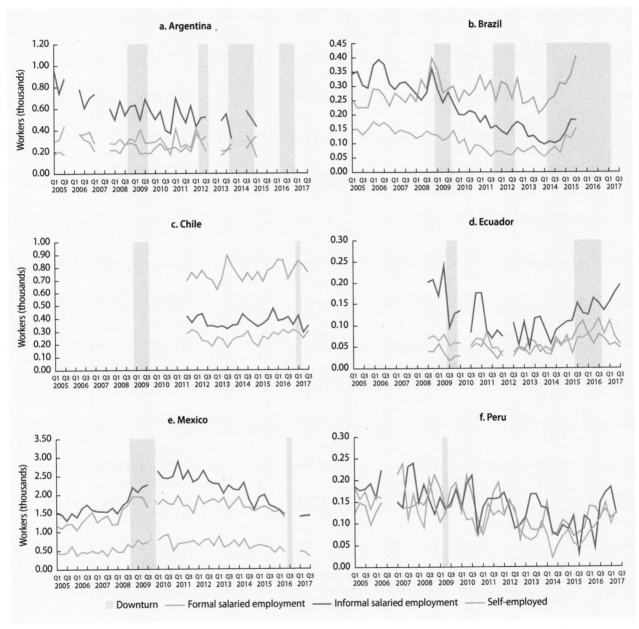

*Source:* Sousa 2021.
*Note:* This figure shows the quarterly numbers of workers experiencing job loss, defined as transitioning from employment to unemployment. The analysis is limited to full-time workers, and the trends are seasonally adjusted. The shaded areas labeled "downturn" represent quarters of negative gross domestic product growth according to estimates from national authorities.

TABLE 2.3  **Correlation of job loss across sectors**

| Country | Formal and informal wage work | Informal sector | |
|---------|------------------------------|------------------|---|
| | | Independent work | Informal wage work |
| Argentina | −0.094 | 0.167 | 0.277 |
| Brazil | 0.594 | 0.458 | 0.566 |
| Chile | 0.428 | −0.087 | 0.335 |
| Ecuador | 0.227 | 0.272 | 0.323 |
| Mexico | 0.402 | 0.022 | 0.355 |
| Peru | 0.136 | 0.519 | 0.082 |

*Source:* Sousa 2021.
*Note:* This table reports the correlation coefficients between seasonally adjusted detrended quarterly job loss flows, by sector of employment. The analysis is limited to full-time workers.

Figure 2.5 shows the lower net job finding rates in the formal sector across the six countries throughout the business cycle. That is, as a share of the workforce, new job growth is lower in the formal sector than in the informal sector.

## Job creation and job destruction during economic downturns

In the formal sector, decomposing the contributions of job creation and job destruction across small and large firms shows that employment adjustments are driven by lower job creation and higher volatility of employment in large firms. The employment response to crises by small firms is more muted. However, this difference between small and large firms goes away when firm births and deaths—which are substantially more common among small firms—are taken into account. The following analysis is done using administrative data sets from Brazil and Ecuador on repeated cross sections and employer panels with full longitudinal information. These data span the past four decades in Brazil and the past two decades in Ecuador and include several business cycles.

As shown in figure 2.6, a reduction in gross job creation is what drives lower employment in the formal sector during downturns in Brazil and Ecuador—job creation falls faster and more significantly than job destruction. Notably, during the recent

slowdown that hit commodity-exporting economies in South America beginning in 2015, gross job destruction surpassed gross job creation, resulting in a net destruction of formal employment. In other words, upon entering a period of slower growth, employers first stop generating new positions. As the downturn continues or worsens, they then begin to reduce overall employment (through layoffs, early retirements, or simply not filling vacant positions).[10] In contrast, during periods of growth, gross job creation exceeds gross job destruction as existing firms grow and new firms enter the labor market.

But how do different types of employers adjust across the business cycle? Literature from the OECD and other high-income countries has found significant differences in how small and large firms respond to crises, with implications for the quality of employment for workers. Moscarini and Postel-Vinay (2009, 2013) argue that less attractive firms (those that pay less or provide lower quality employment, often smaller firms) are better able to retain good workers during downturns because they face less competition for talent during those periods. This finding is consistent with Moscarini and Postel-Vinay (2012), who find that employment growth is more cyclical in large firms than in small firms across several high-income economies, a surprising result because small firms are more credit constrained. They also posit that large firms can poach workers from smaller

**FIGURE 2.5    Quarterly net job finding rates, formal and informal sectors, 2005–17**

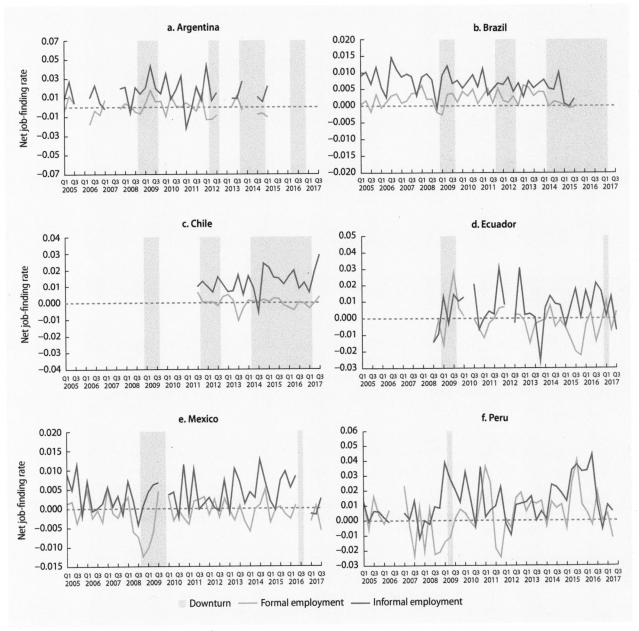

*Source:* Sousa 2021.
*Note:* This figure shows the net job finding rates for the formal and informal sectors, calculated as the quarterly job finding rate (the flow out of unemployment into the sector) minus the quarterly job loss rate (the flow from the sector into unemployment) as a share of employment in that sector. The analysis is limited to full-time jobs, and the net job finding rate is seasonally adjusted. The shaded areas labeled "downturn" represent quarters of negative gross domestic product growth according to estimates from national authorities.

FIGURE 2.6   **Gross job flows in Brazil and Ecuador, formal sector**

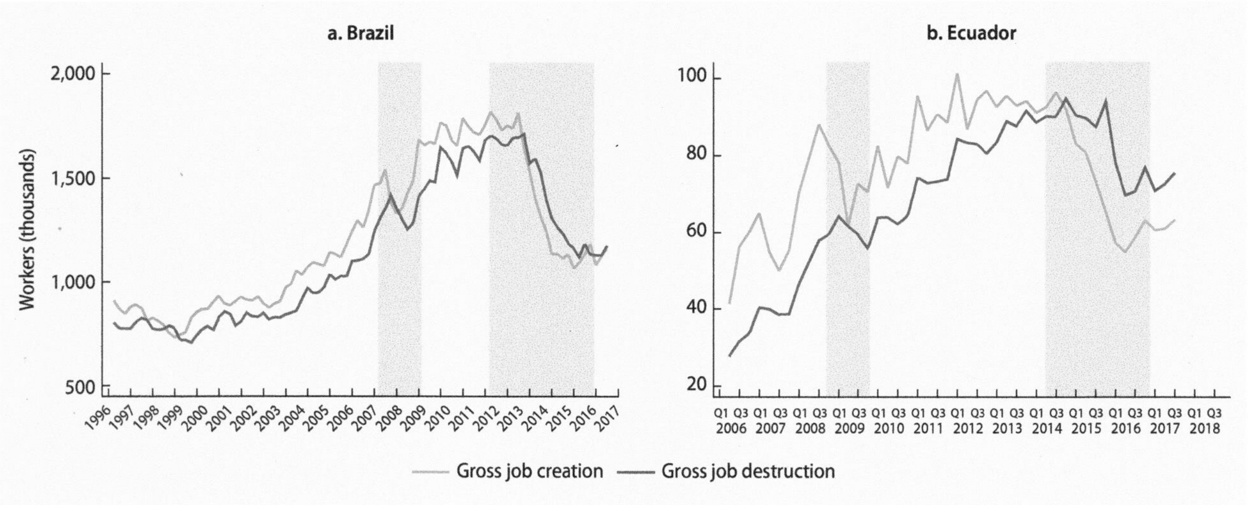

*Source:* Silva and Sousa 2021.
*Note:* This figure is based on a balanced panel of private sector firms. The shaded areas indicate economic downturns. Series are seasonally adjusted. In panel a, the data are from the first quarter of all years shown.

firms during high-growth periods, when labor markets are tight. Haltiwanger et al. (2018) find that large firms are more sensitive to unemployment levels than small firms in the United States. Additionally, they find evidence of a "cyclical firm wage ladder" wherein workers are more able to move to better employers (defined as firms that pay higher wages) during good times and less able during bad times.

Applying a similar empirical approach to formal sector employment information from Brazil and Ecuador, Silva and Sousa (2021) differentiate job creation and job destruction rates between large and small firms in the formal sector. Panels a and b of figure 2.7 show the gross job creation and job destruction rates of large and small firms in each country—in both countries, large firms increasingly account for more of gross job flows. This trend is partially by construction, because as large firms grow, they account for an increasing share of total employment (large firms account for 40 percent and 35 percent of formal employment in Brazil and Ecuador, respectively, and small firms account for 30 percent and 32 percent). Although the

magnitude of their effects differs, both types of firms follow broadly similar patterns in terms of job creation, suffering large swings across the business cycle.

To assess the relative contributions of large and small firms to overall unemployment, these gross job flows are converted into job creation and job destruction rates—calculated as total job creation or destruction as a share of employment. Panels c and d of figure 2.7 show the net job creation rates for large and small firms in Brazil and Ecuador.[11] They show that large firms exhibit particularly sharp peaks and valleys across the business cycle: that is, large firms are more cyclical in employment than small firms. Even taking into account their larger employment level, the fluctuations in the net employment of large firms are more responsive to demand factors than those of small firms.

Finally, this report applies the methodology of Moscarini and Postel-Vinay (2012) to estimate the differential gross job creation rate and differential gross job destruction rate between large and small firms. A positive differential rate indicates that large firms have higher rates (of job creation or job destruction) than small firms, while a negative differential rate indicates that large employers have lower rates. In accordance with the sharper peaks and valleys of employment in large firms, differential job creation rates in both Brazil and Ecuador show greater cyclicality in job creation for large firms (figure 2.7, panels e and f).

**FIGURE 2.7** **Gross job flows and differential rates in large and small firms in the formal sector**

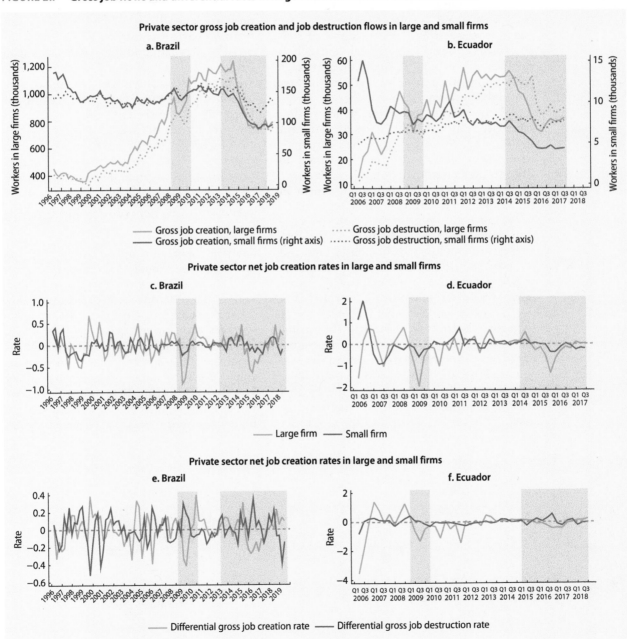

*Source:* Silva and Sousa 2021.
*Note:* This figure is based on a balanced panel of private sector firms. Small firm job flows are reported on the right axis in panels a and b. Firm size is defined each year: small firms are those with 20 or fewer employees, and large firms are those with more than 250 employees. The shaded areas indicate economic downturns. Series are seasonally adjusted. In panels a, c, and e, the data are from the first quarter of all years shown.

However, the mechanisms of job loss differ across countries, as is illustrated by the differential job destruction rates in Brazil and Ecuador. In Brazil, differential job destruction rates show significant variation. During downturns they are positive, reflecting higher job destruction rates in large firms than in small firms, and during recoveries they are negative, suggesting the opposite. In Ecuador, however, the differential job destruction rate is stable around 0, implying that large and small firms destroy jobs at similar rates across the business cycle.

Taken together, these results show that among formal firms, job losses are substantially higher for large firms than for small firms during downturns. In other words, in Brazil and Ecuador, employment in large firms is more cyclical than employment in small firms. However, deconstructing job flows into job creation and job destruction shows that the mechanisms underlying changes in employment in small firms and large firms differ across the two countries. In Brazil, large firms both create and destroy jobs at higher rates than small firms. In Ecuador, the higher employment response among large firms is driven by these firms' more dramatic swings in job creation over the course of the business cycle relative to small firms.

Large firms are thought to be more resilient than small firms, and, partially for this reason, to be better employers that provide more job security. This idea appears to be

contradicted by the results above: the biggest job losses in the formal sector are in large firms, in both absolute and relative terms. However, it is important to differentiate between firm resilience and job security. The results above do not take into account firm births and deaths. Births and deaths are disproportionately likely to happen among small firms (in part by construction, because firms often begin small and may gradually shrink before death). Once firm births and deaths are taken into account, the difference in job losses between large firms and small firms becomes less noticeable (figure 2.8). The lower resilience of small firms, exhibited by their higher fluctuations in deaths and births, explains a significant part of their fluctuations in net job creation during downturns.

## Job transitions across different types of workers

Another source of complexity in job creation and destruction trends is heterogeneity across workers. Because more experienced workers may be more productive and more expensive for firms to replace (Jovanovic 1979), losing workers with lower levels of human capital (including firm-specific human capital) would result in lower transaction costs for employers. For example, Robertson and Dutkowsky (2002) find that adjustment costs in the manufacturing sector in Mexico are higher for nonproduction workers (who are

FIGURE 2.8    **Net job creation rates in Brazil and Ecuador's formal sectors**

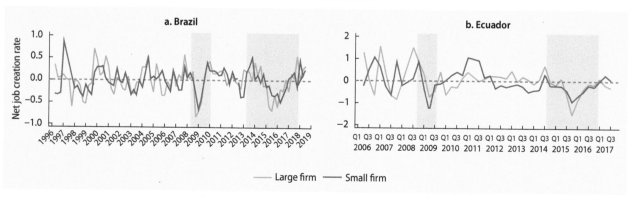

*Source:* Silva and Sousa 2021.
*Note:* This figure shows the net job creation rates in the private sector, including firm births and deaths. It is based on a balanced panel of private sector firms. The shaded areas indicate economic downturns. Series are seasonally adjusted. In panel a, the data are from the first quarter of all years shown.

typically higher-wage workers), workers with more job-specific training, and workers in more unionized sectors. As a result, when a firm experiences falling demand, lower-wage production workers are laid off at higher rates than these higher-wage workers.

This finding implies that quantitative adjustment will tend to take place through reductions in employment of workers with lower adjustment costs. In high-income economies, low-earning workers exit the labor force during downturns at disproportionate rates (Carneiro, Guimarães, and Portugal 2012; Solon, Barsky, and Parker 1994), and displacement is higher for low-skilled and young workers than for other types of workers (Devereux 2004; Teulings 1993). Research in LAC countries suggests that similar trends hold there. Studying the 2009 economic crisis in Mexico, Campos-Vazquez (2010) and Freije, López-Acevedo, and Rodrí-guez-Oreggia (2011) both find larger job loss rates for young and unskilled workers.

The LAC region's combination of large informal sectors and workers of varying skill levels suggests there may be a hierarchy in adjustment costs, in which informal workers, who have fewer job protections, face a greater likelihood of job loss regardless of skill. Among formal workers, lower-income workers would be more likely to experience job loss than higher-income workers. Indeed, in five of the six countries analyzed and across the business cycle, lower-wage workers are more likely to enter a spell of unemployment than higher-wage workers regardless of whether they are in the formal or informal sectors (figure 2.9). Mexico is the only exception: in that country, transitions into unemployment are higher in the middle of the wage distribution than at the bottom or the top.

However, low-skilled workers' increased likelihood of transitioning into unemployment does not indicate that their employment is more vulnerable to fluctuations in economic growth. Instead, cyclical employment transitions—those that are correlated with lagged economic growth—are more common among skilled workers than among unskilled workers. (See table 2A.1 of annex 2A.) This

result holds for both men and women. None of the job transitions analyzed was cyclical for low-skilled women in any of the six countries studied.

## A changing employment structure and the disappearance of good jobs

Crises translate into fewer job opportunities over time, beyond the business cycle (Artuc, Bastos, and Lee 2021). Crises reduce worker churning, that is, job-to-job flows, leading to a reduction in job match quality. The rationale for this effect is that when fewer job opportunities are available, workers are less able and less willing to leave their current jobs for new jobs. Using a structural model for Brazil, Artuc, Bastos and Lee (2021) find that adverse external shocks lower internal mobility across jobs, which in turn reduces worker welfare over the life of the worker.

Crises are also gradually shrinking the number of good job opportunities in the LAC region. This effect occurs because crises in the region do not just shape worker flows temporarily; they also have significant after-crisis effects on the structure of employment that last for several years (Regis and Silva 2021). In many macroeconomic studies of crises, the analysis focuses on short-term impacts, such as negative deviations in employment or real wages in the short run (concomitant or the following year). This focus is to be expected, given that direct measures on the basis of aggregate data at the national level from past crisis episodes are generally not available. Quarterly data on employment in LAC countries are available only from the late 1990s, and these data are not separated into formal and informal employment. Long monthly time series for employment are even more limited. An alternative strategy to measure longer-term effects would be to examine high-quality administrative data combined with national accounts. This was the path that Regis and Silva (2021) followed.

Regis and Silva (2021) investigate the longer-term effects of crises on jobs by compiling time series of total, formal, and informal employment dating back as far

FIGURE 2.9 **Quarterly share of workers entering unemployment per wage decile, formal and informal sectors, 2005–17**

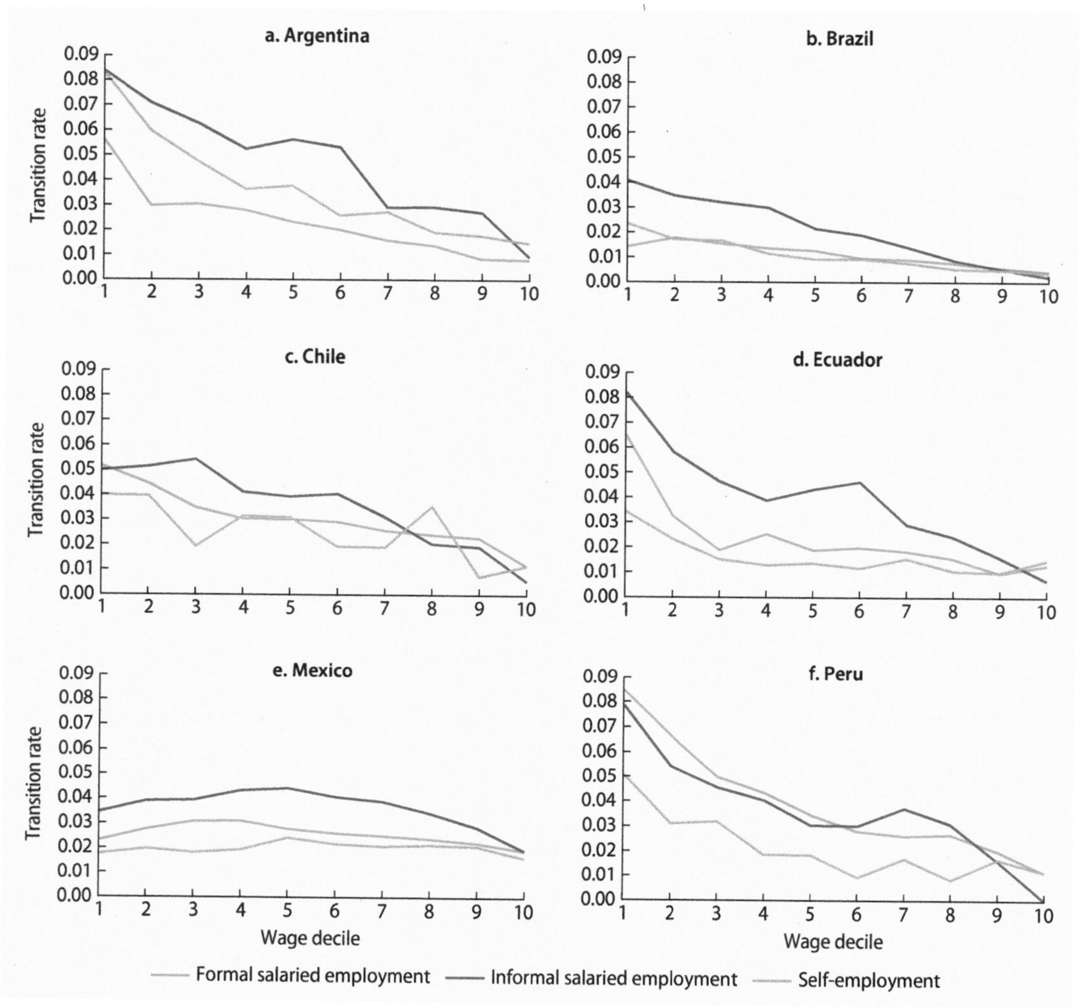

*Source:* Sousa 2021.
*Note:* The quarterly transition rate from employment to unemployment is defined as the share of workers employed in quarter t who transition into unemployment in quarter t+1.

as the 1980s for three countries: Brazil (1985–2019), Chile (2006–19), and Mexico (1994–2019). Following Jorda (2005) and Jorda, Singh, and Taylor (2020), the study estimates impulse response functions of total, formal, and informal employment to crises. The authors created a new monthly linked employer-employee database using annual administrative data from the social security records of each country (which include administrative longitudinal data on the countries' formal labor markets). To create these data, information on the months of hiring or

separation of each formal worker was used. Because these data cover all formal workers, the team took the employment series available from the national accounts, harmonized it across time with their database, and inferred, through the difference between the two, the countries' total informal employment.[12] In the context of this study, crises were defined on the basis of quarterly GDP for each country, which was standardized on the interval [0,1] (where 0 represents the deepest recession and 1 represents the largest expansion) and used to define the economy's long-run trend.

GDP was below or above its long-run trend as the cycle approached the values of 0 or 1, respectively. The business cycles thus defined were then used to obtain a recession dummy. Its duration corresponded to the time between the cycle's peak and trough.

This study has three key results. First, crises have caused multi-year reductions in employment in Brazil, Chile, and Mexico (figure 2.10). Second, in these three countries, formal employment is shrinking in a strong and lasting manner. It takes LAC economies multiple

**FIGURE 2.10  Impulse response functions, by type of employment, during the 30 months after the beginning of the recession**

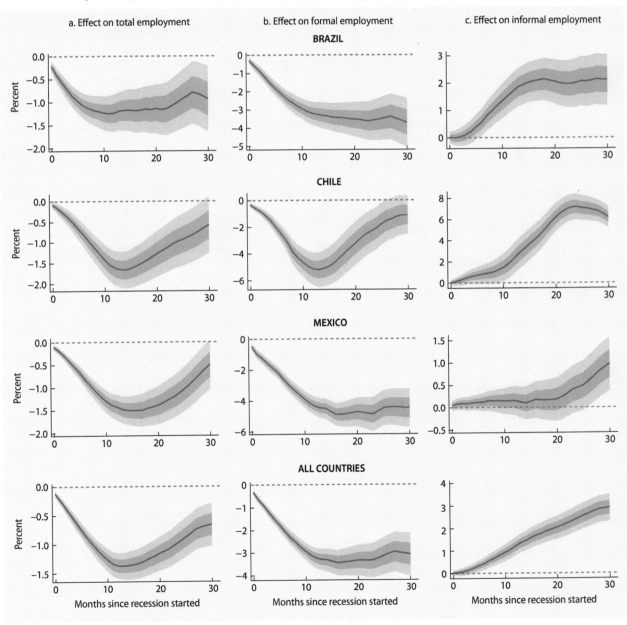

*Source:* Regis and Silva 2021.
*Note:* Lags are measured in months after the beginning of a crisis. Shaded areas correspond to the 95 percent confidence intervals (1.96 standard-error-bands, lighter blue) and 68 percent confidence intervals (1 standard-error-bands, darker blue) around response estimates.

years to recover from the contraction in formal employment induced by a crisis. In Brazil, more than 30 months after the beginning of a recession, formal employment remained well below its initial level and—especially concerning—showed little in the way of recovering. Overall employment remained lower for 20 months after the start of a recession, with signs of movement toward recovery only in Chile and Mexico; formal employment also remained lower for more than 20 months, with a recovery trend only in Chile; and informality remained higher, showing little in the way of reversal in Brazil or Chile. These findings suggest that exposure to sluggish labor markets not only moves people temporarily into informality but also leads to more fundamental structural changes. After a severe crisis, employment may not recover to what it had been before; the crisis may very well push the labor market into a new equilibrium. Third, whereas in Brazil and Chile informality works as a shock absorber in terms of employment from the outset of a crisis, this is not the case in Mexico, where informal employment stagnates for about 20 months before it starts to increase. The delayed effect on informality may be caused by formal workers looking for other formal work before eventually giving up and shifting to informality. Overall, after three years, the average recession in Brazil, Chile, and Mexico causes a net loss of 1.5 million jobs, with a 3% contraction of formal work and an expansion of the informal. The current crisis could be even worse and cause a contraction in formal employment of up to 4%.

This study's findings help us to rationalize the differences across the LAC countries in the lag between a change in output and its effect on the unemployment rate. In Colombia, unemployment exhibits a fast and elastic reaction to output shocks: on average, the unemployment rate decreases by 45 basis points following a 1 percent increase in output. In Brazil, unemployment is also sensitive to output shocks, but it reacts more slowly: on average, the unemployment rate decreases by 10 basis points following a 1 percent increase in output, but the accumulated change after one year is around 40 basis points. Unemployment in Argentina, Chile, and Peru, in contrast, is strongly inelastic to changes in output: the accumulated change after one year is 10 or fewer basis points (IMF 2019).

## Conclusion

The results presented in this chapter show that in general, and despite the presence of large informal sectors, unemployment is a significant margin of adjustment for labor markets in the LAC region during economic downturns. Although job loss is present in both the formal and informal sectors, a significant driver of unemployment is a slowdown in job creation in the formal sector. At the same time, there is evidence that the informal sector acts as a buffer for employment during downturns, absorbing workers who might otherwise enter the formal sector or become unemployed. A third potential margin of adjustment, reduction in hours, does not seem to be important in most countries in either the formal or informal sectors.

Economic crises impact workers' welfare not only through these margins of adjustment but also by reducing the number of job opportunities available. Fewer opportunities mean reduced churning, which in turn means lower-quality job matches. These inferior matches reduce the productivity growth and lifetime earnings of workers, resulting in real welfare reductions. Also, the impact of a crisis on the employment level can last long after the recession ends, and the crisis may cause permanent adjustments to the structure of employment in an economy.

This chapter exploited key sources of available data to provide empirical measures of labor market adjustments throughout the LAC region. The first section of the analysis was based on labor flows, using labor force survey data for six LAC countries (Argentina, Brazil, Chile, Ecuador, Mexico, and Peru), while the second and third sections featured analysis of monthly linked employer-employee databases that were newly developed for this study using information on the months of hiring or separation for individual workers in Brazil, Chile, Ecuador, and Mexico. Although the administrative data from the first section provide rich detail on worker flows and job destruction in the formal sector, the new survey data paint a broader picture of the full labor market, including the unemployed and the significant proportion of workers in the LAC region who work informally.

Because of the large amounts of data required for these analytics, many of the smaller or more impoverished countries in the LAC region cannot be included in this analysis. However, estimates of Okun's Law for a wider set of LAC countries show that the countries included in this analysis run the gamut of results in the region. The relationship between economic growth and unemployment rates varies widely across the region (figure 2.11). The estimate of Okun's Law is relatively high in Bolivia (–0.63) but close to 0 in neighboring Paraguay, while Chile and Jamaica have estimates comparable to that of the United States (–0.48) (Aguiar-Conraria, Martins, and Soares 2020; Ball, Leigh, and Loungani 2017). Although the lack of data prevents a detailed examination of the mechanisms of labor market adjustment in each of the LAC countries, the countries that are included in this chapter's

**FIGURE 2.11** **Estimates of Okun's Law for countries in the LAC region, 1991–2018**

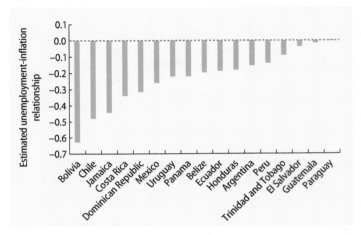

*Source:* Authors' calculations on the basis of IMF indicators.
*Note:* Okun's Law estimates represent the inverse relationship between inflation and unemployment. These estimates represent the slope of that relationship.

analysis, like Chile, Mexico, and Peru, can perhaps shed some light on the adjustment mechanisms in other countries in the region with similar Okun's Law values.

## Notes

1. These statistics are according to the Instituto Salvadoreño de Seguro Social and the Inter-American Development Bank Labor Market Observatory.
2. These statistics were computed by the authors using SEDLAC (Socio-Economic Database for Latin America and the Caribbean) data (World Bank and CEDLAS).
3. In this table and in subsequent figures, the standard measure of the cyclicality of a variable is used, which is the unconditional correlation of its deviations from the trend with a filtered measure of GDP. To detrend a series, we use a Hodrik-Prescott filter.
4. Indeed, research in high-income countries has found that job match quality is lower during downturns; that is, individuals take shorter-lasting and lower-paying jobs during such periods (Bowlus 1995), and employment reallocates to lower-paying industries and firms (Moscarini and Postel-Vinay 2012).
5. These values are for 2018 and are based on LAC Equity Lab tabulations using SEDLAC data (World Bank and CEDLAS).

6. Formal self-employment work is becoming more common in some countries in the LAC region, notably Brazil. However, this study combines such workers with informal dependent workers when discussing informality, because the vast majority of formal self-employed workers in the region do not pay taxes on their earnings, contribute to social security, or receive employment benefits.
7. As part of its response to the COVID-19 crisis, Brazil introduced a temporary wage subsidy program that allowed the reduction of hours for formal sector workers under certain conditions.
8. Brazil, Ecuador, and Peru show weaker correlations, with coefficients of 0.10, 0.15, and –0.14, respectively.
9. Okun's so-called Law gives the elasticity between unemployment and output. This elasticity is typically negative but less than one in absolute terms, which means that labor markets do not fully adjust to every shock in cyclical output in the first year after it occurs. A sensible explanation for this partial adjustment

is the expectation by employers that these cyclical changes are, by definition, temporary. Also, whereas this paper's results on cyclicality are derived from the analysis of individual-level transitions, Okun's Law simply compares the macro series of the unemployment rate with that of real GDP growth.

10. Lower job creation can also result from fewer firm births, and higher job destruction can also result from more firm deaths. Figure 2.5 is a balanced panel, so it does not include these effects, but the patterns of gross job creation and destruction are similar when using unbalanced panels in both countries.

11. Net job creation equals job creation minus job destruction as a share of employment.

12. Although this study reports results from the impulse response function to crises, it also covers the effects of other large exogenous shocks, including import growth among trading partners, changes in the terms of trade for commodities, and movements in the exchange rate.

## References

Abras, A., R. K. Almeida, P. Carneiro, and C. H. L. Corseuil. 2018. "Enforcement of Labor Regulations and Job Flows: Evidence from Brazilian Cities." *IZA Journal of Development and Migration* 8 (1).

Aguiar-Conraria, L., M. M. F. Martins, and M. J. Soares. 2020. "Okun's Law across Time and Frequencies." *Journal of Economic Dynamics and Control* 116.

Arias, J., E. Artuc, D. Lederman, and D. Rojas. 2018. "Trade, Informal Employment and Labor Adjustment Costs." *Journal of Development Economics* 133: 396–414.

Artuc, E., P. Bastos, and E. Lee. 2021. "Trade Shocks, Labor Mobility, and Welfare: Evidence from Brazil." World Bank, Washington, DC.

Ball, L., D. Leigh, and P. Loungani. 2017. "Okun's Law: Fit at 50?" *Journal of Money, Credit and Banking* 49 (7): 1413–41.

Belloc, F., and M. D'Antoni. 2020. "The Elusive Effect of Employment Protection on Labor Turnover." *Structural Change and Economic Dynamics* 54: 11–25.

Bosch, M., and J. Esteban-Pretel. 2012. "Job Creation and Job Destruction in the Presence of Informal Markets." *Journal of Development Economics* 98 (2): 270–86.

Bosch, M., and W. Maloney. 2008. "Cyclical Movements in Unemployment and Informality in Developing Countries." Policy Research Working Paper 4648, World Bank, Washington, DC.

Bosch, M., and W. F. Maloney. 2010. "Labor Dynamics in Developing Countries: Comparative Analysis using Markov Processes: An Application to Informality." *Labour Economics* 17 (4): 621–31.

Bowlus, A. J. 1995. "Matching Workers and Jobs: Cyclical Fluctuations in Match Quality." *Journal of Labor Economics* 13 (2): 335–50.

Campos-Vazquez, R. 2010. "The Effects of Macroeconomic Shocks on Employment: The Case of Mexico." *Estudios Economicos* 25 (1): 177–246.

Carneiro, A., P. Guimarães, and P. Portugal. 2012. "Real Wages and the Business Cycle: Accounting for Worker, Firm, and Job Title Heterogeneity." *American Economic Journal: Macroeconomics* 4 (2): 133–52.

Castellanos, S. G., R. Garcia-Verdu, and D. S. Kaplan. 2004. "Nominal Wage Rigidities in Mexico: Evidence from Social Security Records." *Journal of Development Economics* 75 (2): 507–33.

David, A., F. Lambert, and F. G. Toscani. 2019. "More Work to Do? Taking Stock of Latin American Labor Markets." IMF Working Paper 19/55, International Monetary Fund. https://www.imf.org/en/Publications/WP/Issues/2019/03/09/More-Work-to-Do-Taking-Stock-of-Latin-American-Labor-Markets-46661.

David, A. C., S. Pienknagura, and J. E. Roldos. 2020. "Labor Market Dynamics, Informality and Regulations in Latin America." IMF Working Paper 20/19, International Monetary Fund. https://www.imf.org/en/Publications/WP/Issues/2020/01/31/Labor-Market-Dynamics-Informality-and-Regulations-in-Latin-America-48893.

Davis, S., and J. Haltiwanger. 1992. "Gross Job Creation, Gross Job Destruction, and Employment Reallocation." *Quarterly Journal of Economics* 107 (3): 819–63.

Devereux, P. J. 2004. "Cyclical Quality Adjustment in the Labor Market." *Southern Economic Journal* 70 (3): 600–15.

Dix-Carneiro, R., and B. K. Kovak. 2019. "Margins of Labor Market Adjustment to Trade." *Journal of International Economics* 117: 125–42.

Elsby, M. W., B. Hobijn, and A. Sahin. 2013. "Unemployment Dynamics in the OECD."

*Review of Economics and Statistics* 95 (2): 530–48.

Erten, B., J. Leight, and F. Tregenna. 2019. "Trade Liberalization and Local Labor Market Adjustment in South Africa." *Journal of International Economics* 118: 448–67.

Freije, S., G. López-Acevedo, and E. Rodríguez-Oreggia. 2011. "Effects of the 2008–09 Economic Crisis on Labor Markets in Mexico." Policy Research Working Paper 5840, World Bank, Washington, DC.

Haltiwanger, J. C., H. R. Hyatt, L. B. Kahn, and E. McEntarfer. 2018. "Cyclical Job Ladders by Firm Size and Firm Wage." *American Economic Journal: Macroeconomics* 10 (2): 52–85.

IMF (International Monetary Fund). 2019. *Regional Economic Outlook: Stunted by Uncertainty.* https://www.imf.org/en /Publications/REO/WH/Issues/2019/10/22 /wreo1019.

Jaramillo, M., and H. Nopo. 2020. "COVID-19 and External Shock: Economic Impacts and Policy Options." COVID-19 Policy Document 5, United Nations Development Program in Latin America and the Caribbean, New York.

Jorda, O. 2005. "Estimation and Inference of Impulse Responses by Local Projections." *American Economic Review* 95 (1): 161–82.

Jorda, O., S. R. Singh, and A. M. Taylor. 2020. "Longer-Run Economic Consequences of Pandemics." Working Paper 26934, National Bureau of Economic Research, Cambridge, MA.

Jovanovic, B. 1979. "Job Matching and the Theory of Turnover." *Journal of Political Economy* 87 (5): 972–90.

Kaur, S. 2019. "Nominal Wage Rigidity in Village Labor Markets." *American Economic Review* 109 (10): 3585–3616.

Liu, Y. 2018. "Job Creation and Destruction in Japan: Evidence from Division-Level Employment Data." *Journal of Asian Economics* 58: 59–71.

Maloney, W. F. 1999. "Does Informality Imply Segmentation in Urban Labor Markets? Evidence from Sectoral Transitions in Mexico." *World Bank Economic Review* 13 (2): 275–302.

Moscarini, G., and F. Postel-Vinay. 2009. "Large Employers Are More Cyclically Sensitive."

Working Paper 14740, National Bureau of Economic Research, Cambridge, MA.

Moscarini, G., and F. Postel-Vinay. 2012. "The Contribution of Large and Small Employers to Job Creation in Times of High and Low Unemployment." *American Economic Review* 102 (6): 2509–39.

Moscarini, G., and F. Postel-Vinay. 2013. "Stochastic Search Equilibrium." *Review of Economic Studies* 80 (4): 1545–81.

Ochieng, H. K., and B. Park. 2017. "The Heterogeneity of Job Creation and Destruction in Transition and Non-Transition Developing Countries: The Effects of Firm Size, Age and Ownership." *East Asian Economic Review* 21 (4): 385–432.

Regis, P., and J. Silva. 2021. "Employment Dynamics: Timeline and Myths of Economic Recovery." World Bank, Washington, DC.

Robertson, R., and D. H. Dutkowsky. 2002. "Labor Adjustment Costs in a Destination Country: The Case of Mexico." *Journal of Development Economics* 67 (1): 29–54.

Shimer, R. 2005. "The Cyclical Behavior of Equilibrium Unemployment and Vacancies." *American Economic Review* 95 (1): 25–49.

Silva, J., and L. Sousa. 2021. "Job Creation and Destruction in Small and Large Firms in Brazil and Ecuador." World Bank, Washington, DC.

Solon, G., R. Barsky, and J. A. Parker. 1994. "Measuring the Cyclicality of Real Wages: How Important Is Composition Bias?" *Quarterly Journal of Economics* 109 (1): 1–25.

Sousa, L. 2021. "Economic Shocks and Employment Adjustments in Latin America." World Bank, Washington, DC.

Taskin, T. 2013. "Intensive Margin and Extensive Margin Adjustments of Labor Market: Turkey versus United States." *Economics Bulletin* 33 (3): 2307–19.

Teulings, C. 1993. "The Diverging Effects of the Business Cycle on the Expected Duration of Job Search." *Oxford Economic Papers* 45: 482–500.

Van Rens, T. 2012. "How Important Is the Intensive Margin of Labor Adjustment? Discussion of Aggregate Hours Worked in OECD Countries: New Measurement and Implications for Business Cycles by Lee Ohanian and Andrea Raffo." *Journal of Monetary Economics* 59 (1): 57–63.

## Annex 2A: Additional analysis of employment transitions

FIGURE 2A.1  **Quarterly net flows into part-time work, formal and informal sectors, 2005–17**

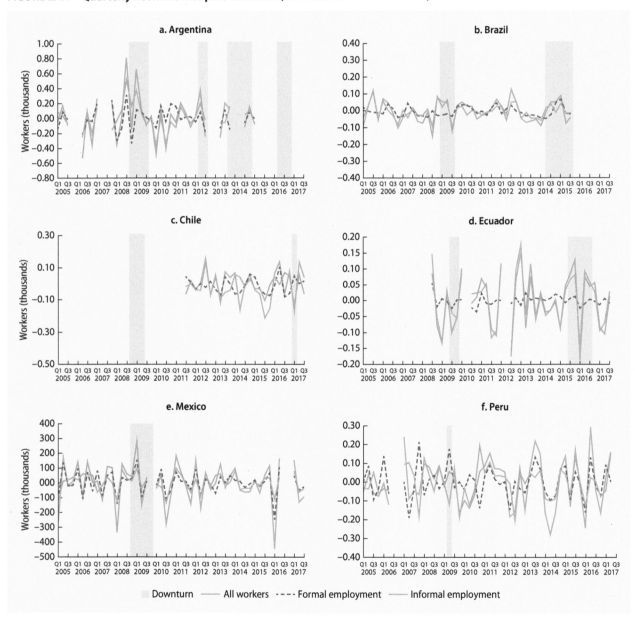

*Source:* Sousa 2021.
*Note:* These panels show the cyclical components of net flows into part-time work (the number of workers moving from full-time to part-time work minus the number of workers moving from part-time to full-time work) among workers employed in formal dependent employment or informal employment (dependent or self-employed). This analysis is limited to workers who did not transition between formality and informality at the same time as they transitioned from part-time to full-time work and who did not change sectors. Flows are estimated as the number of workers who transitioned between two consecutive quarters of observation. The cyclical component is estimated with seasonal adjustments and a Hodrik-Prescott filter. The shaded areas labeled "downturn" represent quarters of negative gross domestic product growth according to estimates from national authorities.

**TABLE 2A.1    Cyclicality of employment transitions, by gender and skill level**

| Country | Initial state | Final state | Women | | Men | |
|---|---|---|---|---|---|---|
| | | | High-skilled | Low-skilled | High-skilled | Low-skilled |
| Argentina | Formal | Informal | 0.19 | 0.12 | 0.17 | 0.14 |
| | Formal | Unemployed | −0.04 | −0.01 | −0.06 | −0.15 |
| | Informal | Formal | 0.09 | 0.23 | 0.45 | 0.93* |
| | Informal wage | Formal | 0.09 | 0.31 | 0.41 | 0.71 |
| | Informal wage | Unemployed | −0.34 | −0.29 | −0.69** | 0.09 |
| | Self-employed | Formal | 0.08 | −0.02 | 0.22 | 0.81* |
| | Self-employed | Unemployed | 0.40 | 0.17 | −0.33 | −0.41 |
| Brazil | Formal | Informal | 0.29 | 0.19 | 0.30 | 0.15 |
| | Formal | Unemployed | 0.02 | 0.05 | −0.22* | −0.20 |
| | Informal | Formal | 0.86** | 0.80 | 0.60* | 0.93* |
| | Informal wage | Formal | 0.94 | 0.93 | 0.28 | 0.94 |
| | Informal wage | Unemployed | −0.10 | −0.41 | −0.28 | −0.04 |
| | Self-employed | Formal | 0.88** | 0.80 | 0.78** | 0.77 |
| | Self-employed | Unemployed | −0.01 | 0.09 | −0.29* | −0.11 |
| Chile | Formal | Informal | 0.13 | 0.00 | −0.72 | −0.23 |
| | Formal | Unemployed | 0.22 | 0.58 | −0.03 | −0.13 |
| | Informal | Formal | 1.14 | 1.25 | 0.33 | 1.03 |
| | Informal wage | Formal | 0.27 | 0.78 | 0.53 | 1.15 |
| | Informal wage | Unemployed | −0.09 | −0.65 | 0.69 | 0.44 |
| | Self-employed | Formal | 2.43 | 2.45 | 0.51 | 1.66 |
| | Self-employed | Unemployed | −0.53 | −0.73 | 0.95 | 0.87 |
| Ecuador | Formal | Informal | 0.12 | 0.72 | −1.25 | 0.29 |
| | Formal | Unemployed | −0.58 | −0.79 | 0.14 | 0.16 |
| | Informal | Formal | 0.47 | 0.40 | −0.33 | −0.53 |
| | Informal wage | Formal | 0.62 | 0.08 | −0.03 | −0.82 |
| | Informal wage | Unemployed | 0.34 | −0.93 | 0.33 | −0.75 |
| | Self-employed | Formal | −0.09 | −0.21 | −0.20 | −0.08 |
| | Self-employed | Unemployed | −0.27 | 0.10 | 0.08 | −0.07 |
| Mexico | Formal | Informal | −0.11 | −0.44 | 0.22 | −0.17 |
| | Formal | Unemployed | −0.38** | 0.02 | −0.19 | 0.07 |
| | Informal | Formal | 0.17 | 0.25 | 0.86*** | 1.04** |
| | Informal wage | Formal | −0.06 | 0.28 | 0.72** | 0.90 |
| | Informal wage | Unemployed | −0.10 | −0.14 | −0.47** | −0.06 |
| | Self-employed | Formal | 0.29 | 0.86 | 0.59* | 0.71 |
| | Self-employed | Unemployed | 0.00 | −0.40 | 0.00 | −0.34 |

*table continues next page*

**TABLE 2A.1   Cyclicality of employment transitions, by gender and skill level *(Continued)***

| Country | Initial state | Final state | Women | | Men | |
|---|---|---|---|---|---|---|
| | | | High-skilled | Low-skilled | High-skilled | Low-skilled |
| Peru | Formal | Informal | 1.71 | 2.83 | 2.65** | 1.78 |
| | Formal | Unemployed | 0.67 | 0.80 | 0.09 | −0.07 |
| | Informal | Formal | −0.48 | −1.27 | −1.26 | −1.32 |
| | Informal wage | Formal | −1.27 | −1.65 | −1.18 | −0.88 |
| | Informal wage | Unemployed | 0.86 | 0.98 | 1.37 | 0.29 |
| | Self-employed | Formal | 0.48 | −0.23 | −0.90 | −0.86 |
| | Self-employed | Unemployed | 0.63 | 0.52 | −0.55 | 0.06 |

*Source:* Sousa 2021.
*Note:* This table shows the coefficients of an ordinary least squares regression of quarterly transition rates on lagged gross domestic product growth rate, by gender and skill group. "Low-skilled" workers have secondary education or less, and "high-skilled" workers have tertiary or higher education. Transition rates are defined as the share of workers with one type of employment in quarter t who transitioned into another type of employment in quarter t+1.
Significance level: * = 90 percent, ** = 95 percent, *** = 99 percent.

# The Impact on Workers, Firms, and Places | 3

## Introduction

The previous chapter showed how crises in Latin America and the Caribbean (LAC) change aggregate employment dynamics and the employment structure. Crises lead to higher unemployment (more than they lead to increases in informality), with particularly prominent job losses in the formal sector. As good job opportunities shrink, the overall economic structure is altered. Job loss caused by crises is particularly painful in the LAC region because of its sluggish recovery processes. The region's slow job creation depends on demand-side factors, like firms and locations, not just on workers. Although the evidence presented thus far suggests that crises have detrimental impacts at the aggregate level, how severe are their impacts on individual workers? How do sectors and firms adjust employment and wages in response to crises? Which margins of adjustment are used, beyond shedding jobs, and what are their medium- to long-run effects on efficiency? And how do the characteristics of localities shape crisis impacts?

These questions are important to the LAC region's crisis response agenda, particularly because of their long-lasting implications.

If unemployment is persistent, the associated human capital decay will be greater and will lead to a larger decrease in long-term growth potential. Notwithstanding the size of a shock, if its effects are largely heterogeneous across workers, with some losing much more than others, targeting scarce support toward the workers who lose the most may yield larger gains. The stakes are very high for Latin America in terms of not only growth potential but also social stability; some recent studies have linked job displacement with rising violence (Dell, Feigenberg, and Teshima 2019). Furthermore, the previous chapter showed that quantitative adjustments to crises affect lower-skilled workers more than higher-skilled workers. Scarring can amplify this effect, further eroding the earnings of lower-skilled workers and increasing inequality in an already highly unequal region.

Crises can decrease individual welfare, but they can also increase efficiency in the short and medium run. During a crisis, employer-employee matches and the job-specific human capital arising from them, which often take a long time to build and would regain viability when the economy goes back to normal, may be permanently dissolved because of the temporary shock. This loss may slow the ramping up of production later on, and it implies a loss in productivity. However, job loss spurred by an economic crisis can also have an important cleansing effect and lead to increased productivity at both the firm and market levels. It can be a good thing—provided that new jobs are created after the crisis is over.

This chapter begins with a careful characterization of the scarring caused by involuntary and exogenous job loss—that is, job loss unrelated to the worker's performance or preferences—by looking at the long-term wage losses of displaced workers following firm closures. The literature on the LAC region finds large, short-run effects of such displacements; for example, Amarante, Arim, and Dean (2014) find wage losses in excess of 14 percent one year after job separation for high-tenure Uruguayan workers. Arias-Vázquez, Lederman, and Venturi (2019) add to this growing literature, finding large and long-lasting wage effects of displacement caused by firm closure. Two years after the closure of a plant, wages tend to be 11 percent lower for displaced workers than for nondisplaced workers. Four years after the closure, the wage gap is 6 percent. Wages do not fully recover until nine years later.

Next, this chapter considers the scarring caused by the initial conditions faced by new entrants into the labor force in the LAC region. It considers whether there are long-term employment and wage consequences of entering the labor market during a downturn, generating what the popular press calls "a lost generation." This question is particularly salient for the LAC region, given its high rates of youth unemployment and its investments in increasing and improving educational outcomes at the secondary and tertiary levels. Are these investments in the region's human capital stock undermined by frequent crises? Previous research that has found evidence of long-term effects of economic downturns on labor market entrants has focused on high-income economies.[1] Studies of countries such as Japan, Sweden, and the United States find evidence of negative long-term wage effects for new graduates.

But to what extent do these results apply to labor markets in the LAC region, where the share of college-educated workers is far smaller and where informality continues to be a significant employment option? Moreno and Sousa (2021) estimate the extent of the scarring caused by the initial labor conditions new entrants face in the first decade of their working lives in four Latin American economies. Their findings confirm that entering the labor market during a crisis does have long-term consequences in the LAC region. However, this scarring is found in employment outcomes (lower participation rates, higher unemployment rates, and higher likelihood of informality) rather than in a long-term effect on earnings, and it is most prominent among workers with only secondary education. Similarly, Fernandes and Silva (2021) find stronger scarring effects in employment and wage outcomes for lower-skilled workers than for higher-skilled workers in the formal sector in Brazil and Ecuador. One explanation for this effect is that competition is lower for skilled jobs because of the relative scarcity of college graduates in the LAC region. That is, the analysis suggests that scarring is likely exacerbating the region's high level of wage inequality.

Switching gears to consider efficiency, this chapter shows that there are three main ways in which LAC firms and sectors adjust to crises that can alter their efficiency in the long term. First, worker adjustment varies depending on workers' employer or firm characteristics: workers for larger, better-managed firms cope better with crisis effects (Fernandes and Silva 2021). This finding has implications for firms' productivity and labor demand. In the LAC region, the adjustment mechanisms to crises include cleansing effects; scarring, which reflects a lack of opportunities; and shocks to distortions that led to rents, with potential positive effects on efficiency in the long run.

In addition, the results presented in this chapter lead to questions about how institutional and market factors external to workers affect scarring and, in general, long-run prospects for job recovery. The chapter's results show that employment in protected firms, defined as those that face less competition, is less affected by crises than is employment in less-protected firms. In sectors where a few firms hold a large percentage of the market, shocks do not lead to any downward real wage adjustments. Instead, they can lead to increases in employment, the opposite of what normal economic mechanisms would bring about. By the same logic, employment responds less to negative export shocks in state-owned firms than in private-owned firms.

The chapter closes by considering the third piece of the triangle, places. Findings indicate that workers in less formal localities cope better in the wake of crises than workers from other localities. The presence of a large informal sector may protect some workers against shocks. For instance, this study finds smaller employment and wage losses in response to crises for formal, private sector workers who live in localities with higher rates of informality (Fernandes and Silva 2021). This finding suggests that informality can be an important buffer for employment in the medium to long run, when workers may transition from unemployment to informality; such an effect was shown by Dix-Carneiro and Kovak (2019) in the case of adjustment to trade liberalization. Indeed, transitions from unemployment to informality are two times more likely in the Brazilian data than transitions from unemployment to formality.

Finally, findings indicate that workers in localities with more (alternative) job opportunities bounce back better from crises. Losses in employment (and sometimes wages) for formal workers are larger and longer-lasting in localities with larger primary sectors, smaller service sectors, fewer large firms, and production highly concentrated in the same sector where the workers were employed before the crisis (Fernandes and Silva 2021). In such cases, these workers' persistent losses of earnings may reflect the lack of opportunities for them in the rebound, not just scarring in the traditional sense of a persistent loss of human capital associated with a period of unemployment or lower-quality employment.

## Workers: A bigger toll on the unskilled

The goal of this section is to improve understanding of the long-term implications of crises for workers in the LAC region. A primary focus of the chapter is characterizing the incidence and magnitude of labor scarring in the region. Scarring refers to the long-run effects of job loss on a worker's earnings through the decay of the worker's human capital and changes in the worker's quality of employment. Since the lasting wage effects of job losses were first documented in the United States by Jacobson, LaLonde, and Sullivan (1993a, 1993b), studies from around the world have found that the wage effects of losing a job are long-lasting. Decay of human capital and reallocation of workers and firms across sectors are two important channels through which crises can have long-term implications on the welfare and economic growth prospects of the LAC region.

This section answers two sets of questions. First, how extensive is scarring in Latin America and the Caribbean, and what forms does it take? The section looks at scarring across three dimensions that can cause it: job loss, worse initial conditions at workforce entry, and crisis-driven adjustment. And second, how does scarring vary across different types of workers?

Scarring implies a reduction in human capital and worker productivity, leading to worse employment outcomes and lower wages over time. Human capital can be thought of as taking two forms. General human capital includes skills that are valuable in many sectors of the economy (such as general education, literacy, and some computer skills). Specific human capital is related to a specific industry or firm and is generated through employment experience and on-the-job training that make a worker more productive in that firm or industry. Scarring results from a decay of either (or both) of these types of human capital. When workers lose their jobs, they lose the firm-specific skills and relationships they had learned and built in those jobs. Burdett, Carrillo-Tudela, and Coles (2020) find that lost human capital is the most important factor in determining the costs of job loss to workers, but Carrington and Fallick (2017) suggest that additional research is necessary to assess the extent of this factor's contribution.

However, scarring does not strictly require job loss. To the extent that on-the-job training and experience generate human capital, keep existing human capital from eroding, and signal a worker's quality to other employers, the quality of workers' early job matches can have significant effects on their human capital accumulation and career trajectories. Workers who first enter labor markets in bad times have been shown to have lower earnings than otherwise similar workers who first enter labor markets in good times.

This section reviews the literature and reports the results of two new background papers, developed in the context of this flagship research project, on labor market scarring in Latin America. Two of the papers use matched worker-firm data to look at scarring following job loss and scarring caused by firms' exposure to crises. The third uses labor force surveys to look at scarring beyond those employed in the formal sector and consider how conditions at the time of entry into the labor market impact workers' employment outcomes over the first decade of their working lives.

This section also examines whether different types of workers are affected in different ways by crises. Scarring-based losses will not be incurred by every worker; rather, they will be concentrated among certain groups of workers. This section identifies some of those groups, who merit special attention from policy makers in order to reduce the economic and social costs of crises. Understanding the differences in responses to crises across types of workers is important, because it allows governments to target support where it is needed most.

## Severity of long-term effects

### Scarring caused by job loss

Losing a job has significant costs in the short term and the long term. The earliest studies on this topic focused on the United States.

Jacobson, LaLonde, and Sullivan (1993a, 1993b) show that US workers incur prolonged periods of lost wages after losing their jobs. They also demonstrate that a sample of workers in Pennsylvania experienced losses of approximately 25 percent of their predisplacement earnings that lingered for five to six years after the loss of their jobs (Jacobson, LaLonde, and Sullivan 1993a). Other studies find the same phenomenon in other countries.[2] Longer or more frequent spells of unemployment have larger negative wage consequences (Arulampalam 2001; Gregg and Tominey 2005; Gregory and Jukes 2001). In addition, scarring from job loss can last across generations. Oreopoulos, Page, and Stevens (2008) find that Canadian sons whose fathers were displaced had annual earnings 9 percent lower than those of similar children whose fathers did not experience similar employment shocks. However, most of the research in this area has focused on developed countries.

One of the more arresting symptoms of economic crises is mass layoffs caused by firm closures. Looking at mass layoff events helps address the potential endogeneity of workers who leave firms voluntarily, because the reason for leaving a firm (even in the context of a mass layoff) has a significant effect on subsequent earnings and employment (Flaaen, Shapiro, and Sorkin 2019). However, there are surprisingly few studies on scarring of displaced workers following firm closures in Latin America. Amarante, Arim, and Dean (2014) and Kaplan, González, and Robertson (2007), studying Uruguay and Mexico, respectively, are important exceptions. Amarante, Arim, and Dean (2014) find wage losses in excess of 14 percent one year after job separation for high-tenure Uruguayan workers. The reduction in wages is even greater for workers who separated during downturns. In Mexico, Kaplan, González, and Robertson (2007) use administrative matched firm-worker data to follow workers who left firms during "mass layoffs"—events in which a large share of the firms' employment leaves the firms. They find large reductions in wages for these workers and greater reductions for workers who separated during downturns.

Building on this approach, Arias-Vázquez, Lederman, and Venturi (2019), in a background analysis for this report, find that workers who were displaced from their jobs when their plants closed suffered large and long-lasting wage losses. They use Mexican data from 2005 to 2017 (retrospective information on employment at the worker level from Mexico's National Survey of Occupation and Employment) that allow them to identify job losses resulting from firm closures. Their results indicate that it took an average of 10 years for workers who were displaced by a plant closing to recover their wages. This period is significantly longer than the average recovery period for workers who voluntarily quit (three years) or for workers who closed their own businesses (four years). Figure 3.1 illustrates the magnitude and duration of the impact of a plant closing on the real wages of displaced workers compared with nondisplaced workers. Initially, in their first two years after displacement, wages are 11 percent lower for the displaced workers than for nondisplaced workers. The wage gap narrows to 6 percent after the fourth year following the plant closing, and the displaced workers' wages recover completely only after ten years.

### Scarring caused by entering the labor market during a downturn

As mentioned earlier in this chapter, scarring does not strictly require job loss. To the extent that on-the-job training and experience generate human capital, keep existing human capital from eroding, and signal a worker's quality to other employers, the quality of workers' early job matches can have significant effects on their human capital accumulation and career trajectories. In this way, young workers may be especially vulnerable to the impacts of crises on local labor markets, because entering the labor market is more difficult in bad times and doing so has long-term effects on earnings (Hardoy and Schone 2013).

Workers who first enter labor markets in bad times have been shown to have lower earnings than otherwise similar workers who first enter labor markets in good times (as shown by Brunner and Kuhn [2014] for

Austria and Kahn [2010] for the United States). Liu, Salvanes, and Sørensen (2016) find that the mechanism behind these long-term negative effects for college-educated workers is cyclical skill mismatch—that is, the dearth of job opportunities when these workers enter the job market leads them to accept worse employment matches. The study finds that the match quality of these workers' first jobs explains most of their losses of long-term earnings from graduating in a recession.

There is scant research on the scarring of new labor force entrants in the LAC region. Cruces, Ham, and Viollaz (2012) use pseudopanels and birth cohorts to find a strong but short-lived negative impact on wages for Brazilian workers exposed to downturns early in their labor market experience. Martinoty (2016) finds that downturns lead to changes in the composition of youth employment (because some youth choose to remain in education longer). All education groups who enter the labor market during a downturn show evidence of long-term scarring.

To build more evidence on the topic of scarring in the LAC region, Moreno and

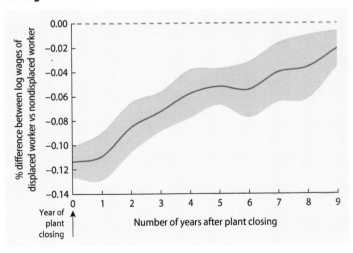

FIGURE 3.1    **Effect on wages of displacement caused by plant closings in Mexico**

*Source:* Arias-Vázquez, Lederman, and Venturi 2019.
*Note:* This figure plots the percentage difference between the log wages of displaced workers and nondisplaced workers (i.e., the estimated coefficient on the lagged displacement variable) on the vertical axis against the year since job displacement on the horizontal axis (where 0 is the year in which the plant closed). The solid line plots the coefficients (the wage gap). The dotted lines plot the 95 percent confidence intervals. Standard errors are clustered at the state level. All regressions control for years of education, gender, marital status, age, age squared, state, survey period, and industry fixed effects.

FIGURE 3.2 **Unemployment rates by cohort, Argentina and Colombia**

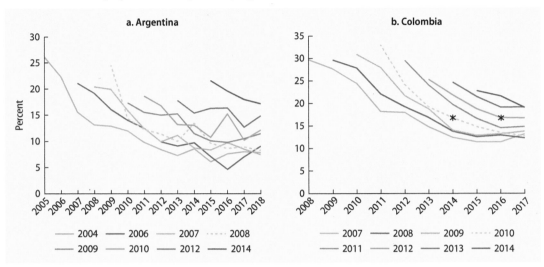

*Source:* Moreno and Sousa 2021.
*Note:* This figure reports national unemployment rates by year of entering the labor market. The stars on the lines for the 2010 and 2012 cohorts in Colombia show their unemployment rates four years after entry.

Sousa (2021) test for cohort effects on labor market outcomes related to the economic conditions during the year of entry into the labor force. Figure 3.2 shows the unemployment rates for cohorts in their first years of labor market participation in Argentina and Colombia. Initial unemployment levels differed noticeably across these cohorts: Colombian youth entering the labor market in 2010 faced significantly higher unemployment rates than those entering in 2012. The figure also illustrates that this difference can continue for years after entry. The 2010 cohort did not catch up to the 2012 cohort's lower unemployment rate until four years after entering the labor market.

Following the methodology of Genda, Kondo, and Ohta (2010), Moreno and Sousa (2021) exploit spatial and temporal variations in local unemployment rates at the time a cohort enters the labor market. By using repeated cross-sections and subnational unemployment rates, the same cohort is observed over time and across different initial labor market conditions. Because this methodology relies on survey data, it can be used to consider informality as an outcome, which is not possible when using administrative records.

Across the four countries with subnational series long enough to use for this analysis—Argentina, Brazil, Colombia, and Mexico—Moreno and Sousa (2021) find that initial employment conditions can lead to scarring, which is experienced as a combination of higher unemployment, lower labor market participation, and higher informality, depending on the country. However, their results do not reflect significant scarring through wage effects; such effects are noticeable only in the first three years of labor market participation and only for specific subsets of workers (Brazilian women and low-skilled Mexican men). Figure 3.3 presents the results for low-skilled workers in Mexico. In Mexico, new entrants with only secondary education who enter the labor market during worse periods have lower participation rates and potentially higher rates of discouragement, as suggested by the combination of lower participation and a lower unemployment rate. This result continues for these workers' first

**FIGURE 3.3** **Employment and wage effects of higher local unemployment at labor market entry in Mexico**

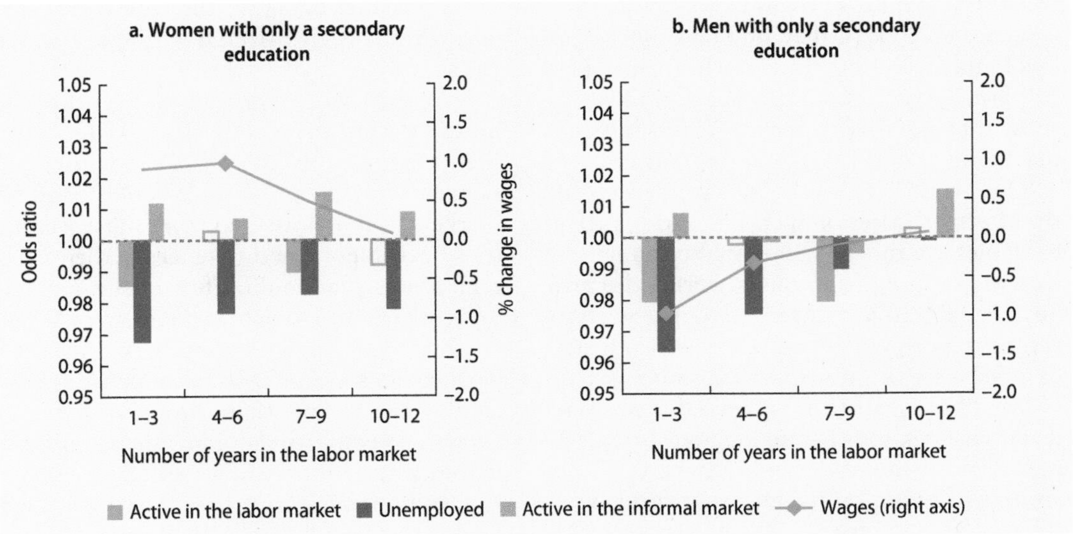

Source: Moreno and Sousa 2021.
Note: The logistic odds ratio is reported for binary outcomes, and Heckman coefficients are reported for log wages. The solid bars (and solid dots) indicate that the corresponding coefficient is statistically significant. The standard errors are calculated by bootstrapping (rep = 50) and are clustered by year and region. The model used includes individual characteristics and fixed effects for region, cohort, and year. The open bars and portions of line without a solid dot are not statistically significant.

nine years in the labor market. Interestingly, despite a significant difference in labor force participation rates between men and women in Mexico, this result holds for both groups.

The results for Mexico also show higher rates of informality in later years for workers who enter the labor market during a downturn. This same result is found in Colombia and for some types of workers in Brazil. Although, as discussed in the previous chapter, informality is not necessarily an inferior employment option in the LAC region, this result echoes the theory mentioned earlier that informality serves as a buffer for employment during economic crises. One role of that buffer is to absorb new entrants into the labor market who might, in better times, find formal employment. By contrast, in Argentina, informality rates for men who enter the labor market during downturns are lower and unemployment rates are higher, suggesting that informality is not an effective buffer for this group.

### Scarring passed through from crisis-affected firms

Most of the existing research on scarring focuses on the overall effects of displacements in both good and bad economic times. However, there are many reasons to suspect that displacement during a crisis may not have the same effects as displacement during better times. This distinction is particularly relevant to the LAC region, where crises are frequent. Davis and von Wachter (2011) find that earnings losses from job displacement are higher in recessions than in expansions, and Amarante, Arim, and Dean (2014) find larger wage reductions for workers who separated during downturns than for other workers. McCarthy and Wright (2018) find that Irish workers who lost their jobs during the global financial crisis of 2008–09 incurred much larger and long-lasting earnings losses than workers who lost their jobs between 2005 and 2007. Focusing on the US labor market, Carrington (1993); Farber (2003); Howland and Peterson

(1988); and Jacobson, LaLonde, and Sullivan (1993b, chapter 6) suggest that labor market conditions can affect the wages workers earn in their new jobs (if they find new jobs) after involuntarily leaving their previous jobs. And Kaplan, González, and Robertson (2007) show that scarring in Mexico is much worse during times of crisis than at other times.

One of the key challenges in identifying the effects of crises on worker scarring is that examples are rare of firm-specific changes in demand ensuing from crises. Fernandes and Silva (2021), in a background paper written for this report, exploit heterogeneity in firms' exposure to the global financial crisis of 2008–09 to measure the potential of a severe demand shock to generate long-term employment and wage effects on workers. Their strategy is based on the idea that firms were differentially exposed to the external shocks caused by the crisis given the differences in their predetermined portfolios of export destinations. Using full-population longitudinal employer-employee data from social security records linked with firm export customs data by destination, for two LAC countries (Brazil and Ecuador), they compared the employment outcomes of formal workers initially in firms that faced larger labor demand shifts with those of workers in firms that faced smaller shifts over the eight years following the crisis.

They find that the effect of the global financial crisis was stronger and longer-lasting for workers initially in more negatively affected firms. Figure 3.4 shows the study's results. The effects of the global financial crisis on workers' average number of months formally employed are shown in panel a, and the effects on workers' average real monthly wages are in panel b. Each point in the figure represents the regression coefficient on the crisis for the relevant year.

The response in Brazil differs from that in Ecuador. The effect on months worked in Brazil is more negative at first but fades over time (although never fully disappearing). In Ecuador, the opposite is true: the immediate negative effect grows over time. Employment did not recover in Brazil or in Ecuador (nor did real wages in Brazil) even nine years after

the crisis. One possible reason for this difference has to do with wage flexibility. Figure 3.4, panel b, shows that the real wages of more adversely affected workers in Brazil fell significantly after the crisis. This reduction in real wages meant that workers in more affected firms took pay cuts (either at their original firm or at their new jobs). In Ecuador, however, real wages did not fall for workers in more affected firms. These countries have important differences in their labor regulations that could affect crises' impacts on workers. In particular, rigidity of wages implies that any adjustment in the labor market must occur through quantities (i.e., employment) rather than through prices (i.e., wages), so employment adjustments in labor markets with more rigid wages may be larger.

Other papers find long-lasting effects from other shocks as well. Increased competition from China, for example, has led to long-lasting losses in employment and wages in high-income countries (for the United States, Autor, Dorn, and Hanson [2013] and Autor et al. [2014]; for Denmark, Utar [2014]; and for Germany, Dauth, Findeisen, and Suedekum [2016] and Yi, Müller, and Stegmaier [2016]). The international trade literature shows that the dynamics of labor market adjustment to trade shocks are different in developed countries than they are elsewhere (Autor et al. 2014; Dauth, Findeisen, and Suedekum 2017; Dauth et al. 2019; Utar 2018). For Brazil, Dix-Carneiro and Kovak (2017, 2019) focus on the adverse effects of a large tariff liberalization reform. They find that a worker whose region initially faced a 10-percentage-point-larger decline in tariffs compared with other regions worked, on average, 9.9 fewer months in the formal sector between 1990 and 2010. This effect is large: those months represent 8 percent of the average number of total months worked in the formal sector during that 21-year period (125 months). Like Fernandes and Silva (2021), Dix-Carneiro and Kovak (2017, 2019) find that average employment and wage outcomes fail to recover even a decade and a half after an initial shock. It is striking that the temporary shock studied by

**FIGURE 3.4**  **Dynamic effects of the global financial crisis on workers**

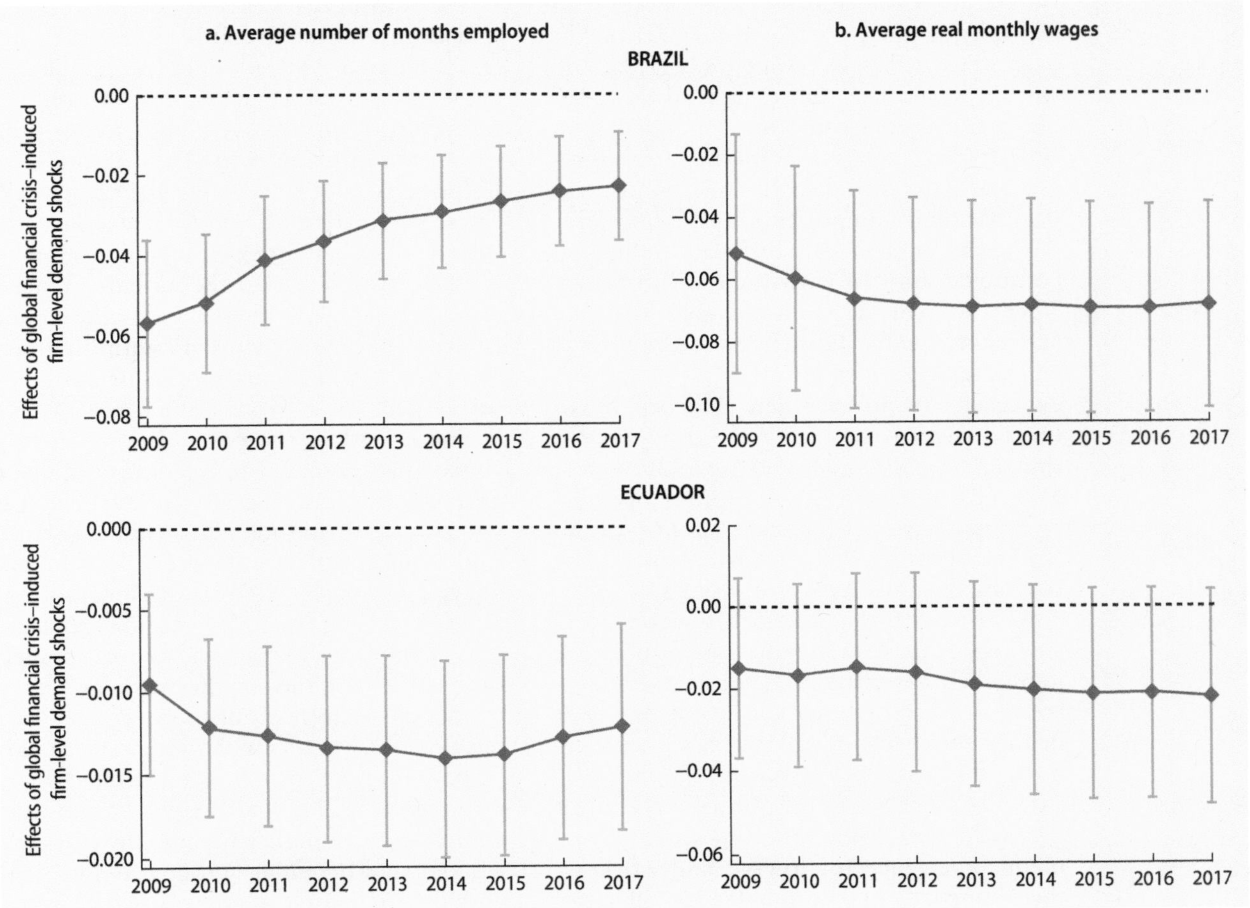

Source: Fernandes and Silva 2021.
Note: This figure shows the effects of global financial crisis–induced firm-level demand shocks (experienced from 2008 to 2009) on workers' average number of months formally employed in the years 2009 to 2017 (panel a) and average real monthly wages from 2009 to 2017 (panel b). More negative estimates imply larger reductions in the respective outcome among workers employed at the time of the global financial crisis in firms facing larger external demand reductions (relative to those employed in less affected firms). The vertical lines represent 95 percent confidence intervals on the basis of robust standard errors clustered by firm. The samples include about 3 million worker-year observations for Brazil and about 800,000 worker-year observations for Ecuador.

Fernandes and Silva (2021) led to the type of effects normally associated with large, permanent shocks such as trade liberalization.

## Incidence of long-term effects

As shown in chapter 2, the job losses caused by crises are not evenly spread across types of workers. In related recent research, Yagan (2019) shows that localized shocks during the global financial crisis were associated with rising (wage) earnings inequality within types of workers in the United States. Workers who were initially similar experienced different employment and earnings outcomes after exposure to different crisis-related local shocks. Yagan (2019) finds that low earners initially bore more of the employment effects of those shocks. The literature has also shown that the long-term impact on labor markets of China's export explosion was large and that the job losses it caused were concentrated among low-skilled workers in high-income countries (Autor et al. 2014; Autor, Dorn, and Hanson 2013; Dauth, Findeisen, and Suedekum 2016; Utar 2014; Yi, Müller, and Stegmaier 2016). The evidence on this phenomenon's effects on women versus men and young workers versus old workers is more mixed.

Job and worker characteristics—especially the skill distribution, but also the occupational composition and labor force participation rates—are different in the LAC countries than in high-income countries. Therefore, this section considers scarring across workers with different demographic characteristics and levels of labor market experience. It presents new evidence, drawing on two of the background papers for this report, Fernandes and Silva (2021) and Moreno and Sousa (2021). Both papers disaggregate scarring across different types of workers, thus providing a closer look at how scarring operates across these types.

To the extent that low-skilled workers and workers from low-income households are more likely to experience quantitative adjustments leading to unemployment or lower quality employment, scarring can have long-term implications for wage inequality. If slowdowns imply disproportionately lower access to on-the-job training and employment experience for low-skilled workers, their human capital accumulation will suffer more than that of high-skilled workers. This effect could lead to lower wage growth for low-skilled workers, exacerbating the wage inequality between the two groups. The results presented below suggest that scarring may contribute to increasing inequality in the already highly unequal LAC region. Low-skilled workers, at any given moment, are more likely to experience not just job loss and higher unemployment but also longer-term impacts from shocks.

What do this research project's findings suggest? Fernandes and Silva (2021) estimate the differences in changes in employment and wages following the global financial crisis–induced drop in demand for individuals working for Brazilian and Ecuadorean firms across occupation and demographic groups. They follow the employment outcomes of

each of these individuals from 2009 to 2017. Figure 3.5 summarizes their results.

The results for Brazil indicate that only less educated workers experienced strong employment and wage responses to the crisis, whereas workers with higher education were not significantly affected (figure 3.6). Relative to older workers, younger workers saw significantly smaller responses to the firm export shock in terms of months worked. Responses to the global financial crisis were similar across male and female workers and across workers with high and low previous participation in formal labor markets.

For Ecuador, the paper finds a strong employment response to the global financial crisis only for less educated workers, whereas workers with higher education were not significantly affected (figure 3.6). Interestingly, the wages of workers with low previous participation in the formal sector showed a significant negative response to gross domestic product declines in the workers' firms' export destinations, but there was no such response for workers with high previous participation in the formal sector. Employment responses to the global financial crisis were similar across male and female workers, workers in different age groups, and workers with different levels of previous participation in the formal sector. Taken as a whole, these findings suggest that less skilled workers in Brazil and Ecuador and older workers in Brazil were most severely hurt by the global financial crisis.

Turning back to the scarring of new entrants on the basis of initial labor market conditions, Moreno and Sousa (2021) find that workers with only secondary education experienced the most negative long-term effects on their employment outcomes because of initial labor market conditions (table 3.1). Although the specific mechanisms that cause scarring and the length of the scarring may vary across men and women, the overall story is similar. For both men and women, scarring occurs for those with lower levels of schooling, is unlikely for those who are college-educated, and is far

**FIGURE 3.5**    **Heterogeneity in effects of the global financial crisis across workers**

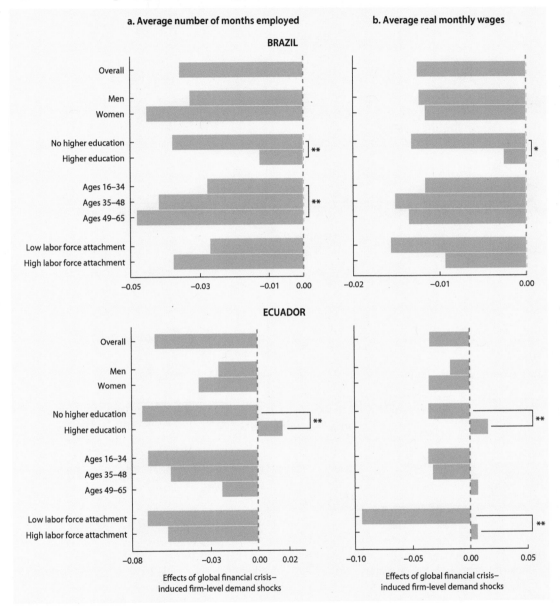

Source: Fernandes and Silva 2021.
Note: This figure shows the effects of global financial crisis–induced firm-level demand shocks (experienced from 2008 to 2009) on Brazilian and Ecuadorian workers' average number of months formally employed from 2009 to 2017 (panel a) and average real monthly wages from 2009 to 2017 (panel b). More negative estimates imply larger reductions in the respective outcome among workers employed at the time of the global financial crisis in firms facing larger external demand reductions (relative to those employed in less affected firms). Each bar shows the coefficient from a regression for the subsample on the basis of the worker characteristic listed on the y-axis in each subsample. The full samples have about 3 million worker-year observations for Brazil and about 800,000 worker-year observations for Ecuador.
***, **, and * indicate the significance levels, 1 percent, 5 percent, and 10 percent, respectively, of the t-test that indicates whether the difference in coefficients across worker categories is significant.

**FIGURE 3.6  Dynamic effects of the global financial crisis on workers by skill**

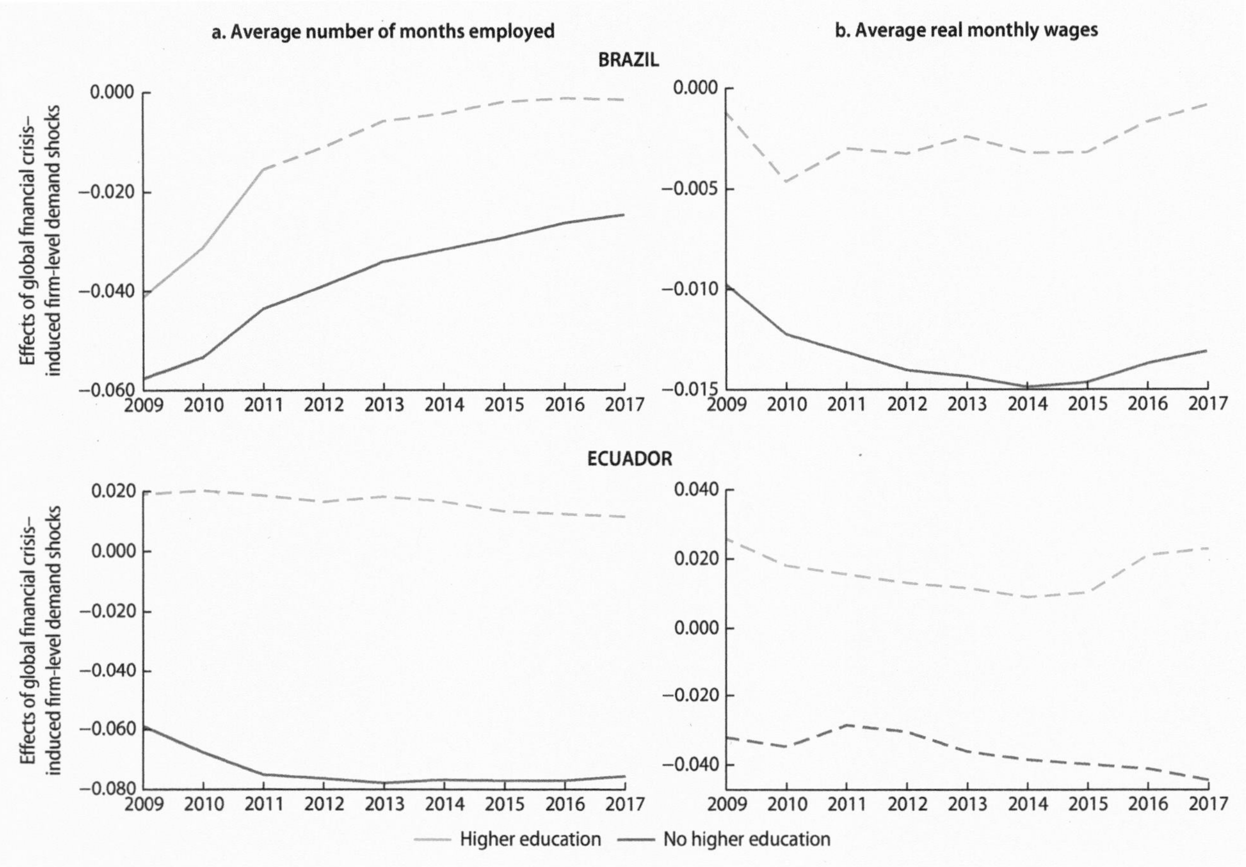

a. Average number of months employed

b. Average real monthly wages

BRAZIL

ECUADOR

—— Higher education    —— No higher education

*Source:* Fernandes and Silva 2020.
*Note:* The figure shows the effects of global financial crisis–induced firm-level demand shocks (2008–09) on Brazilian and Ecuadorian workers' with and without higher education in terms of average number of months formally employed from 2009 to 2017 (panel a) and average real monthly wages from 2009 to 2017 (panel b). Negative estimates imply larger reductions in the respective outcomes among workers employed at the time of the global financial crisis in firms that face larger external demand reductions (relative to less affected firms). The lines join the coefficients for each year. Dashed lines mean that the coefficient on the global financial crisis effect is not statistically significantly different from zero. The full samples have about three million worker-year observations for Brazil and about 800,000 worker-year observations for Ecuador.

more likely to occur through employment outcomes than through lower wages.

These results are in line with research on high-income countries. Because more experienced workers may have higher productivity and be more expensive for their firms to replace (Jovanovic 1979), losing workers with lower levels of human capital (including firm-specific human capital) implies lower transaction costs for employers. In high-income economies, low-earning workers exit the labor force in disproportionate numbers during downturns (Carneiro, Guimarães, and Portugal 2012; Solon, Barsky,

and Parker 1994), and displacement is more likely for low-skilled and young workers than for other types of workers (Devereux 2004; Teulings 1993). Research in LAC countries suggests similar trends. Studying the 2009 economic crisis in Mexico, Campos-Vazquez (2010) and Freije, López-Acevedo, and Rodríguez-Oreggia (2011) find larger job loss rates for young and unskilled workers than for other workers.

The LAC region's combination of large informal sectors and workers of varying skill levels suggests there may be a hierarchy in adjustment costs, in which informal

**TABLE 3.1  Presence of negative effects on employment and wage scarring, by gender and education**

|  | Women | | Men | |
| --- | --- | --- | --- | --- |
|  | Secondary education | Tertiary education | Secondary education | Tertiary education |
| Lower labor force participation | Colombia [4–12] Mexico [1–9] | N.A. | Brazil [4–6] Mexico [1–3] | N.A. |
| Higher unemployment | Argentina [1–6] Brazil [4–12] | Colombia [1–3] | Argentina [4–6] Brazil [4–9] | N.A. |
| Higher informality | Brazil [4–9] Colombia [4–12] Mexico [7–9] | N.A. | Colombia [4–12] Mexico [10–12] | Colombia [10–12] |
| Lower wages | Brazil [1–3] | Brazil [1–3] | Mexico [1–3] | N.A. |

*Source:* Moreno and Sousa 2021.
*Note:* This table reports the countries and years (in brackets) since entering the labor market for which there is evidence of scarring (defined as a statistically significant coefficient). N.A. indicates that no evidence of scarring was found.

workers, who have fewer job protections, face a greater likelihood of job loss regardless of skill. Among formal workers, low-skilled and low-income workers would be more likely to experience job loss than high-skilled or high-income workers.

## Firms: The cost of limited market competition

The previous section established that crises affect welfare in the long run. This section will discuss how crises also affect efficiency. Economists are increasingly coming to appreciate the importance of firm heterogeneity in determining and driving workers' outcomes. Some studies suggest that industry structure (Koeber and Wright 2001) and local wage bargaining practices (Janssen 2018) matter to these outcomes, but the relationship between firm and local labor market characteristics and labor market scarring has received very little attention. This section focuses on the roles of two topics that are particularly important in the LAC region: market power and labor market conditions.

As a crisis ripples through an economy, the supply side and the demand side of the labor market are affected. On the supply side, less skilled and more vulnerable workers bear larger costs and lasting adverse effects. On the demand side, firm-level responses depend on the structure of the local market.

That structure can indicate the prevailing degree of market power held by certain firms. Market power is a function of factors both outside a firm, such as market concentration, and inside a firm, such as productivity. This section highlights frontier research in this area in Latin America and the Caribbean and presents new results.

### Cleansing effects

Job loss spurred by an economic crisis can reduce productivity by destroying employer-employee matches and the job-specific human capital arising from them. However, macroeconomic shocks result in microeconomic reallocation at the worker and firm levels. At these defining moments, workers' and firms' fates are linked. Firms can adjust their number of employees, the number of hours worked by these employees, and the wages offered to them, and workers can choose either to accept these offers or to search for other options. From these interactions, a new short-run equilibrium is formed. This study shows that this equilibrium depends on local labor market conditions as well as on the ability of firms to adjust jobs and wages, which is linked to labor market regulations. Because firms are a key transmission channel of the effects of crises to individual workers, these effects also depend on the structure of the product market, existing rents, and rent-sharing mechanisms.

In the transition to a new equilibrium, many workers will lose their jobs or see their earnings fall, some firms will go out of business, and new entrants to the labor market will face more challenging starts to their careers. As explored earlier in this chapter, the impacts of a crisis leave scars on workers and firms. Many workers do not fully recover even in the long run: their earnings do not bounce back, and their careers follow different, worse tracks. The losers lose a lot. Less-skilled workers and those with lower earnings are the most adversely affected in the LAC region. In the labor market, employer-employee matches and the job-specific human capital arising from them may be permanently dissolved because of a temporary shock. This dissolution may slow the ramping up of production later, and it implies a loss in productivity. A crisis can also have persistent effects on technology inputs, which can be a margin of adjustment for firms, and on the structure of the economy, if the crisis kills off some firms and increases the market share of others. Large economic disruptions can free workers and other inputs of production from low productivity firms, allowing them to move to more productive firms as the economy recovers. Similarly, crises can spur reallocation of firms out of sectors with very low productivity. These changes can have persistent effects on the economy.

Because of these types of effects, crises can decrease individual welfare, but they can also increase efficiency and increase productivity (at both the firm and market levels) in the short and medium runs.

Although the Covid-19 crisis, because of its nature, has led to increasingly rapid technological advances driven by digitization (Beylis et al. 2020), how can crises without this characteristic also have persistent effects on technology? Evidence from Brazil shows that firms adjust to external demand shocks through changes in productivity, skill demand, product appeal, and markups (Mion, Proenca, and Silva 2020). Firm-level demand shocks during the global financial crisis caused more-affected firms to reduce their capital-to-worker ratio in countries such as Ecuador, whereas in Brazil firms simply adjust employment and wages in response to these shocks (Fernandes and Silva 2021). Negative external demand shocks also increase the skill content of production—the share of skilled labor in total employment increases—in countries such as Argentina (Brambilla, Lederman, and Porto 2012), Brazil (Mion, Proenca, and Silva 2020), and Colombia (Fieler, Eslava, and Xu 2018).

Through different mechanisms, crises in Latin America impact the structure of the overall economy. Firm-level demand shocks during the global financial crisis induced firm exit—not on impact, but around two years after the crisis in Brazil and Ecuador (Fernandes and Silva 2021). Debt overhang problems have also been documented, with the potential to kill off less resilient firms and increase the market share of more resilient ones. In addition to their effects on already-existing firms, crises have persistent effects on firms that are created during bad times. Demand is a key driver of firms' capabilities, and if firms start while demand is low, they will have more difficulty developing their networks of clients and learning how to work well with them. New evidence from the United States indicates that firms that are born in times of crisis end up stunted—that is, they grow slowly throughout their life cycles even when times improve (Moreira 2018). These changes have persistent implications for the economy that firms cannot revert.

By inducing the exit of less efficient firms, bad economic times can have a cleansing effect. Suppose a labor market is subject to large friction, so that very-low-productivity firms can survive by hiring workers for very low wages. Given the market's large friction, workers who receive these firms' low-wage offers take them, because the other option of continuing to look for work despite the low job-matching rate is worse. Therefore, low-productivity firms can essentially trap resources that could be more efficiently used elsewhere. In this context, large economic disruptions can have a cleansing effect by freeing workers from such firms and allowing them to reallocate themselves into more productive firms as the economy recovers. Similarly, crises could allow reallocation out of low-productivity sectors that have been living at the margin of survival. But these effects are possible only if jobs are created after the crises are over. Hence, the positive effects of crises on aggregate productivity are not guaranteed.

Importantly, the positive effects of crises on firm-level productivity are also not guaranteed. New evidence produced in the context of this report shows that the global financial crisis of 2008–09 led to a reduction in firm productivity in Brazil and Ecuador (contrary to evidence from the United States of job recovery because of increases in total factor productivity [TFP]) (Fernandes and

Silva 2021). Figure 3.7 shows that in Brazil, a drop in demand for a firm's exports caused by the crisis was associated with significantly lower productivity for that firm, regardless of whether this productivity was measured using value added per worker or TFP. In Ecuador, the relationship between productivity and decreases in export demand caused by the crisis goes in the same direction. One possible reason for the difference in productivity effects across the two countries—long-lasting decline in Brazil versus temporary decline in Ecuador—is the documented difference in the countries' employment adjustment: the

**FIGURE 3.7   Dynamic effects of the global financial crisis on firms**

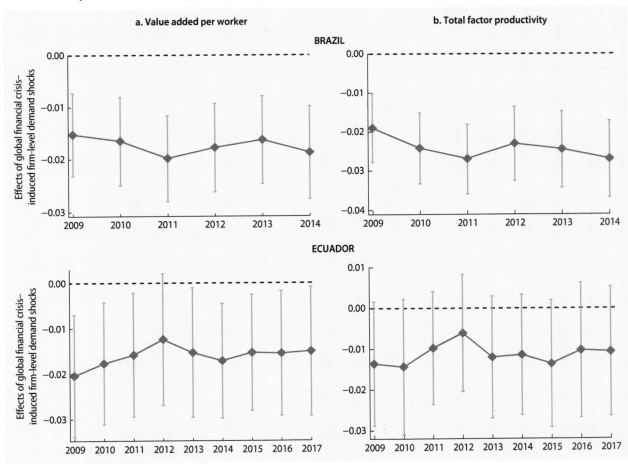

*Source:* Fernandes and Silva 2021.
*Note:* This figure shows the effects of global financial crisis–induced firm-level demand shocks (experienced from 2008 to 2009) on firms' productivity from 2009 to the year listed on the x-axis. More negative estimates imply larger reductions in the respective outcomes for firms facing larger external demand reductions (relative to less affected firms). Vertical lines represent 95 percent confidence intervals on the basis of robust standard errors clustered by firm. Each graph shows the coefficients from a single regression that is based on about 90,000 firm-year observations for Brazil and about 23,000 firm-year observations for Ecuador.

recovery was more "jobless" in Ecuador. This difference is also consistent with possible stronger labor hoarding by Ecuadorean firms in anticipation of a recovery in demand, caused by the difficulty of firing and then rehiring workers or the overhead character of some types of labor. Two other mechanisms were also at play. First, results show that firms in Brazil increased their share of skilled workers during the crisis, but such adjustment did not take place in Ecuador. Second, Brazilian firms did not adjust their capital-to-worker ratios, but firms in Ecuador registered a strong and lasting reduction in this measure.

## Protected sectors and firms: Market concentration dampens positive cleansing

Less competitive market structures may dampen the positive cleansing effects described earlier in this chapter. If protected firms, defined as those facing less competition, adjust less during a crisis, their opportunity to experience a cleansing effect is smaller. Rather than becoming more agile and productive, if these firms gain more market share and further crowd out the competition during economic downturns, they may trap additional resources that could be used more efficiently elsewhere. This dynamic is particularly concerning in the LAC region, which exhibits high inequality and low productivity growth.

It is well accepted that perfect competition is rare in output and factor markets. The imperfect competition in output markets often implies that firms have some market power. Market power is often measured with concentration indices, such as the Herfindahl-Hirschman index, which calculates the sum of the squares of the market shares of each firm in a defined market. Economists often associate higher measures of concentration—resulting from the presence of fewer firms with larger market shares—with more market power held by those firms. Although firms with more market power tend to make the same kinds of input choices (such as capital-labor ratios) as firms facing stronger competition, firms with more market power have an incentive to reduce their

output in order to increase the market price of their goods. In the extreme case, a market served by a monopolist has less output than a market served by a large number of tiny competitive firms. As such, total employment in a concentrated market may be lower than it would be in a more competitive market.

At the same time, market concentration is associated with larger differences between output prices and firm-level costs (i.e., higher markups). In some cases, higher markups generate rents that firms may share with their workers. A firm-specific "premium" is the term used to describe what happens when a firm shares higher-than-competitive earnings with its workers in the form of additional pay. Firms might also offer workers higher-than-competitive wages in order to retain them or to encourage loyalty to the firm and reduce shirking. Recent work demonstrates the importance of firm-specific premiums that can be shared with workers through bargaining (Card, Cardoso, and Kline 2016).

Several studies suggest that higher market concentration is associated with lower wage inequality because firms earning premiums pass those premiums along to their workers. For example, Magalhães, Sequeira, and Afonso (2019) find that inequality (measured as the ratio of "skilled" workers' wages to less-skilled workers' wages) is lower when the local industry is more concentrated (as measured by the Herfindahl-Hirschman index).

However, lower product market concentration may also be correlated with more competition among workers—but it can help cushion the adverse effects of job loss and scarring. When there are more firms in an area that value a specific set of skills, workers with those skills incur fewer losses following job loss (Green 2012; Neffke, Otto, and Hidalgo 2018). Additionally, Yang (2014) finds that increased agglomeration, defined as an increase in the number of firms within a given sector in a region, reduces unemployment rates within that sector but is associated with higher unemployment rates within the region. A smaller number of studies focus on employment adjustment in response to shocks in the presence of wage premiums. Orazem, Vodopivec, and Wu (2005) show that, at least for Slovenia, firms with higher profits shed fewer workers than less profitable firms when exposed to negative output shocks.

In this context, product market concentration can affect the size and distribution of labor market adjustments to crises. This effect is particularly relevant in Latin America, where there is some evidence of resource misallocation in favor of politically connected firms. The value of political capital has been studied in different contexts in the region. For example, during the Pinochet regime in Chile (1973–90), firms with links to the dictatorship were relatively unproductive and benefited from resource misallocation, and these distortions persisted as the country transitioned into democracy (González and Prem 2020). In Brazil, after anticorruption audits, municipalities experienced an increase in economic activity concentrated in the sectors that were most dependent on government relationships. Evidence of patronage in Brazil was also found in the selection of workers into public sector organizations (Colonnelli, Prem, and Teso 2020). In Ecuador, where political connections have been shown to cause misallocation of procurement contracts, firms that form links with the bureaucracy experience an increased probability of being awarded a government contract (Brugués, Brugués, and Giambra 2018). In Costa Rica, Alfaro-Urena, Manelici, and Vasquez (2019) find large changes in rents collected by a firm when the firm starts supplying multinational corporations. Overall, De Loecker, Eeckhout, and Unger (2020) show that markups are very high in Latin America compared with other continents.

Although the existing literature shows a link between product market concentration (and agglomeration), wages, and unemployment, few studies focus on the relationship between concentration and labor market scarring. To fill this gap, Fernandes and Silva (2021) use detailed, microlevel data to

**FIGURE 3.8** **Effects of the global financial crisis on Brazilian workers depending on sectoral concentration and state ownership**

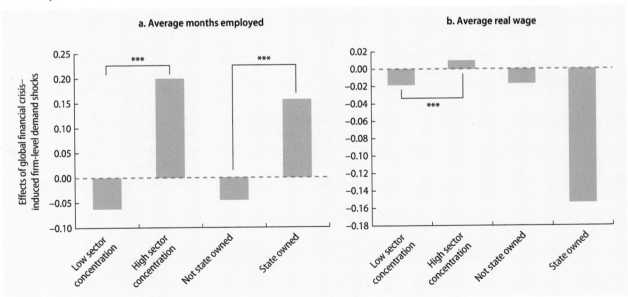

*Source:* Fernandes and Silva 2021.
*Note:* The figure shows the effects of global financial crisis–induced firm-level demand shocks (2008) on Brazilian workers' average number of months formally employed and average real monthly wages from 2009 to 2017 in low- and high-concentration sectors in the first set of bars. High-concentration sectors have a Hirshman-Herfindahl index of employment concentration within the sector above the median. The second set of bars in the figure show the effects of global financial crisis–induced firm-level demand shocks (2008–09) in firms that are publicly owned and in firms that are privately owned. Negative estimates imply larger reductions of the respective outcome among workers employed at the time of the global financial crisis in firms that face larger external demand reductions (relative to less affected firms). Each graph shows the coefficients from two different regressions, one for the first set of two bars, and one for the second set of two bars.
*** , ** , and * indicate the significance levels, 1 percent, 5 percent, and 10 percent, respectively, of the t-test that indicates whether the difference in coefficients across worker categories is significant.

evaluate changes in worker-level employment and wages according to the type of market structure and the type of firm. The results are presented in figure 3.8. They show, for example, that workers who at the time of the crisis work in markets with low market concentration incur larger scarring effects. In these less concentrated sectors, lower wages and lower employment are seen in response to shocks, as economic theory predicts. Conversely, in sectors in which a few firms control a large share of the market, a negative demand shock does not result in employment losses—rather, it increases employment—and wages do not adjust. These results are consistent with the idea that firms with more market power are more protected from negative shocks. Although the workers in these sectors are better insulated from crises than other workers, the costs of this protection are borne by the economy as a whole.

The existence of imperfect competition in output markets is well accepted by economists (as asserted by Card et al. 2018), and concerns about imperfect competition in Latin American product markets have emerged in policy discussions (OECD 2015). These policy discussions hinge critically on the source of the concentration in these product markets. There are several potential sources, including economic barriers to entry (such as large fixed costs), political barriers to entry (such as government protections or regulation), and firm-level productivity differences that result in the most productive firms driving out less productive firms (Melitz 2003).

Recent work suggests that firm rents are prevalent in developing countries and that they are frequently associated with political connections, both in Latin America (Brugués, Brugués, and Giambra 2018) and elsewhere (Rijkers, Freund, and Nucifora 2017). State-owned firms are an extreme example of firms with strong political connections. These firms are less profitable in general and have higher labor-to-capital ratios than private firms (Dewenter and Malatesta 2001). Although a large literature describes the differences in employment choices between state-owned and

private firms, little empirical evidence compares the differences in employment adjustment to shocks between state-protected firms and unprotected firms.

To fill this gap, Fernandes and Silva (2021) compare the change in employment following a negative shock in state-owned firms and in private firms. They find that state-owned firms adjusted less along the intensive margin (workers' months worked) in response to the global financial crisis of 2008–09 because these firms were shielded from the shock.

## Places: The role of local opportunities and informality

So far, this chapter has explored the potential differences in scarring caused by differences in personal (demographic) characteristics and firm characteristics. A third dimension that could affect labor market scarring is the properties of the local labor markets in which workers live and work. Recent research has paid increasing attention to the significant costs workers bear when moving between cities or industries. Dix-Carneiro (2014) estimates that the median direct mobility cost that workers face when switching sectors ranges from 1.4 to 2.7 times the average annual wage. Artuc, Chaudhuri, and McLaren (2010) and Artuc and McLaren (2015) obtain similar estimates for the cost of changing sectors. The costs of changing locations, by some estimates, can be as high as 7 times the average annual income (Bayer, Keohane, and Timmins 2009; Bishop 2008; Kennan and Walker 2011).[3] As a result, workers, especially low-wage workers, tend to be more closely tied to their local labor markets than was previously thought.

Such ties to local labor markets means that the characteristics of those markets might play a significant role in shaping labor market scarring. For example, Meekes and Hassink (2019) show that the local housing market significantly affects workers following job losses—the effect of displacement on their probability of changing homes is negative. Lessons from the previous section already suggest that the amount of concentration in an industry might affect employment and wages. Living in a "company town" offers very different opportunities than does living in a large and diversified metropolitan area. The degree of informality in the local labor market also matters.

Informality might affect scarring in several important ways, and not all of them point in the same direction. For many workers, especially in the LAC region, the informal labor market is considered to be a safety net that replaces the traditional role of social insurance. Workers who lose formal sector jobs and find themselves without family or government support have little choice but to accept any available job opportunity. When the legal requirements for starting or operating a business are not strictly enforced, these workers may have an easier time setting up informal businesses (such as the street market shops, or *tianguis*, often seen in Mexico) than regaining formal employment. Informal sector employment can therefore offer opportunities for human capital accumulation through experience and entrepreneurship.

However, the presence of a large informal sector may indicate imperfect enforcement of the minimum wage or other employment laws. In many cases, informal sector entrepreneurs offer services to exporting firms and formal sector firms that help those firms smooth out demand fluctuations. Because of the various firm-level costs to adjust employment, formal sector firms prefer to keep relatively constant formal labor forces. In some cases, employment laws even motivate firms to hire fewer workers during peak times than they otherwise would. Instead, when demand increases, exporting formal sector firms subcontract with informal firms or hire workers informally to meet the surge in demand. When demand contracts, the formal sector firms simply reduce their orders and employment for the informal sector or reduce their use of informal workers, keeping their formal employment more or less constant. Therefore, formal workers in areas with high informality may find wage growth elusive, because the essentially infinite supply of informal workers available to perform unfilled jobs

weakens the link between increased labor demand and the need for their firms to raise wages. This effect generates results similar to those of labor market scarring—but, on the other hand, job losses in the formal sector might be lower in these localities than in those with less informality.

Recent work for this study sheds light on this apparent contradiction in several ways. First, Fernandes and Silva (2021) find that formal workers in municipalities with higher levels of informality lost less in the global financial crisis. In particular, within a given country, the paper finds smaller employment and wage losses for formal workers hit by shocks who live in less formal local labor markets, suggesting that the medium-run effects of crises on unemployment are lower for formal workers in places where informality is higher. Ironically, the effects of crises may even shift from negative to positive for workers in municipalities with high informality rates. These results are consistent with the idea that (a) in the presence of informality, formal firms may employ informal workers and (b) those firms reduce their employment of informal workers, rather than formal workers, in the face of negative export shocks (figure 3.9). In this context, informality may provide de facto flexibility for firms and workers to cope with adverse shocks. This result is in line with findings on the effect of trade liberalization in Brazil by Dix-Carneiro and Kovak (2019) and Ponczek and Ulyssea (2018).

This study also finds that workers in localities with more (alternative) job opportunities bounce back better from crises. Specifically, larger and longer-lasting losses in employment (and sometimes wages) in response to a crisis are found for formal workers in localities with larger primary sectors, smaller service sectors, fewer large firms, and production highly concentrated in the same sector where they were employed precrisis (Fernandes and Silva 2021). These workers' persistent earnings losses may reflect their lack of opportunities in the rebound, not just "scarring" in the traditional sense of a persistent loss of human capital associated with a period of unemployment or lower-quality employment.

**FIGURE 3.9** **Effects of the global financial crisis on Brazilian workers depending on local labor market informality**

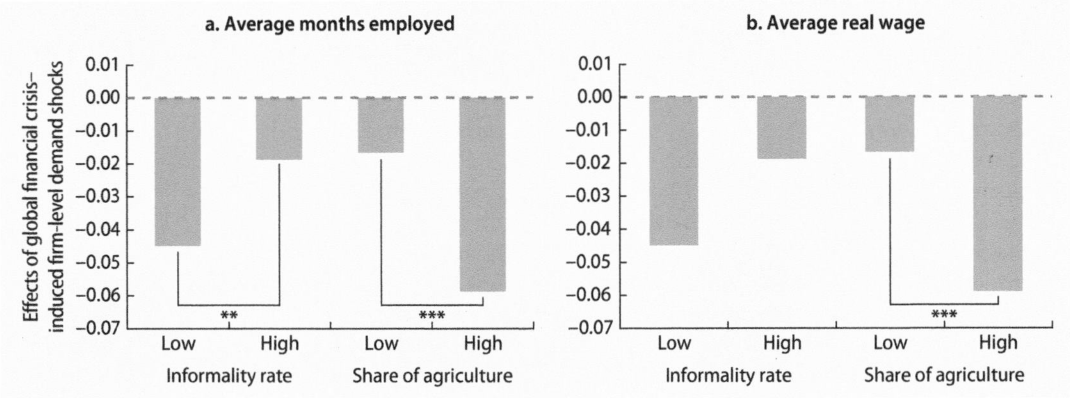

a. Average months employed

b. Average real wage

*Source:* Fernandes and Silva 2021.
*Note:* The figure shows the effects of global financial crisis–induced firm-level demand shocks (2008) on Brazilian workers' average number of months formally employed and average real monthly wages from 2009 to 2017 in high and low informality. High informality municipalities are those with a level of informality above the median. The share-of-agriculture bars in each panel show the effects of global financial crisis–induced firm-level demand shocks (2008–09) in firms that are located in municipalities with high and low shares of employment in agriculture. Negative estimates imply larger reductions of the respective outcome among workers employed at the time of the global financial crisis in firms that face larger external demand reductions (relative to less affected firms). Each panel shows coefficients from two different regressions, one for the first set of two bars, and one for the second set of two bars. ***, **, and * indicate the significance levels, 1 percent, 5 percent, and 10 percent, respectively, of the t-test that indicates whether the difference in coefficients across worker categories is significant.

## Conclusion

Crises can lead to long-term effects on labor markets through two key channels. First, to the extent that crises lead to interruptions in employment that destroy or reduce the human capital stock of a region, they may have long-run effects on that region's growth prospects.[4] The accumulation of human capital is integral to the continued economic growth and social gains of a region. Although a country's human capital stock is a key determinant of growth through its role as an input into production (Mincer 1984), researchers have also emphasized its contribution to growth through increasing innovation, productivity, and technological uptake (Benhabib and Spiegel 1994; Nelson and Phelps 1966; Romer 1990).

The second channel by which crises can lead to employment changes with long-term effects on growth is by inducing a reallocation of workers and firms (for example, across sectors or occupations) or altering firms' use of technology (for example, the way firms combine their various inputs). Such reallocation results both in job destruction (which hits at once) and in job creation being

slowed by market friction. The findings presented in this chapter suggest that both channels are in play in Latin America.

The evidence presented in this chapter indicates that crises leave scars—not on every worker, but on many of them. Some workers recover from displacement and other livelihood shocks, while others end up permanently scarred. For example, in Brazil and Ecuador, the effects of a crisis on worker employment and wages are still present for an average of nine years after the beginning of the crisis. It is striking that a temporary shock can lead to the type of effects normally associated with large permanent shocks, such as trade liberalization.[5] This finding suggests that success in raising the LAC region's long-term economic growth rate will depend on whether the region's crisis-response measures effectively prevent unnecessary destruction of human capital and business capabilities.

For lower-skilled workers (those with no college education), the earnings losses caused by crises are persistent. Workers with higher education suffer minimal impacts from crises on their wages and very short-lived impacts on their employment. Interestingly, however, the responses to the global financial crisis of 2008–09 were similar across male and female workers and across workers with high and low previous participation in the formal labor market. New entrants to the labor market during a crisis face a worse start to their careers, from which it is difficult to recover. Although the specific mechanisms for and the lengths of scarring may vary between men and women, the overall story across the LAC countries is similar—for both men and women, scarring is more likely for those with lower levels of schooling compared with those with college educations, and it is far more likely to occur through employment outcomes than through lower wages.

In this context, the extent to which resources are targeted toward those most affected by crises and whether those resources can effectively reach them is crucial. However, if workers in localities with more job opportunities bounce back better from crises, as this study finds—either because they have more informal job opportunities or because the set of employers available to them (more large firms and larger service sectors with compatible jobs) is more amenable to them finding new jobs—the observed losses in earnings among other workers may not be so much scarring, in the traditional sense of a loss of human capital, but rather a symptom of those workers' lack of opportunities. In this case, approaching the issue solely from a worker-based perspective will not solve the issue.

The effects on workers described above have important implications for equity and poverty. And, as this report shows, they can also affect efficiency in the long run. Crises do more than just destroy jobs; they also alter productivity down the road. Consistent with the slow pickup of jobs after a crisis are two facts. First, crises can have persistent effects on the technology use of preexisting firms and on the size and capability of new firms formed during the crisis. Preexisting firms adjust their skill demand, product appeal, and markups in response to demand shocks. For example, Fernandes and Silva (2021) find that in response to the global financial crisis, Brazilian and Ecuadorian firms increased their capital per worker ratio. Crises also increase the skill content

of production: the share of skilled labor in total employment has been shown to increase in the presence of negative external demand shocks in countries such as Argentina (Brambilla, Lederman, and Porto 2012), Brazil (Mion, Proenca, and Silva 2020), and Colombia (Fieler, Eslava, and Xu 2018). Second, firms that are born in times of crisis end up stunted, growing slowly throughout their life cycles even when times improve. If firms start in a period when demand is low, they are less able to develop client relationships and to learn how to work well with clients, and this impairment stays with them for a long time. If jobs are slow to recover after a crisis because of firm scarring in this broader sense, policies to address labor-market scarring may not be enough to solve the problem, as discussed in the next chapter.

Another key mechanism at play is cleansing. Less productive firms can more easily turn unprofitable and be scrapped in a recession than can highly productive ones. However, the units in place may not experience the full impact of a fall in demand if the fall is made up for with a reduction in the job creation rate. Destruction and reallocation effects are a good thing, but only as long as new jobs are created after the crisis is over. Once the firm and spatial dimensions of labor market adjustment to crises are included, the importance of the demand side is clear. Importantly, results show that protected sectors and firms adjust less during a crisis (Fernandes and Silva 2021), suggesting that these sectors experience less of a cleansing effect.

## Notes

1. See, for example, Brunner and Kuhn (2014) for evidence on Austria; Genda, Kondo, and Ohta (2010) for Japan and the United States; Kwon, Milgrom, and Hwang (2010) for Sweden and the United States; and Kahn (2010) for the United States.
2. These studies include Burda and Mertens (2001); Couch (2001); Davis and Von Wachter 2011; Fallick (1996); Flaaen, Shapiro, and Sorkin 2019; Hyslop and Townsend (2019); Kletzer (1998); Krolikowski 2017; Lachowska, Mas, and Woodbury 2018; Menezes-Filho (2004); and Ruhm (1991a, b).

3. There are important differences in the determinants of mobility across the diverse countries of the LAC region. A "spatial development" flagship report analyzing these determinants in the region is under way.

4. Crises can also lead to firm scarring by imposing a fixed cost on firms, from which financially constrained firms might not be able to recover, and a loss of firm-specific human capital.

5. The international trade literature shows large and lasting dynamic labor market adjustments to trade shocks (see, for example, Autor et al. 2014; Dauth, Findeisen, and Suedekum 2017; Dauth et al. 2019; Dix-Carneiro and Kovak 2017, 2019; and Utar 2018).

## References

Alfaro-Urena, A., I. Manelici, and J. P. Vasquez. 2019. "The Effects of Multinationals on Workers: Evidence from Costa Rica." Unpublished paper.

Amarante, V., R. Arim, and A. Dean. 2014. "The Effects of Being out of the Labor Market on Subsequent Wages: Evidence for Uruguay." *Journal of Labor Research* 35 (1): 39–62.

Arias-Vazquez, FJ, D. Lederman, and L. Venturi. 2019. "Transitions of Workers Displaced due to Firm Closure." Unpublished paper.

Artuc, E., and J. McLaren. 2015. "Trade Policy and Wage Inequality: A Structural Analysis with Occupational and Sectoral Mobility." *Journal of International Economics* 97: 278–94.

Artuc, E., S. Chaudhuri, and J. McLaren. 2010. "Trade Shocks and Labor Adjustment: A Structural Empirical Approach." *American Economic Review* 100: 1008–45.

Arulampalam, W. 2001. "Is Unemployment Really Scarring? Effects of Unemployment Experiences on Wages." *Economic Journal* 111 (475): 585–606.

Autor, D. H., D. Dorn, and G. H. Hanson. 2013. "The China Syndrome: Local Labor Market Effects of Import Competition in the United States." *American Economic Review* 103 (6): 2121–68.

Autor, D. H., D. Dorn, G. H. Hanson, and J. Song. 2014. "Trade Adjustment: Worker-Level Evidence." *Quarterly Journal of Economics* 129 (4): 1799–1860.

Bayer, P., N. Keohane, and C. Timmins. 2009. "Migration and Hedonic Valuation: The Case of Air Quality." *Journal of Environmental Economics and Management* 58: 1–14.

Benhabib, J., and M. M. Spiegel. 1994. "The Role of Human Capital in Economic Development: Evidence from Aggregate Cross-Country Data." *Journal of Monetary Economics* 34 (2): 143–73.

Beylis, G., R. Fattal Jaef, M. Morris, A. Rekha Sebastian, and R. Sinha. 2020. *Going Viral: COVID-19 and the Accelerated Transformation of Jobs in Latin America and the Caribbean.* World Bank Latin American and Caribbean Studies. Washington, DC: World Bank.

Bishop, K. C. 2008. "A Dynamic Model of Location Choice and Hedonic Valuation." Unpublished, Washington University in St. Louis, 5.

Brambilla, I., D. Lederman, and G. Porto. 2012. "Exports, Export Destinations, and Skills." *American Economic Review* 102 (7): 3406–38.

Brugués, F., J. Brugués, and S. Giambra. 2018. "Political Connections and Misallocation of Procurement Contracts: Evidence from Ecuador." Research Department Working Papers 1394, CAF Development Bank of Latin America, Caracas, Venezuela.

Brunner, B., and A. Kuhn. 2014. "The Impact of Labor Market Entry Conditions on Initial Job Assignment and Wages." *Journal of Population Economics* 27 (3): 705–38.

Burda, M. C., and A. Mertens. 2001. "Estimating Wage Losses of Displaced Workers in Germany." *Labour Economics* 8 (1): 15–41.

Burdett, K., C. Carrillo-Tudela, and M. Coles. 2020. "The Cost of Job Loss." *Review of Economic Studies* 87 (4): 1757–98.

Campos-Vazquez, R. 2010. "The Effects of Macroeconomic Shocks on Employment: The Case of Mexico." *Estudios Economicos* 25 (1): 177–246.

Card, D., A. R. Cardoso, J. Heining, and P. Kline. 2018. "Firms and Labor Market Inequality: Evidence and Some Theory." *Journal of Labor Economics* 36 (S1): 13–70.

Card, D., A. R. Cardoso, and P. Kline. 2016. "Bargaining, Sorting, and the Gender Wage Gap: Quantifying the Impact of Firms on the Relative Pay of Women." *Quarterly Journal of Economics* 131 (2): 633–86.

Carneiro, A., P. Guimarães, and P. Portugal. 2012. "Real Wages and the Business Cycle: Accounting for Worker, Firm, and Job Title Heterogeneity." *American Economic Journal: Macroeconomics* 4 (2): 133–52.

Carrington, W. J. 1993. "Wage Losses for Displaced Workers: Is It Really the Firm That Matters?" *Journal of Human Resources* 28 (3): 435–62.

Carrington, W. J., and B. Fallick. 2017. "Why Do Earnings Fall with Job Displacement?" *Industrial Relations* 56 (4): 688–722.

Colonnelli, E., M. Prem, and E. Teso. 2020. "Patronage and Selection in Public Sector Organizations." *American Economic Review* 110 (10): 3071–99.

Couch, K. A. 2001. "Earnings Losses and Unemployment of Displaced Workers in Germany." *Industrial and Labor Relations Review* 54 (3): 559–72.

Cruces, G., A. Ham, and M. Viollaz. 2012. "Scarring Effects of Youth Unemployment and Informality: Evidence from Brazil." Center for Distributive, Labor and Social Studies (CEDLAS) working paper, Economics Department, Universidad Nacional de la Plata, Argentina.

Dauth, W., S. Findeisen, and J. Suedekum. 2016. "Adjusting to Globalization: Evidence from Worker-Establishment Matches in Germany." Düsseldorf Institute for Competition Economics (DICE) Discussion Paper 205, Heinrich Heine University, Düsseldorf, Germany.

Dauth, W., S. Findeisen, and J. Suedekum. 2017. "Trade and Manufacturing Jobs in Germany." *American Economic Review* 107 (5): 337–42.

Dauth, W., S. Findeisen, J. Suedekum, and N. Woessner. 2019. "The Adjustment of Labor Markets to Robots." University of Würzburg, Würzburg, Germany.

Davis, S. J., and T. M. Von Wachter. 2011. "Recessions and the Cost of Job Loss." Working Paper 17638, National Bureau of Economic Research, Cambridge, MA.

De Loecker, J., J. Eeckhout, and G. Unger. 2020. "The Rise of Market Power and the Macroeconomic Implications." *Quarterly Journal of Economics* 135 (2): 561–644.

Dell, M., B. Feigenberg, and K. Teshima. 2019. "The Violent Consequences of Trade-Induced Worker Displacement in Mexico." *American Economic Review: Insights* 1 (1): 43–58.

Devereux, P. J. 2004. "Cyclical Quality Adjustment in the Labor Market." *Southern Economic Journal* 70 (3): 600–15.

Dewenter, K., and P. Malatesta. 2001. "State-Owned and Privately Owned Firms: An Empirical Analysis of Profitability, Leverage, and Labor Intensity." *American Economic Review* 91: 320–34.

Dix-Carneiro, R. 2014. "Trade Liberalization and Labor Market Dynamics." *Econometrica* 82: 825–85.

Dix-Carneiro, R., and B. K. Kovak. 2017. "Trade Liberalization and Regional Dynamics." *American Economic Review* 107 (10): 2908–46.

Dix-Carneiro, R., and B. K. Kovak. 2019. "Margins of Labor Market Adjustment to Trade." *Journal of International Economics* 117: 125–42.

Fallick, B. C. 1996. "A Review of the Recent Empirical Literature on Displaced Workers." *Industrial and Labor Relations Review* 50 (1): 5–16.

Farber, H. S. 2003. "Job Loss in the United States, 1981–2001." Working Paper 471, Industrial Relations Section, Princeton University, Princeton, NJ.

Fernandes, A., and J. Silva. 2021. "Labor Market Adjustment to External Shocks: Evidence for Workers and Firms in Brazil and Ecuador." Background paper written for this report. World Bank, Washington, DC.

Fieler, A. C., M. Eslava, and D. Y. Xu. 2018. "Trade, Quality Upgrading, and Input Linkages: Theory and Evidence from Colombia." *American Economic Review* 108 (1): 109–46.

Flaaen, A., M. D. Shapiro, and I. Sorkin. 2019. "Reconsidering the Consequences of Worker Displacements: Firm versus Worker Perspective." *American Economic Journal: Macroeconomics* 11 (2): 193–227.

Freije, S., G. López-Acevedo, and E. Rodríguez-Oreggia. 2011. "Effects of the 2008–09 Economic Crisis on Labor Markets in Mexico." Policy Research Working Paper 5840, World Bank, Washington, DC.

Genda, Y., A. Kondo, and S. Ohta. 2010. "Long-Term Effects of a Recession at Labor Market Entry in Japan and the United States." *Journal of Human Resources* 45 (1): 157–96.

González, F., and M. Prem. 2020. "Losing Your Dictator: Firms during Political Transition." *Journal of Economic Growth* 25 (2): 227–57.

Green, C. P. 2012. "Short Term Gain, Long Term Pain: Informal Job Search Methods and Post-Displacement Outcomes." *Journal of Labor Research* 33 (3): 337–52.

Gregg, P., and E. Tominey. 2005. "The Wage Scar from Male Youth Unemployment." *Labour Economics* 12 (4): 487–509.

Gregory, M., and R. Jukes. 2001. "Unemployment and Subsequent Earnings: Estimating Scarring among British Men." *Economic Journal* 111 (475): 607–25.

Hardoy, I., and P. Schone. 2013. "No Youth Left Behind? The Long-Term Impact of Displacement on Young Workers." *Kyklos* 66 (3): 342–64.

Howland, M., and G. E. Peterson. 1988. "Labor Market Conditions and the Reemployment of Displaced Workers." *Industrial and Labor Relations Review* 42 (1): 109–22.

Hyslop, D. R., and W. Townsend. 2019. "The Longer-Term Impacts of Job Displacement on Labour Market Outcomes in New Zealand." *Australian Economic Review* 52 (2): 158–77.

Jacobson, L. S., R. J. LaLonde, and D. G. Sullivan. 1993a. "Earnings Losses of Displaced Workers." *American Economic Review* 83 (4): 685–709.

Jacobson, L. S., R. J. LaLonde, and D. G. Sullivan. 1993b. *The Costs of Worker Dislocation.* Kalamazoo, MI: W. E. Upjohn Institute for Employment Research.

Janssen, S. 2018. "The Decentralization of Wage Bargaining and Income Losses after Worker Displacement." *Journal of the European Economic Association* 16 (1): 77–122.

Jovanovic, B. 1979. "Job Matching and the Theory of Turnover." *Journal of Political Economy* 87 (5): 972–90.

Kahn, L. B. 2010. "The Long-Term Labor Market Consequences of Graduating from College in a Bad Economy." *Labour Economics* 17 (2): 303–16.

Kaplan, D. S., G. M. González, and R. Robertson. 2007. *Mexican Employment Dynamics: Evidence from Matched Firm-Worker Data.* Washington, DC: World Bank.

Kennan, J., and J. R. Walker. 2011. "The Effect of Expected Income on Individual Migration Decisions." *Econometrica* 79 (1): 211–51.

Kletzer, L. G. 1998. "Job Displacement." *Journal of Economic Perspectives* 12 (1): 115–36.

Koeber, C., and D. W. Wright. 2001. "Wage Bias in Worker Displacement: How Industrial Structure Shapes the Job Loss and Earnings Decline of Older American Workers." *Journal of Socio-Economics* 30 (4): 343–52.

Krolikowski, P. 2017. "Job Ladders and Earnings of Displaced Workers." *American Economic Journal: Macroeconomics* 9 (2): 1–31.

Kwon, I., E. M. Milgrom, and S. Hwang. 2010. "Cohort Effects in Promotions and Wages: Evidence from Sweden and the United States." *Journal of Human Resources* 45 (3): 772–808.

Lachowska, M., A. Mas, and S. A. Woodbury. 2018. "Sources of Displaced Workers' Long-Term Earnings Losses." Working Paper 24217, National Bureau of Economic Research, Cambridge, MA.

Liu, K., K. G. Salvanes, and E. Ø. Sørensen. 2016. "Good Skills in Bad Times: Cyclical Skill Mismatch and the Long-Term Effects of Graduating in a Recession." *European Economic Review* 84: 3–17.

Magalhães, M., T. Sequeira, and Ó. Afonso. 2019. "Industry Concentration and Wage Inequality: A Directed Technical Change Approach." *Open Economies Review* 30: 457–81.

Martinoty, L. 2016. "Initial Conditions and Lifetime Labor Outcomes: The Persistent Cohort Effect of Graduating in a Crisis." Mimeo.

McCarthy, N., and P. W. Wright. 2018. "The Impact of Displacement on the Earnings of Workers in Ireland." *Economic and Social Review* 49 (4): 373–417.

Meekes, J., and W. H. J. Hassink. 2019. "The Role of the Housing Market in Workers' Resilience to Job Displacement after Firm Bankruptcy." *Journal of Urban Economics* 109: 41–65.

Melitz, M. J. 2003. "The Impact of Trade on Intra-industry Reallocations and Aggregate Industry Productivity." *Econometrica* 71 (6): 1695–1725.

Menezes-Filho, N. 2004. "Costs of Displacement in Brazil." University of São Paulo, Brazil.

Mincer, J. 1984. "Human Capital and Economic Growth." *Economics of Education Review* 3 (3): 195–205.

Mion, G., R. Proenca, and J. Silva. 2020. "Trade, Skills, and Productivity." Unpublished paper.

Moreira, S. 2017. "Firm Dynamics, Persistent Effects of Entry Conditions, and Business Cycles," Working Papers 17-29, Center for Economic Studies, U.S. Census Bureau.

Moreno, L., and L. Sousa. 2021. "Early Employment Conditions and Labor Scarring in Latin America." Background paper written for this report. World Bank, Washington, DC.

Neffke, F. M. H., A. Otto, and C. Hidalgo. 2018. "The Mobility of Displaced Workers: How the Local Industry Mix Affects Job Search." *Journal of Urban Economics* 108: 124–40.

Nelson, R. R., and E. S. Phelps. 1966. "Investment in Humans, Technological Diffusion, and Economic Growth." *The American Economic Review* 56 (1/2): 69–75.

OECD (Organisation for Economic Co-operation and Development). 2015. "Competition and Market Studies in Latin America: The Case of Chile, Colombia, Costa Rica, Mexico, Panama and Peru." Organisation for Economic Co-operation and Development, Paris.

Orazem, P. F., M. Vodopivec, and R. Wu. 2005. "Worker Displacement during the Transition:

Experience from Slovenia." *Economics of Transition* 13 (2): 311–40.

Oreopoulos, P., M. Page, and A. H. Stevens. 2008. "The Intergenerational Effects of Worker Displacement." *Journal of Labor Economics* 26 (3): 455–83.

Ponczek, V., and G. Ulyssea. 2018. "Is Informality an Employment Buffer? Evidence from the Trade Liberalization in Brazil." Unpublished manuscript.

Rijkers, B., C. Freund, and A. Nucifora. 2017. "All in the Family: State Capture in Tunisia." *Journal of Development Economics* 124 (C): 41–59.

Romer, P. M. 1990. "Endogenous Technological Change." *Journal of Political Economy* 98 (5, Part 2): 71–102.

Ruhm, C. J. 1991a. "Are Workers Permanently Scarred by Job Displacements?" *American Economic Review* 81 (1): 319–24.

Ruhm, C. J. 1991b. "Displacement Induced Joblessness." *Review of Economics and Statistics* 73 (3): 517–22.

Solon, G., R. Barsky, and J. A. Parker. 1994. "Measuring the Cyclicality of Real Wages: How Important Is Composition Bias?" *Quarterly Journal of Economics* 109 (1): 1–25.

Teulings, C. 1993. "The Diverging Effects of the Business Cycle on the Expected Duration of Job Search." *Oxford Economic Papers* 45: 482–500.

Utar, H. 2014. "When the Floodgates Open: 'Northern' Firms' Response to Removal of Trade Quotas on Chinese Foods." *American Economic Journal: Applied Economics* 6 (4): 226–50.

Utar, H. 2018. "Workers beneath the Floodgates: Low-Wage Import Competition and Workers' Adjustment." *Review of Economics and Statistics* 100 (4): 631–47.

Yagan, D. 2019. "Employment Hysteresis from the Great Recession." *Journal of Political Economy* 127 (5): 2505–58.

Yang, X. 2014. "Labor Market Frictions, Agglomeration, and Regional Unemployment Disparities." *Annals of Regional Science* 52 (2): 489–512.

Yi, M., S. Müller, and J. Stegmaier. 2016. "Industry Mix, Local Labor Markets, and the Incidence of Trade Shocks." US Census Bureau, Suitland, MD.

# Toward an Integrated Policy Response | 4

## Introduction

Few doubt that a better policy framework to mitigate, manage, and help people recover from crises is crucial for countries in Latin America and the Caribbean (LAC) to succeed in lifting their long-term growth rates and increasing their people's well-being. Macroeconomic frameworks across the countries in the region changed dramatically in the 1990s, as did social protection and labor policies in the early 2000s. But changes in policy have been relatively limited since then. The COVID-19 pandemic and the associated sluggishness of the global economy may be prolonged, and structural changes in labor markets are ongoing. Given these circumstances, crisis response has moved to the forefront of policy debate in the LAC region.

Considering the evidence presented in earlier chapters on the importance of demand to crisis adjustment and the triangle of workers, sectors and firms, and locations, how can policies mitigate the impacts of crises on workers and promote better recovery? This study shows that crises have a meaningful negative effect on welfare in the LAC region and that the documented labor market scarring is likely to affect the region's economic growth potential. To mitigate this damage, policy makers should design and deploy instruments that cushion the effects of crises on workers in the short run; shock impacts spread unequally across workers and firms, and many will not regain their lost job, wages, or clients. But policy makers should pay just as much attention to efficiency and resilience, promoting peoples' ability to bounce back when exposed to an adverse shock (which can be aided by healthy economic growth).

This chapter builds on the findings from the first three chapters to identify the necessary elements of an effective policy response to crises in Latin America and the Caribbean as revealed by these broader lenses. It discusses the policy implications of the previous chapters' findings, assesses the ability of existing systems to tackle the challenges of crisis response, and discusses potential reforms, although it does not evaluate the impacts of the different policy responses proposed. The reported policy results and implementation details are based on the existing literature, and the new evidence presented on the effectiveness of reforms is based on past crises in the region.

The evidence featured in the previous chapters suggests that the success of policy responses to the crisis triggered by the COVID-19 pandemic will depend on whether response measures effectively prevent unnecessary destruction of human capital and otherwise viable enterprises and on the quality of complementary domestic policies and reforms beyond the labor market. Cushioning the crisis's short-term impact through macroeconomic and social protection and labor policies will be crucial to avoiding poverty and excessive job destruction, given the employment and wage losses documented in this report. Strong, prudent macroeconomic frameworks and automatic stabilizers are the first line of defense to shield labor markets from crises. Prudent fiscal and monetary policies can lower the likelihood and severity of certain types of crises and provide the fiscal space needed to give support and avert system-wide financial strain when crises do occur.

In addition to macroeconomic policies, the typical automatic stabilizer used in Organisation for Economic Co-operation and Development (OECD) countries is reliable unemployment insurance, which many LAC countries still lack. This type of social protection and labor program is key to cushioning the impacts of crises on formal workers. However, many workers in the LAC region earn their living in the informal economy, and the best way to protect their consumption is through responsive cash transfer programs. Targeted on the basis of household need rather than whether the lost job was formal or informal, these programs reduce the extent to which labor market adjustment translates into short- and longer-term impacts on the poor and vulnerable. Because reemployment is crucial to avoid scarring, active labor market programs to support reskilling and job search are a third vital element of effective social protection and labor systems.

Although social protection and labor systems can cushion workers from the impacts of crises, they do not address the structural issues that determine the magnitude of these impacts or the economy's ability to bounce back. This study highlights, for example, the dichotomy between protected and unprotected firms in the LAC region (caused by the former group's market power) and the region's low geographic mobility of workers, both of which magnify the welfare effects of shocks. It also highlights pockets of rigidity in labor regulations that are slowing transitions of workers across jobs. Hence, competition policies, regional policies, and labor regulations are a third key dimension of a policy response to crises. These important structural issues are also causing LAC labor markets' poor adjustment to crises, and might require interventions at the sector and locality levels that interact with social protection needs and incentives.

Local labor markets' characteristics and sector product markets' conditions determine the magnitude of the impacts of crises on workers. In terms of labor market regulations and institutions, this study documents limited adjustment through reductions in hours, more adjustment through unemployment, and an informal sector that serves as a buffer in some countries. With respect to product market conditions, the study finds that initially similar workers experience different employment and earnings outcomes after exposure to the same crisis because of differences in their sectors' competition structures. It also documents that the localities where workers live affect the impacts they face. Its results suggest that employment and wage losses following shocks are smaller for formal workers who live in areas with more informality. Why do crisis effects pass through to workers more in some places than in others? One factor is that the geographic mobility of workers is lower than expected by economists and policy makers. Constraints on movement create friction in the stylized labor market adjustment mechanisms that can magnify welfare losses, as shown in earlier chapters. The policy response to crises needs to tackle these structural issues squarely, according to the weight each issue has in each country or setting.

Given the complexity of labor markets' adjustment to economic crises in the LAC region, this report argues that countries can improve their responses by advancing on three fronts. The combination of policies needed is truly cross-sectoral, including macroeconomic, social protection and labor, competition, and regional policies, and it will determine the speed of adjustment and the trajectory of workers' recoveries.

This chapter starts with a discussion of the public policy "shield" that determines how a crisis affects workers and their families—the country's macroeconomic frameworks and automatic stabilizers. Strong, sound macroeconomic policies can decrease the frequency of crises, for example, by protecting against fiscal imbalances and domestic inflationary pressures. They can also lessen the severity of crises by reducing the size of the needed adjustments and shaping the adjustments' composition. The LAC region has significantly improved its macroeconomic frameworks in the past few decades, resulting in fewer domestic crises and significantly lower inflation rates. Even so, its fiscal policy in particular remains weak and, in many countries, unsustainable, with small tax bases and relatively generous entitlement programs. Many countries in the region also lack social protection and labor programs that provide adequate automatic stabilizers (such as unemployment insurance).

The chapter next turns to the question of how governments can use labor markets and social protection policies to alleviate or revert the impacts of crises on workers and the economy. To begin answering this question, the chapter considers why most people in the LAC region are not covered by any formal income assistance for unemployment. It assesses the region's existing income support programs (including unemployment insurance plans, cash transfers, and other social assistance benefits), their unintended (positive and negative) consequences as currently designed, and how they could be reengineered to provide a more effective crisis response. The chapter's discussion of social protection and labor systems concludes by highlighting

policy options that governments in the region could consider in order to improve the mixed record of their employment support programs and to reduce the (short- and long-term) impacts of crises on workers. A distinction is made between short-term, transitory programs enacted during crises to avoid excessive job losses (including employment retention schemes, temporary employment programs, and demand stimulus programs) and longer-term programs deployed by governments to reskill workers and ease their transitions between jobs. The latter set of programs are discussed in light of the LAC region's mixed track record at reducing the duration of unemployment and improving the quality of job matches. Because even brief crises can leave lasting scars on workers, the formidable challenge for governments is to distinguish the crises requiring only transitory responses from those requiring more sustained support and to respond accordingly as workers and the economy adjust. This chapter also discusses insights from the existing evidence and policy experiences and recommends ways to improve the region's responses to the current COVID-19 crisis.

Next, the chapter shifts its focus to the efficiency effects of crises and how to tackle structural issues that can worsen labor market adjustment—in particular, how to break rigidities, address the insider story, and respond to the lack of opportunities in some places and regions. Chapter 3 showed how factors beyond the labor market affect the magnitude of crises' impacts on workers. Structural challenges in the LAC region act to slow and even prevent necessary labor market adjustments, hence weakening economic recoveries. These structural issues can change the nature—and the impact on people—of systemic shocks from transitory to long-term. The policy implication of these findings and the related literature is that even if a country's macroeconomic policies and its social protection and labor system are in pristine order, the best outcomes for workers in the wake of crises can be achieved by complementing these measures with sectoral and place-based policies to deal with the structural issues that currently impede strong recoveries. This reform agenda would involve addressing inefficiencies in labor market adjustment caused by legislation, product markets' structures, workers' lack of geographic mobility, and depressed areas. Addressing these structural challenges will require changes to legal frameworks and regulations as well as targeted public investment.

## Three key policy dimensions

So far, this report has unpacked the welfare and efficiency stories caused by the triangle of workers, sectors and firms, and localities and has examined from there the mechanisms at play.

An exogenous shock is transmitted to the labor market through shocks in supply and demand, altering the labor market's normal functioning and generating job losses and transitions to informal jobs in excess of those registered in normal times. These excess flows affect the size and composition of employment. Chapter 2 describes this adjustment process in the LAC region, considering the various margins by which the labor market can adjust to shocks and the factors that help determine the severity of the adjustment.

What does this process mean for workers, and how do the characteristics of sectors, firms, and localities affect the size and nature of crisis impacts? A macroeconomic shock results in microeconomic reallocation at the worker and firm levels. At these defining moments, workers' and firms' fates are linked. Firms can adjust their numbers of employees, hours worked, and wages offered, and workers can choose to either accept these offers or search for other options. From these interactions, a new short-run equilibrium is formed. This study shows that the new equilibrium depends on local labor market conditions as well as on the ability of firms to adjust jobs and wages, which is linked to labor market regulations. Because firms are a key channel transmitting the effects of crises to individual workers, these effects also depend on existing rents, rent-sharing mechanisms, and the structure of product markets.

In the transition to a new equilibrium, many workers will lose their jobs or see their earnings fall, some firms will go out of business, and new entrants to the labor market will face more challenging starts to their careers. As explored in chapter 3, the impacts of a crisis leave scars on workers and firms. Many workers do not fully recover even in the long run: their earnings do not come back, and their careers follow different, worse tracks. The losers lose a lot. Less skilled workers and those with lower earnings, are the most adversely affected in the LAC region. From a labor market perspective, employer-employee matches and the job-specific human capital arising from them, which often take a long time to build and would regain profitability when the economy returns to normal, may be permanently dissolved because of a temporary shock. This loss may slow the ramping up of production later, and it implies a loss in productivity. A crisis can also have persistent effects on technology inputs, which can be a margin of adjustment for firms, and on the structure of the economy, as the crisis kills off some firms and increases the market share of others. These changes can have persistent implications for the economy that firms cannot revert.

Considering the triangle of workers, sectors and firms, and locations, how can policies mitigate the impacts described above? Figure 4.1 presents a framework for thinking about the relevant policy areas. Given the characteristics of labor market adjustments in the LAC region identified in chapters 2 and 3, this chapter discusses what policies are needed in the region to mitigate the negative impacts of crises and provide better responses to them. The analysis makes clear that labor market policies alone are insufficient. Strong, prudent macroeconomic frameworks and automatic stabilizers (the shield in figure 4.1) are the first line of defense to protect labor markets from crises. These preventative macroeconomic measures—along with social protection and labor systems—mitigate the impacts of external shocks on a country's economy and reduce the chance of domestic shocks by stabilizing the macroeconomic

**FIGURE 4.1**   **How adjustment works and a triple entry of policies to smooth it**

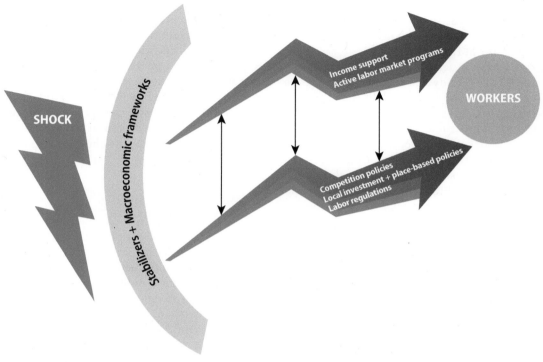

*Source:* World Bank

environment. Prudent fiscal and monetary policies prevent certain types of crises and ensure sufficient fiscal space to provide support and avert system-wide financial strain when other types of crises occur.[1]

In order for economies to effectively protect themselves from external shocks, macroeconomic stabilizers are key. As discussed in later sections of this chapter, countries' social protection and labor systems can include nationally administered income protection arrangements, such as unemployment insurance and other forms of income support for affected individuals. These "safety net" programs ideally function countercyclically, expanding and increasing the support they provide in bad times, in order to safeguard and stimulate consumption, which would provide a demand stimulus to limit the damage from a crisis and help speed recovery.

Overall, automatic stabilizers operating in the aggregate help households smooth their consumption, reducing the immediate impact of a shock on aggregate demand and employment and, therefore, the size and composition of the shock's effects on labor markets. These policies can lessen the severity of crises by shrinking the necessary adjustment and shaping its composition. They will affect both the change in the total size of the labor market caused by a crisis and the labor market dynamics between the formal economy, the informal economy, and outright unemployment (for example, by preventing excessive destruction of formal jobs), as described in chapter 2.[2]

Social protection and labor policies are key to cushioning the impacts of crises on workers. In addition to providing an automatic stabilizer (unemployment insurance), when organized into coherent and coordinated systems, they protect the incomes and consumption of households through safety nets and promote reemployment through active labor market programs. Targeted on the basis of household need rather than whether a lost job was formal or informal, these programs lessen the extent to which labor market adjustment translates into short- and long-term impacts on workers (as illustrated by the top arrow of figure 4.1).

The labor scarring documented in this study and its adverse impact on countries' potential productivity imply that the LAC region could achieve greater long-term growth if crisis-induced, worker-level human capital decay was reduced. This change would require cushioning the short-term impact of crises through both short-term income support to protect welfare and social protection and labor policies to build human capital and promote faster, higher-quality transitions for displaced workers moving into new jobs. The speed and extent of scarring in the region require that social protection and labor systems provide more than just income support. They should also help people to renew and redeploy their human capital. It is in this broader sense that reforms to the region's existing social protection and labor policies and systems are urgently needed. These transformations will, in turn, affect labor market flows and provide a responsive safety net that contributes meaningfully and effectively to countries' automatic stabilizers, as detailed below.

Although social protection and labor programs cushion workers from the impacts of crises, they do not address the structural issues that determine the magnitude of these impacts in the first place. For example, this report highlights the dichotomy between protected and unprotected firms in the LAC region (caused by the lack of contestability and competition, high levels of concentration, and market power held by the former group of firms) and the sluggish mobility of labor across economically lagging and leading localities, both of which serve to magnify the welfare effects of shocks. This study also highlights pockets of labor market rigidity that are slowing transitions between jobs. Hence, competition policies, regional policies, and labor market regulations are a third key policy dimension determining the effects of crises (as illustrated by the bottom

arrow in figure 4.1). These structural issues may also be behind LAC labor markets' poor adjustment to crises, and they might require interventions at the sector and locality levels, in addition to worker-level and economy-wide interventions, and that interact with social protection needs and incentives (as illustrated by the vertical arrows in figure 4.1). LAC countries' policy responses need to tackle these structural issues squarely, according to the weights they hold in each country or setting.

## Aggregate: Stronger macroeconomic stabilizers

As illustrated in figure 4.1, the first shield against a crisis is the strength of a country's macroeconomic frameworks and automatic stabilizers. These policies filter the extent to which an exogenous shock affects the domestic labor market and, especially relevant to Latin America and the Caribbean, the extent to which domestic conditions can lead to a crisis situation. This section looks at how the LAC region has improved in terms of its macroeconomic frameworks, leading to fewer domestic crises, although it still lacks sufficient automatic stabilizers.

### Stronger macroeconomic frameworks

Few would disagree that avoiding crises in the first place is an important priority to limit their effects, which occur at both the aggregate and the individual levels. As documented in this study, the LAC region experiences frequent crises. During one-third of the quarters between 1980 and 2018, one or more countries in the region was in an economic crisis (as mentioned in chapter 1). However, prudent fiscal and monetary policies can lower the likelihood of certain types of crises, and macroeconomic policies, including demand stimulus interventions and exchange rate depreciations, provide a first line of response to them. In recent decades, the LAC countries have made important strides in strengthening their macroeconomic frameworks and improving their governance and institutions.

These efforts have reduced the frequency of crises in the region, especially those of domestic origin. However, some crises persist, most notably the crisis in the República Bolivariana de Venezuela but also recent political or economic crises in Argentina, Brazil, Haiti, and Nicaragua.

In a critical point to understanding how crises impact workers, the region's stronger macroeconomic frameworks have also altered the nature of the region's labor market adjustments. Because of these stronger frameworks, crises in the LAC region now occur in the context of relatively low inflation. In contrast, the 1980s and early 1990s were characterized by high inflation in most countries in the region. Latin American monetary policies in the 1990s and early 2000s were increasingly aimed at keeping inflation low (Céspedes, Chang, and Velasco 2014). For example, following the Tequila Crisis, Mexico moved from a fixed exchange rate policy to a floating exchange rate policy and instituted relatively strict inflation-targeting rules. Since the early 2000s, most countries in the region have succeeded in taming inflation. The unweighted average inflation rate in the region was 69.6 percent in the 1980s and 30.0 percent in the 1990s, but it fell to only 5.4 percent in the 2000s.[3]

Although this new macroeconomic context has reduced the number of domestic crises in the LAC region, it also has implications for how the region's labor markets adjust to the crises that do occur. Low inflation reduces the downward flexibility of real wages, while firms' ability to cut the nominal wages of existing workers is limited by contracts (formal and informal agreements) and by labor legislation, such as binding statutory minimum wages that are set high relative to average earnings.[4] Hence, firms operating in contexts where inflation is low and stable cannot rely on inflation to help erode real wages during a crisis. Rather, firms can reduce their labor costs only through quantitative adjustments, such as reducing their numbers of positions. As a result, the reduction in inflation likely increased the extent to which labor markets adjust to crises along the quantitative margin (employment). In a recent paper, Gambetti and Messina (2018) show that real wage flexibility declined in Brazil, Chile, Colombia, and Mexico from 1980 to 2010. This result is in line with previous research that has found evidence of falling real wage flexibility in LAC countries over this period (see Lederman, Maloney, and Messina [2011] for the region as a whole, Messina and Sanz-de-Galdeano [2014] for Brazil and Uruguay, and Casarín and Juárez [2015] for Mexico).

The resulting changes in LAC labor markets' adjustment to economic shocks can be illustrated by the differences in responses to crises in Brazil and Mexico during the 1990s versus during the 2000s. The panels in figure 4.2 track fluctuations in the real log gross domestic product (GDP), the inflation rate, mean real wages, and the unemployment rate before and after the first quarter of negative growth (identified as $t = 0$ in the graphs) for four crises: the 1994 Tequila Crisis and the 2008–09 global financial crisis in Mexico and the 1990 and 2015 recessions in Brazil. The figure shows that inflation increased significantly during the Tequila Crisis in Mexico, whereas it remained flat during the 2008–09 downturn. Similarly, in Brazil, the recession of 1990 was characterized by a spike in inflation, whereas inflation remained flat in the more recent crisis.

Given the region's lower inflation rates during more recent crises, one would expect that real wages have not adjusted as much in these crises as in earlier crises. As shown in figure 4.2, real wages fell more significantly during the earlier crises in both Brazil and Mexico. This difference suggests that the price margin is becoming less central to labor market adjustments. These findings are confirmed in Robertson (2020).

If real wage adjustment was an important margin of labor market adjustment during earlier growth shocks, then, given the current context of lower inflation rates, quantitative adjustment has likely taken on increased importance, as the cases of Brazil

**FIGURE 4.2** **Wage and unemployment responses during crises in the 2000s versus crises in the 1990s, Brazil and Mexico**

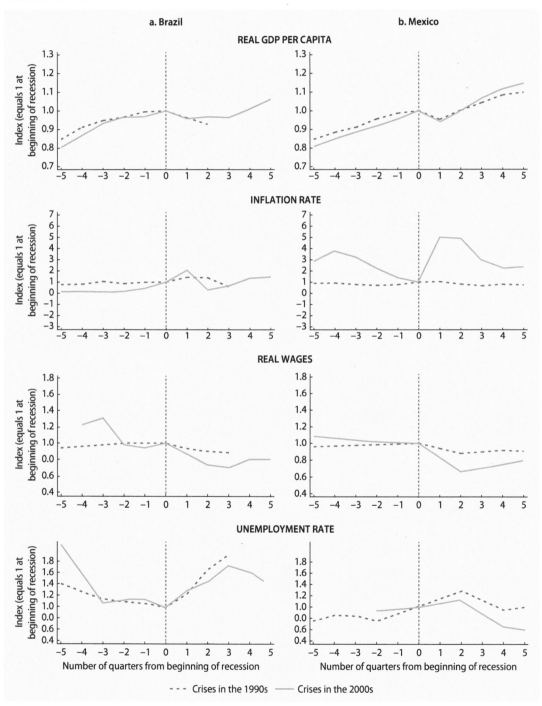

*Source:* World Bank.
*Note:* Episodes of recession in the 2000s were the 2008–09 global financial crisis for Mexico and the 2015 recession for Brazil. Episodes of recession in the 1990s were the Tequila Crisis for Mexico and the 1991 crisis for Brazil. All series are indexed to the year when log real gross domestic product fell, and initial output falls at $t = 0$, which is indicated by dashed lines.

and Mexico suggest. With inflation spiking, unemployment increased only marginally during the Tequila Crisis in Mexico. In contrast, inflation remained relatively flat in Mexico during the 2008–09 crisis while unemployment grew substantially more than in the earlier crisis. In Brazil, the recession of 1990 was also characterized by a spike in inflation and low increases in unemployment, but the recession of 2015 saw lower inflation and a more significant increase in unemployment.[5] The changing importance of wage adjustments relative to quantitative adjustments is reflected in figure 4.3, which reports the sensitivity of unemployment and wages to growth shocks during crisis years for Brazil, Colombia, and Mexico during the 1990s and the 2000s. In line with the results shown in figure 4.2, figure 4.3

suggests that there has been a statistically significant reduction in the sensitivity of wages and a statistically significant increase in the sensitivity of unemployment to output fluctuations.

## Restoring fiscal space

Although the LAC region has made significant strides in reducing inflation, it continues to struggle with another key aspect of the macroeconomic shield—fiscal policy. Prudent fiscal policies prevent certain types of crises and ensure the fiscal space needed to provide support and avert system-wide financial strain when other types of crises occur. This issue is particularly concerning in the face of the fiscal adjustment that might be needed in the LAC region. The region, especially the Atlantic

**FIGURE 4.3** **Sensitivity of unemployment and wages to output fluctuations**

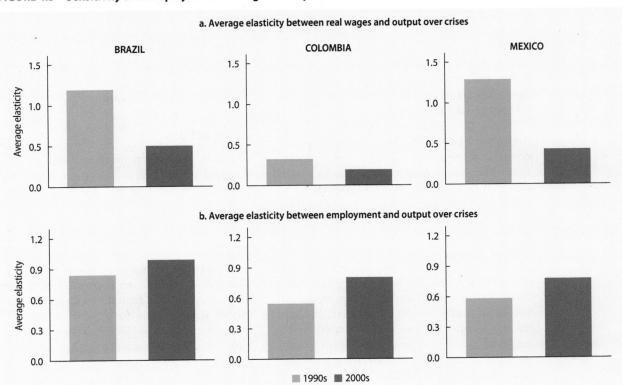

*Source:* World Bank calculations using data on wages and employment from Gambetti and Messina (2018) updated to 2018.
*Note:* This figure reports the dynamic betas during crisis years estimated on the basis of Okun's law by rolling regressions, following the methodology of IMF (2010). The difference in means between crises in the 1990s and crises in the 2000s is statistically significant at the 5 percent level for each country shown.

subregion, has experienced steady growth in public spending in recent years, which has translated into sizable fiscal deficits and public debts (Vegh et al. 2018). Taking a longer-term perspective on fiscal policy will involve tackling complex issues such as removing energy subsidies, modernizing tax policies, and raising the efficiency of social spending, including the financial sustainability of old-age pensions as populations rapidly age.

## Automatic stabilizers (and the lack thereof)

Automatic stabilizers can buffer the impacts of crises on households by increasing disposable income, attenuating the decline in employment and consumption in response to negative demand shocks. In a nutshell, they constitute a de facto demand stimulus. The most intensively used automatic stabilizers in high- and middle-income countries are income support systems for those who lose jobs, including severance pay (lump-sum payments at dismissal) and unemployment insurance (periodic payments contingent on nonemployment and searching for a job). These policies provide liquidity to workers upon dismissal and can smooth their consumption during their job searches.

The LAC region has a long institutional history of providing social insurance to cover threats to income and consumption from old age, disability, and the untimely death of households' primary income earners. However, nationally administered, countercyclical income support plans to cover labor market dislocation (whether pure risk-pooling unemployment insurance or mixed saving and risk-pooling approaches) are relatively rare in the LAC region. Two-thirds of the countries in the region do not yet offer national-level, countercyclical income support plans for displaced workers. And among the few existing programs, only Brazil's, Chile's, and Uruguay's are sufficiently well established or have sufficient coverage and payout volumes to contribute significantly to stabilizing their economies. The landscape of unemployment insurance plans in Latin America, the current

problems with this landscape, and the policy agenda going forward are discussed in detail in the next section. The lack of unemployment insurance adds to the region's lack of effective consumption-smoothing mechanisms, leaving an important gap in the crisis responses countries are equipped to deploy.

Although unemployment insurance is commonly used as an automatic stabilizer, other policies can fill this role. In the COVID-19 crisis, for example, LAC countries' fiscal policies have been strongly countercyclical. Strategies like furloughs, job retention subsidies and the expansion of cash transfer programs have represented an important share of spending in response to the crisis. Making some of these instruments a permanent part of their economies' automatic stabilizers could lower losses and adjustment costs in the wake of future shocks. This change could be implemented by making these programs state-contingent and automatically activated when, for example, unemployment rises above a determined threshold.[6] Indeed, a dynamic, or "adaptive," system of state-contingent support is one of the original motivations for countries to invest in national social protection and labor "safety net" systems (Bowen et al. 2020; Grosh et al. 2008).

## Policy actions

The LAC region has improved significantly in terms of its macroeconomic frameworks in recent decades, and it needs to continue in this direction of prudence and sound macroeconomic management in order to keep up and maintain this progress. Fiscal policy—a key instrument for managing crises and providing demand stimulus to support recovery—remains an area of concern for the region, and the region's more recent track record leaves space for improvement. The reforms still needed involve tackling difficult issues, such as tax policies, energy subsidies, the efficiency of social spending, and the financial stability of old-age pension systems.

In addition, the LAC region still lacks sufficient automatic stabilizers. The need for these stabilizers is made more urgent by the shift in the labor market's main adjustment margin to quantitative adjustment. The limited availability of countercyclical, income support plans for people negatively affected by labor market adjustments is making it more difficult to manage crises and is magnifying crises' effects. Most people who lose their jobs (formal or informal) in downturns are largely unprotected.

Figure 4.4 provides a more complete characterization of the possible policy areas of focus to achieve stronger macroeconomic frameworks and create automatic stabilizers (first policy dimension).

## Social protection and labor systems: Cushioning the impact on workers and preparing for change

The deep and lasting impacts on individuals and economies of labor market adjustments to crises provide a powerful rationale for policy interventions that absorb the impacts of these systemic shocks and cushion households from them. As documented in the previous three chapters, crises often bring about job dislocation or other negative impacts on livelihoods, which come along with long-lasting losses in earnings. In this context, having strong social protection and labor systems in place to protect people's welfare and prevent the depletion of human capital is key. Crises also generate important labor reallocation effects, and effective social protection and labor systems can help people redeploy into new jobs.

Do these systems exist in the LAC region? To answer that question, this section describes the array of publicly provided risk-sharing and coping instruments available in the region and discusses their key gaps. It then presents an agenda for reform to fill these gaps and to increase the coherence and coordination between interventions so that

FIGURE 4.4    **Stabilizers and macroeconomic frameworks: Policy reforms**

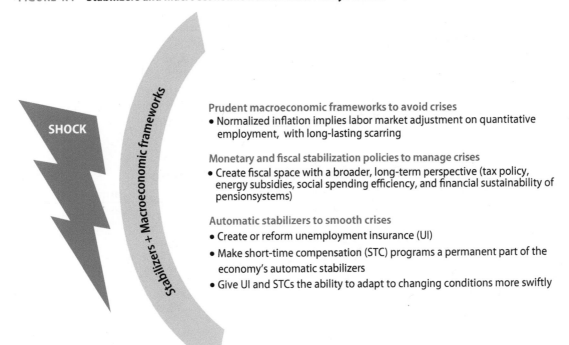

Prudent macroeconomic frameworks to avoid crises
- Normalized inflation implies labor market adjustment on quantitative employment, with long-lasting scarring

Monetary and fiscal stabilization policies to manage crises
- Create fiscal space with a broader, long-term perspective (tax policy, energy subsidies, social spending efficiency, and financial sustainability of pension systems)

Automatic stabilizers to smooth crises
- Create or reform unemployment insurance (UI)
- Make short-time compensation (STC) programs a permanent part of the economy's automatic stabilizers
- Give UI and STCs the ability to adapt to changing conditions more swiftly

*Source:* World Bank.

they can operate as "systems" to cushion the short-term impacts of crises, prevent lasting human capital losses, and facilitate the redeployment of working people through reskilling and reemployment support.

## Cushioning the short-term impact: Income support during unemployment

### *Landscape of income support for unemployment in Latin America and the Caribbean*

Only about a third of the countries in the LAC region offer national unemployment income support plans. Job displacement income support—programs specifically designed to sustain the income and consumption of laid-off workers and their families—in the form of unemployment insurance is, therefore, relatively rare in the region. Workers with formal employment contracts in Brazil, Chile, and Uruguay have access to large risk pools offered by a national unemployment insurance plan (that is, one not specific to a worker's firm, occupation, or sector). In addition, Argentina, The Bahamas, Barbados, Colombia, Ecuador, and the República Bolivariana de Venezuela offer unemployment insurance in the form of contributory risk-pooling plans (table 4.1).

Individual unemployment savings accounts are also available in Chile, Colombia, and Ecuador. Only in Chile are these

various instruments fully integrated into a coherent and coordinated plan: participating workers who lose their jobs make scheduled, limited withdrawals from their individual savings accounts, and a risk-pooling "solidarity fund" underpins their protection should they exhaust their unemployment savings before finding a new job. In Panama and Peru, income support for unemployment is limited to individual savings accounts, with no risk-pooling mechanism. Mexico (with the notable exception of Mexico City and Yucatán) and most other countries in Central America and the Caribbean do not have any form of unemployment insurance, in sharp contrast with countries at similar income levels in other regions. For example, all countries in Europe and Central Asia have mandatory, risk-pooling unemployment insurance (see map 4.1).

Most countries in the LAC region rely instead on severance pay mandates, which are specific to the employment relationship and are financed fully and paid directly by firms (table 4.1). The legal coverage and generosity of this form of protection can be uniform across all regulated employment relationships, or it can vary by contract type, by sector, or even by province. As a risk-sharing instrument, the distinguishing feature of severance pay is that it pools the risk of income loss from involuntary dismissals solely within firms.

**TABLE 4.1  Landscape of formal unemployment income support in the LAC region**

| "Risk-pooling" within firms | Savings (self-insurance) | National risk pooling |
|---|---|---|
| Severance pay mandates on employers | Funded severance and/or individual unemployment savings accounts | Unemployment insurance/benefits |
| Most countries | Argentina<br>Brazil<br>Chile<br>Colombia<br>Ecuador<br>Panama<br>Peru | Argentina<br>The Bahamas<br>Barbados<br>Brazil<br>Chile<br>Colombia<br>Ecuador<br>Uruguay<br>Venezuela, RB |

*Sources:* Fietz 2020; Packard and Onishi 2020.
*Note:* Argentina's individual unemployment savings accounts are available only to registered workers in the construction sector. The government of Mexico City administers a job-seeker benefit, but only to residents and certain groups deemed vulnerable.

**MAP 4.1    Unemployment insurance throughout the world**

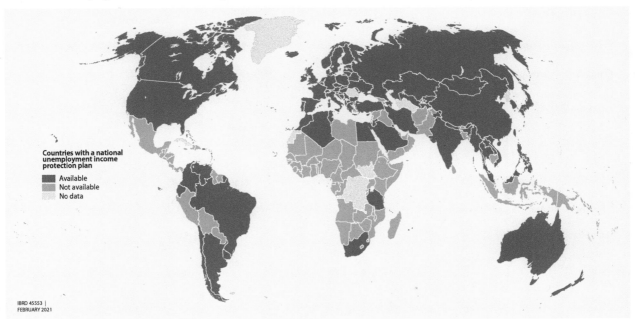

Countries with a national
unemployment income
protection plan

Available
Not available
No data

IBRD 45553 |
FEBRUARY 2021

### Unemployment insurance: Falling short of an adequate crisis response

Job displacement support is effectively out of reach for most workers in the LAC region. Only about 12 percent of unemployed workers in the region have received unemployment benefits (ILO 2019). This rate of effective coverage falls far below that observed in developing and emerging-market countries in Central and Eastern Europe and in some countries in Asia and the Pacific (see figure 4.5).

Widespread, unregulated informal employment practices are the principal culprit for the small share of workers who can access unemployment income support in the LAC region. This low rate of access is the case even in countries with comprehensive sets of unemployment insurance instruments, such as Argentina, Brazil, and Ecuador (ILO 2020). For informal workers, any kind of displacement income support is generally weak—informal urban workers often fall into poverty during crises—and 55 percent of all workers in the LAC region hold this status (Messina and Silva 2020).

However, informal employment practices are only part of the problem. Workers with formal but more precarious contracts may be statutorily excluded from coverage by unemployment income support programs (Fietz 2020). And even among formally employed workers with "standard" employment contracts, effective coverage is disappointingly low. Demanding eligibility requirements that fail to reflect the patterns of employment and tenure achieved even by many formal workers impede effective coverage. Regulatory and administrative failures often mean that contributions are not received. And the transaction costs of securing benefits can be prohibitively high, particularly if the benefits are meager. Beyond the exceptional case of Barbados, whose system delivers benefits to 88 percent of unemployed workers, only in The Bahamas, Chile, and Uruguay do national unemployment insurance arrangements appear to provide widespread, effective coverage (figure 4.5, panel b). Outside these three countries, even in the remaining few LAC

FIGURE 4.5   **Effective coverage of unemployment benefits, selected countries, latest available year**

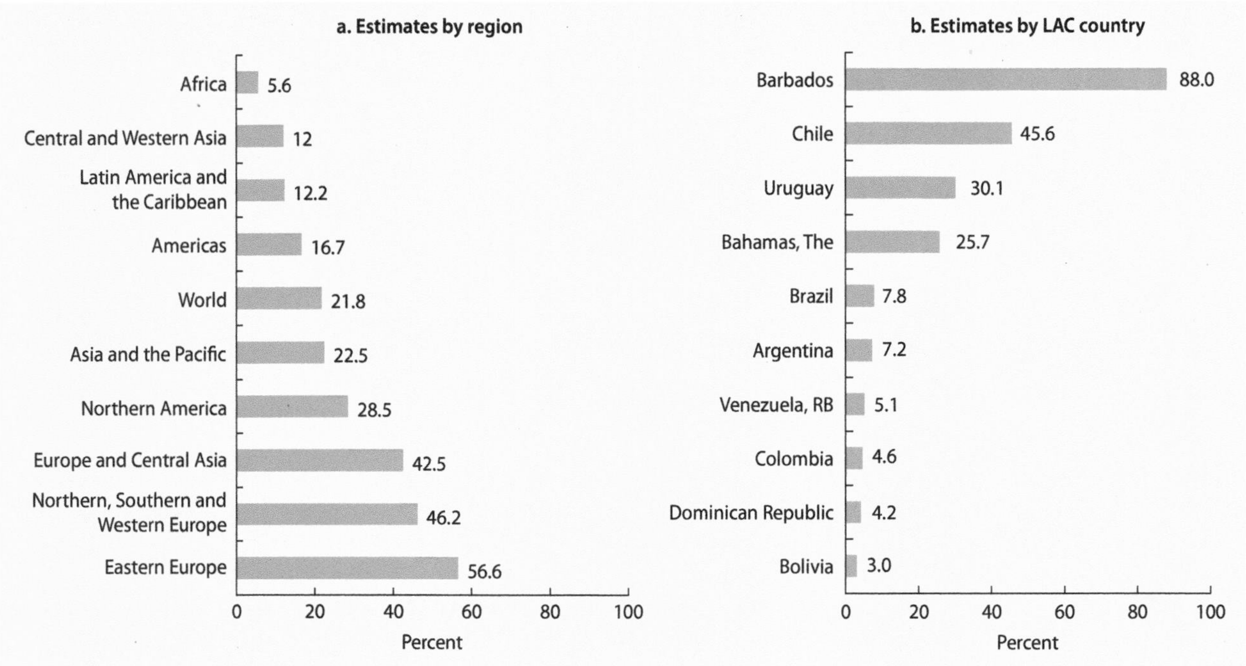

*Source:* ILO 2019.
*Note:* The figures for Bolivia and for the Dominican Republic refer only to mandated severance payments. LAC = Latin America and the Caribbean.

countries that offer unemployment insurance, coverage remains too low.

In addition to limited access and the resulting low levels of effective coverage, unemployment insurance arrangements (whether pure risk pooling or individual savings) in the LAC region have three main flaws as crisis response mechanisms. First, the insurance value of their benefits is limited. In Ecuador, for example, formally employed workers must contribute to the unemployment scheme for at least 24 months before they are eligible for benefits, and upon losing their jobs they are required to wait another 60 days before drawing on their unemployment insurance. This program follows a pattern observed in several middle-income countries where, out of concern for moral hazard, the benefits from the risk-pooling mechanism are set at inadequate levels or the eligibility conditions to receive benefits are made prohibitively stringent and bear little relation to the actual patterns of formal employment in the

economy (Fietz 2020). Furthermore, in countries that offer plans centered around individual savings, low-income workers with limited saving capacity will find it difficult to manage long unemployment spells. Only in Chile's national *Seguro de Cesantia* are parameters set that effectively combine protection and positive incentives for unemployed workers to find new jobs. (Holzmann et al. 2012; Hartley, van Ours, and Vodopivec 2012).

Second, in most LAC countries that have unemployment income support arrangements, these arrangements are offered as an array of overlapping and uncoordinated instruments. For example, a formally employed worker in Brazil with a standard contract is entitled to receive severance pay, an unemployment insurance benefit, and access to the full balance in the worker's individual employer-sponsored severance savings account. Access to the risk-pooling benefit is not sequenced with savings, nor is access to the savings account limited by a schedule of withdrawals. For workers who earn the statutory minimum wage—or close to it—this lack of coordination combines with the benefits' parameters to deliver a total payment upon dismissal well above what they were earning from their job (Almeida and Packard 2018; Fietz 2020). As a result, there is growing evidence of collusion between employees and employers and of induced dismissals: Pinto (2015) shows that the rate of dismissal spikes at the de jure vesting period for unemployment insurance and that 6 percent of those dismissed "without just cause" return to the same firm after a period similar to the maximum payout period for unemployment insurance. The prospect of this "unemployment bonanza" has been identified as the source of Brazil's high rates of employee turnover (Da Silva Teixeira, Balbinotto Neto, and Soares Leivas 2020; Portela Souza et al. 2016). Brazil's unemployment insurance appears to have a very limited consumption smoothing effect to support job searching: Gerard and Naritomi (2019) show that as soon as covered unemployed workers in Brazil receive the benefit, their consumption spikes, although their displacement still generates a long-term loss of consumption of around 14 percent.

Third, when poorly designed and uncoordinated, unemployment insurance has contributed to perverse aggregate outcomes, delivering only a muted "stabilizer" response during downturns and surges in spending during sustained periods of economic growth. If quantitative adjustments have come to predominate labor markets' responses to crises and are leading to long-run consequences through the scarring they cause, the lack of accessible, state-contingent unemployment support programs becomes an even bigger problem. As automatic stabilizers, these programs should also contribute to countercyclical fiscal policy. Indeed, in many OECD countries, spending on unemployment insurance and other transfer programs automatically falls in good times and increases in bad times (as unemployment and poverty experience their cyclical increases), cushioning workers. By contrast, in three

LAC countries with broad-based national unemployment insurance plans—Argentina, Brazil, and Uruguay—spending on unemployment insurance benefits is only weakly correlated with detrended GDP growth (figure 4.6).

### Severance pay mandates: Shallow and unreliable risk pools

In contrast to the dearth of national unemployment insurance, almost all LAC countries rely heavily on mandated, employer-financed severance pay. In the early stages of their economies' structural shift away from agriculture, LAC governments—like those of many developing countries—lacked the capacity to collect taxes and administer risk-sharing programs. Mandating instead that employers pay severance had three substantial social advantages: (a) it discouraged frivolous or unfair dismissals; (b) it gave employees greater bargaining power in negotiations with dominant employers in what are still relatively concentrated and oligopolistic markets (tending toward monopsony in the rural, large-scale agriculture and resource extraction sectors); and (c) it provided households with some protection from destitution at a time when social assistance transfers were rarely provided or meager in size.

However, as the capacity of LAC governments to collect taxes and administer risk-sharing arrangements has grown, the deficiency of mandated severance pay as the sole or even the primary instrument of income protection for unemployment has become apparent. The deficiencies of severance pay are particularly clear in the context of systemic shocks such as the LAC region's crises, whose impacts overwhelm these relatively shallow, firm-level risk-pooling arrangements. In Argentina, according to workers' reported reasons for their employment ending, of the 22.8 percent who reported firm bankruptcy as the reason in 2018, only 33.1 percent actually received severance pay (World Bank 2020). This rate is about the same as in 2010 and is an improvement on earlier coverage rates. However, it leaves two-thirds of the workers covered by law effectively without the income

**FIGURE 4.6  Economic cycle, unemployment, and spending on labor policies and programs**

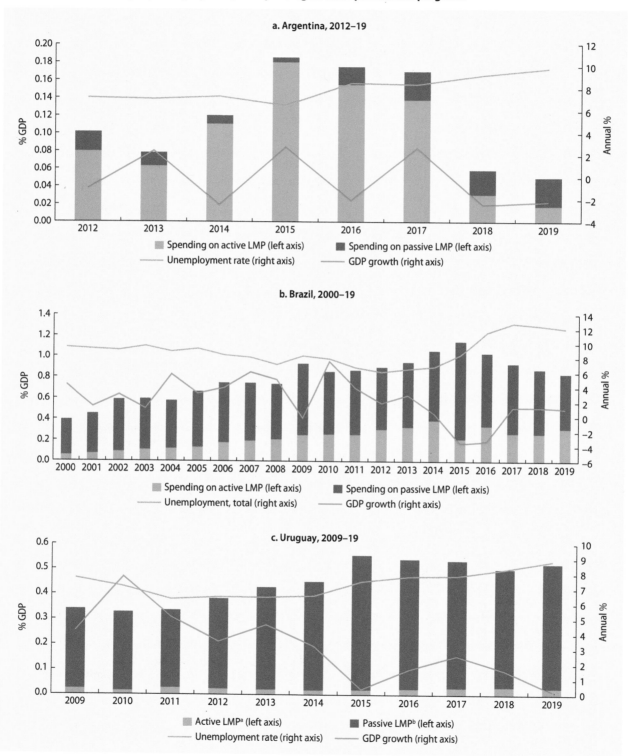

*Source:* Social Protection and Jobs Global Practice, with data from Brazil's Ministry of the Economy, Argentina's Administración Nacional de Seguridad Social and Ministry of Labor and Employment, and Uruguay's Banco de Previsión Social.
*Note:* GDP = gross domestic product; LMP = labor market programs.
a. Projoven, Proimujer, Trabajadores en Seguro Desempleo, etc.
b. Seguro de Desempleo.

support during unemployment they were promised. In countries where the labor code and specialized labor courts impose the burden of proof on firms in disputes over severance pay and where severance liabilities are borne by business owners rather than businesses themselves, large severance mandates combine with restrictions on contracting and dismissals to have a chilling effect on new formal job offers (Holzmann et al. 2012). This effect can partly explain the LAC region's pattern of formal employment shrinking during crises mainly through a reduction in new job offers.

Relying solely on severance pay or unemployment insurance is not as good of a risk-sharing arrangement as using a combination of both (Schmieder and von Wachter 2016). More reliable, robust, and incentive-compatible income support for job displacement can be achieved when employers' severance obligations are prefunded and prudently managed; when their regular contributions to this prefunding can be made transparently in the form of individual savings accounts (preferably managed by independent third parties); and when this prefunding can be integrated with a larger, country-level risk-pooling mechanism, as is the case in several OECD member countries. Many countries, including Chile in Latin America (as discussed in detail later in this chapter), combine severance, individual savings, and risk-pooling plans into effective protection systems that discourage frivolous dismissals, eliminate collusive gaming of the system by firms and employees, tolerate systemic as well as idiosyncratic shocks, and strongly incentivize job search efforts (Castro, Weber, and Reyes 2018; Robalino and Weber 2014).

### What can be done?
A history of frequent systemic shocks combined with the emergence of a significantly sized middle class has created more demand for robust unemployment insurance mechanisms in Latin American countries than in other regions (De Ferranti et al. 2000). Among the handful of national unemployment plans

available in Latin America, two were introduced following the crises of the late 1990s. Past crises and the 2020 pandemic shock dramatically demonstrated the usefulness of having unemployment income support systems with deep and extensive risk pools and that provide a platform and channel for additional, extraordinary support measures when these are needed. The pandemic crisis is likely to motivate proposals for national unemployment insurance plans in the countries that do not have them yet and proposals to expand coverage in those that do. Augmenting unemployment support through the creation or redesign of unemployment insurance is therefore a key policy action to be considered.

In Latin America and the Caribbean, several countries have recently implemented changes to social insurance plans that ease eligibility requirements and increase benefits (ILO 2020). In Brazil and Chile, for example, the unemployment insurance system has also served as the platform for implementing subsidized furlough measures and other employee-retention programs. These systems make all the difference in the quality of labor markets' adjustment to crises. For example, in the United States, extensions of unemployment insurance benefits introduced during deep recessions have been shown to improve the quality of worker-job matches—and the impact on match quality is greater among people who are more likely to be liquidity constrained, such as women, nonwhites, and less educated workers (Farooq, Kugler, and Muratori 2020). In the pandemic-induced contraction of 2020, the United States has used unemployment insurance top-ups and benefit extensions more intensively than subsidized furloughs or other retention subsidies, more so than in other OECD member countries (Furman et al. 2020). Given the burden it forces onto individual firms, as well as the possibly irrecoverable loss of viable businesses and business-specific human capital, this policy choice is controversial. But the expansion of access to (already widespread) unemployment insurance has contained the human costs of this sharp contraction and prevented its unprecedented rates of job destruction from leading to destitution (Furman et al. 2020).

Why have even administratively sophisticated middle- and upper-middle-income countries in the LAC region held back from offering nationally administered income support plans for the unemployed? Setting aside the valid concerns that arise in most countries over moral hazard and other distortions to incentives, the reluctance to offer unemployment income support is usually based on three arguments. First is a fiscal justification: offering unemployment insurance could be costly, especially in a time of sizable fiscal deficits, and the contingent liabilities could be fiscally explosive in light of the region's relatively frequent crises. On average, the LAC countries that offer unemployment insurance spend about 0.3 percent of their GDP on these plans. In the OECD, spending on such plans ranges from about 0.3 percent to 1.8 percent of GDP.[7] This level of spending on a single social protection program could indeed be prohibitive for some LAC countries, given their smaller tax bases, limited enforcement capacity, and ongoing struggles to extend poverty-relief programs and human capital–building services. The trade-off is more acute for the low-income countries in the region. However, evidence suggests that the introduction of some key features can reduce the cost of such programs while still keeping their level of support and responsiveness to crises at acceptable levels. Chile's *Seguro de Cesantia* is an exemplary case of a well-established national income support plan in Latin America that is responsive in times of crisis and financially robust.[8]

Furthermore, concerns for fiscal costs in the immediate term can be myopic, ignoring the true, full costs of prolonged labor market adjustment and forgone productivity from: (a) workers clinging to jobs that are no longer viable or that they are not particularly good at for fear of losing acquired rights to severance; (b) firms' incentives to dismiss newer, younger, possibly better-skilled employees rather than older workers with costlier severance entitlements; (c) job searches driven solely by the urgent need for income, which

often result in poor employment matches; and (d) the unanticipated costs incurred out of pocket or from postponing health and education investments by unemployed people without effective income support as they look for new employment.

Second, in the LAC region, the reluctance to augment unemployment income support is often anchored in the argument that such a scheme is unnecessary given the ample work opportunities in the informal economy and the expectation that informal employment operates as a countercyclical income safety net. Historically, Latin American labor markets have been characterized by high levels of informality (Perry et al. 2007). Indeed, the LAC region is more informal than expected given its level of development (Robertson 2020). However, changes in the size of the region's informal economy are not always countercyclical, nor is relying on informal employment as a safety net without costs: growing evidence shows that spells of informal employment can cause scarring (Cruces, Ham, and Viollaz 2015). Furthermore, the 2000s saw important growth in the number of formal jobs in the region. Between 2002 and 2015, the share of formal employees in total employment increased from 47 percent to 55 percent. This change was caused by a reduction in the share of self-employed, from 24 percent to 20 percent, and of informal employment from 29 percent to 25 percent. In contrast, between 1995 and 2002, the share of self-employed workers had remained stable (Messina and Silva 2020). Hence, although informality remains high in the region, a large share of the labor market is formal in most LAC countries. This shift has changed the aspirations of the Latin American middle class.

Moreover, as pointed out by Antón, Trillo, and Levy (2012) and by Levy (2018), further formalization might be discouraged by the region's current architecture of social protection and labor systems. These systems may not yet offer the protection that working people really value, making them a tax that workers and firms seek to avoid or evade. Although the extent of mandated nonwage costs in most LAC countries—the "tax wedge"[9]—leaves little room to add benefit programs, the perception that the "effective" benefits of formality are low can lead to increased informality.

The third argument for the reluctance to augment unemployment income support is that it is not necessary in countries where labor laws make employee dismissals almost impossible. Indeed, some of the world's existing employment protection laws and institutions were designed when displacement from formal employment was relatively rare. But in a growing number of middle-income and high-income countries, the emphasis of unemployment support programs has shifted from preserving employment relationships to protecting working people as they transition from job to job. Pursued most ambitiously by several countries in Europe, this policy shift entails loosening restrictions on dismissals, aligning protections for workers on different types of employment contracts, and considerably augmenting unemployment income support and public employment services. The general direction of reform has been to shift from protecting workers from change to supporting them for and throughout labor market changes. In Europe, several countries have combined reforms of labor regulations with improvements in the reliability of non–firm-specific income support for unemployment.

This shift has occurred in several countries. For example, from 2011 to 2015, Portugal reduced its severance mandates and considerably improved the reliability of non–firm-specific income support for unemployment as it eased the restrictions and penalties around employee dismissals (OECD 2017). Labor policy reforms in Spain in 2012 took the country's worker protection, unemployment, and reemployment support in a similar direction, substantially loosening restrictions on dismissals and severance entitlements, although these entitlements remain some of the highest among OECD member countries (OECD 2013). Italy's labor policy reforms in 2014–15 also shifted the objectives of the country's social protection and labor regulation from protecting jobs to protecting working people, facilitating the reallocation of workers into more productive occupations (Pinelli et al. 2017). Labor reforms in France from 2016 to 2018 substantially reduced restrictions on the dismissal of permanent workers and brought the mandatory total financial compensation for dismissed workers in 2018 below the average for OECD member countries, comparable to the level offered in the Scandinavian countries (OECD 2019).

Finally, in the current crisis, several countries that have well-established unemployment insurance systems have offered retention subsidies rather than direct support of workers through expanded unemployment insurance. The argument for doing so is that if workers are displaced, human capital, and therefore long-term growth potential, may be permanently lost. The magnitude of the human capital destruction (scarring effects) avoided thanks to these programs depends on (a) the estimated losses in productivity caused by periods of unemployment or nonemployment; (b) the unemployment permanently averted, that is, the workers in the employment retention program who would otherwise have been dismissed (either directly or indirectly when their firm went bankrupt or closed for lack of liquidity); and (c) the unemployment temporarily averted, that is, the workers who are supported now by the program but will be let go after the program support period, or even before then if their firm goes bankrupt. In terms of the government's costs per worker, without this program, unemployment insurance would have to be paid in full to each laid-off worker. With the employment retention program, however, some of the costs are supported by the firm (and part by wage reductions assumed by workers). In addition to the size of these programs, a second key choice when designing them is their duration and their coordination with unemployment insurance. Costs and potential distortions to the economy increase as the effects of a crisis extend from transitory to permanent or accelerate structural changes that were only incipient prior to the crisis.

### Social assistance cash transfers: A vital but overstretched source of income support in crises

In the LAC region's context of pervasive informality and difficult-to-access or missing unemployment insurance, social assistance transfers have become the key instruments to smooth the consumption of most people coping with livelihood shocks and to protect them from impoverishment or deeper poverty. Conditional cash transfer (CCT) programs have become a foundation of social protection systems in most LAC countries; consequently, they are intensively used for crisis response. Introduced in the late 1990s, they have grown considerably since the turn of the century (World Bank 2015). Despite a substantial increase in spending and innovations in targeting and delivery, these programs remain a resource primarily for households living in poverty or close to the poverty line. Another prominent feature of LAC countries' safety nets is their "unconditional" cash transfers, most of which are also targeted. In addition to poverty-targeted programs, many governments in the region have added "categorical" transfers (such as child allowances and social pensions)—cash payments targeted to all members of dependent groups, such as children, the elderly, and people of all ages living with disabilities.

Figure 4.7 presents a breakdown of selected LAC countries' spending on social assistance transfers by program type. In all countries featured except Colombia and Nicaragua, where spending on price subsidies dominates, CCTs and other cash and food transfers are the largest categories of spending on social assistance. For people who are informally employed or who earn their livelihoods in the informal economy, these "noncontributory" transfers are the only protection. In this context, it is not surprising that social assistance and labor-intensive public works ("workfare") are the main

responses to crises in the LAC region (Grosh, Bussolo, and Freije 2014; Packard and Onishi 2020). Although these programs are not meant to serve as the lone source of insurance nor to act as a channel for large-volume fiscal stimulus, even in the LAC countries that have national unemployment insurance plans, governments responded to the global financial crisis of 2008–09 by rapidly and substantially expanding these programs (Grosh, Bussolo, and Freije 2014), much as they have done in 2020 in response to the COVID-19 pandemic (Gentilini et al. 2020).

For people who work informally and their dependents, social assistance transfers are vitally important—and they are typically the only access these people have to an effective, efficient risk-pooling mechanism, albeit through governments' general tax and expenditure systems rather than through explicit social insurance arrangements (Packard et al. 2019). But as consumption-smoothing instruments in the wake of a shock to livelihoods, these transfers fall short. This should not come as a surprise, because most of these programs were not set up for crisis management, even if they have succeeded in preventing poor people from falling deeper into poverty, divesting precious assets, or postponing human capital investment (World Bank 2018).

In general, existing cash transfer programs have four structural limitations that makee it difficult to quickly increase the support they offer in response to a shock: (a) tight poverty targeting using "static" beneficiary registries, (b) meager benefit amounts relative to recipient households' incomes, (c) de jure budget restrictions on the number of eligible households who are admitted to the programs, and (d) LAC countries' lagging investment in identification and delivery systems.

*Tight poverty targeting and static identification systems:* Most social assistance cash transfer programs in Latin America were designed to alleviate poverty rather than prevent impoverishment. As such, eligibility for them is based on whether the household is already poor and whether it includes

**FIGURE 4.7**    **Level and composition of government spending on social assistance transfer programs, selected LAC countries**

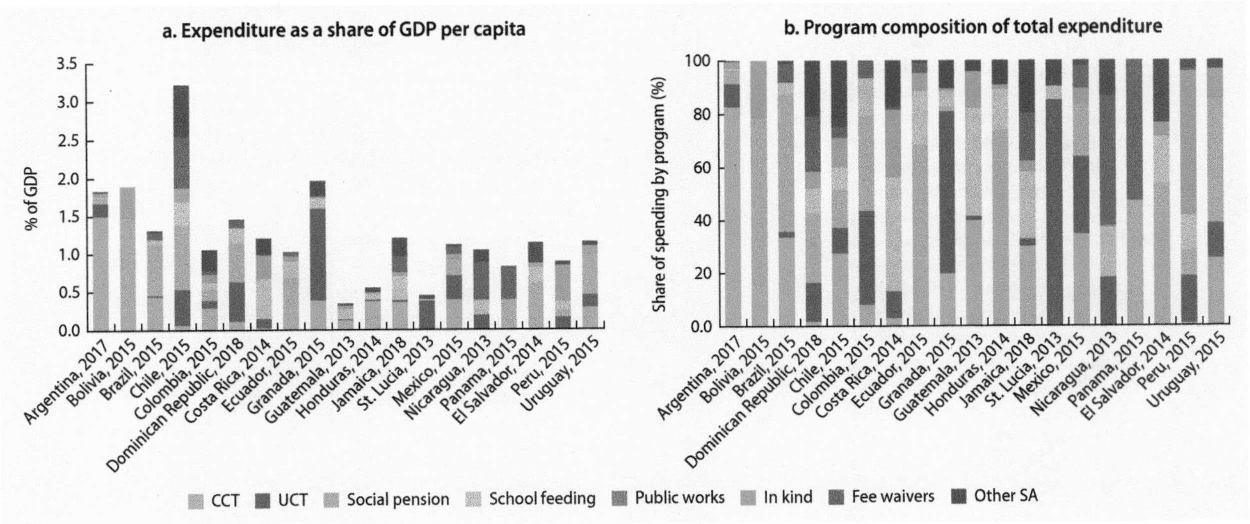

*Source:* World Bank ASPIRE data set: https://www.worldbank.org/en/data/datatopics/aspire.
*Note:* The data shown are from the latest year for which comparable data are CCT = conditional cash transfer; GDP = gross domestic product; LAC = Latin America and the Caribbean; SA = social assistance; UCT = unconditional cash transfer.

members in a dependent group (such as children, the elderly, or the disabled).

Although these programs, as they have been designed and administered by most countries in the LAC region, provide a lifeline to many households, they are not the best suited to helping households manage the risks associated with transitory systemic shocks. The programs cover too few households even among the lowest-earning segments of the population; their registries and delivery systems cannot cope well with rapid increases in the number of households that need support; and their benefit amounts are low relative to conventional levels of consumption-smoothing social insurance (figure 4.8).

The recent policy push to make social assistance cash transfer programs responsive ("adaptive") to natural disasters (Bowen et al. 2020; Williams and Berger-Gonzalez 2020) has substantially loosened these constraints. In earlier crises, labor-intensive public works—also known as "workfare" programs—helped smooth the consumption of some workers, mainly those employed in the informal economy and earning

livelihoods above but close to the poverty line (De Ferranti et al. 2000; Jalan and Ravallion 2003; Subbarao et al. 2013). These programs were the de facto unemployment insurance for the majority of such workers worldwide during the crises of the 1980s and 1990s, and even in the global financial crisis of 2008–09 in several European countries (Packard and Weber 2020). But outside Argentina and Chile, the capacity to deploy these programs quickly and effectively is still limited in the LAC region.

*Meager benefits:* Social assistance cash transfers are typically designed to complement rather than replace earned income. They are typically much lower than the level of income replacement conventionally considered adequate for consumption smoothing (anywhere from 40 to 70 percent of prior income). In light of the explicit aim of enabling and even incentivizing households to make human capital investments (such as taking up and maintaining good nutrition, timely preventative health care, and regular school attendance), these benefit amounts are low relative to the households' earned

FIGURE 4.8   **Insufficient support, with many left behind**

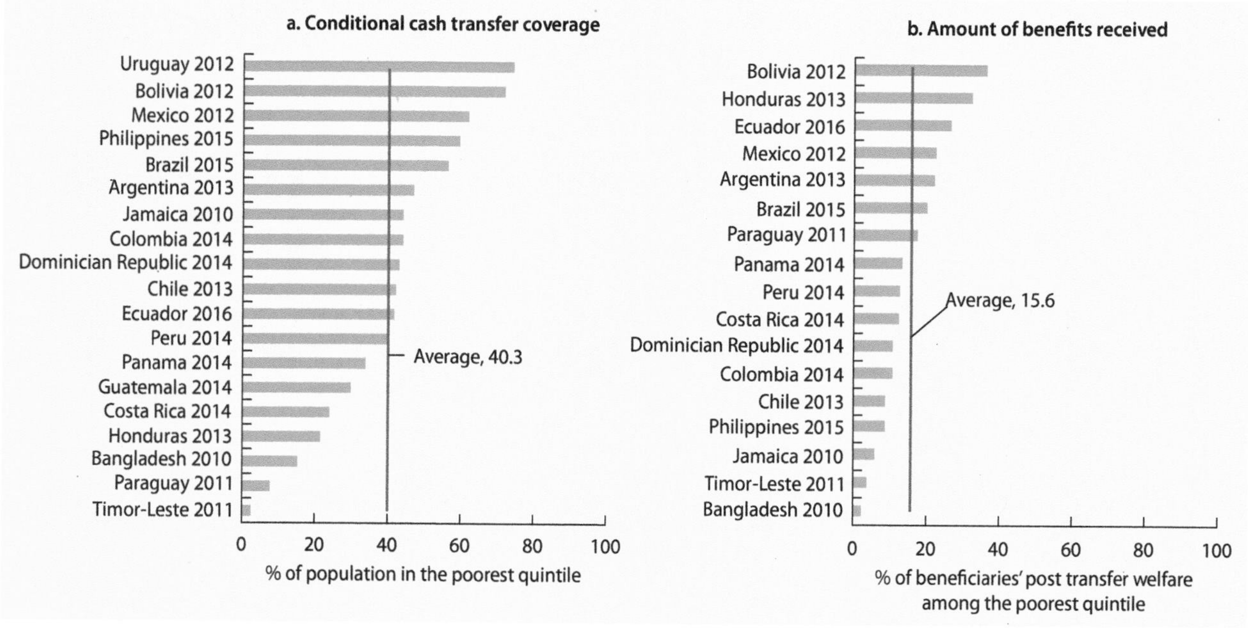

a. Conditional cash transfer coverage

b. Amount of benefits received

*Source:* World Bank 2018.

income. A large body of research suggests that, on the whole, these benefits support positive incentives to return to work (Fiszbein and Schady 2009; Garganta and Gasparini 2015). However, this finding may imply that the amounts transferred are insufficient to robustly smooth consumption when livelihoods are destroyed by a crisis.[10]

*Rationed benefits:* Few social assistance cash transfer programs in Latin America and the Caribbean are entitlements. This distinction matters because budget allocations for most of these programs are discretionary, imposing limits on the amount of benefits that can be paid out to eligible households in any given year. Being eligible does not guarantee entry; there have to be slots available in the program, which depends on other households' entry and exit into the program and on the government's budget. In Argentina and Chile, this aspect of the programs has been changed. But even in Brazil—which is famous for its *Bolsa Familia* CCT program—prior to the recent expansion in coverage in response to COVID-19, more than one million eligible families were waiting for the rations on

benefits to be loosened or lifted altogether. Because these rations are politically and even legislatively cumbersome to loosen quickly, and because policy makers have many other demands to manage with limited fiscal space, it is difficult for social assistance cash transfers, as they exist today in most countries in the LAC region, to substitute for coverage by unemployment insurance plans. Argentina's family allowance program is an instructive exception (box 4.1).

*Lagging investment in identification and delivery systems:* The foundations of most social assistance programs are identification databases, known in most countries as social registries, which enable these programs to identify those in need. However, the share of the population covered by these registries in the LAC region is low and limited to the chronically poor and vulnerable. In the 2020 pandemic, the LAC countries have relied heavily on cash transfers to get money into the hands of vulnerable people quickly, some in more effective ways than others. A key determinant of the success of these efforts is the share of the population covered by the

## BOX 4.1 Family allowances as de facto unemployment insurance

Argentina's safety net is particularly effective at mitigating impoverishment, especially among families with children and those that depend on informal livelihoods (World Bank 2020). For a growing majority of Argentine working people and their dependents, family allowances, specifically the noncontributory *Asignación Universal por Hijo* (AUH), have become de facto unemployment insurance. Indeed, for microentrepreneurs, other self-employed workers, and informal employees with children, AUH is effectively the only rapidly available means of sustaining consumption in the wake of shocks.

But even for people who have formal jobs, AUH can act as a more reliable instrument for consumption smoothing than Argentina's official unemployment support program. This is ironic, because Argentina is one of the few countries in Latin America to offer nationally administered unemployment income protection. A growing scarcity of formal job offers and a trend toward shorter employment spells

make it difficult for workers to gain coverage under that program, and even if they do, benefit levels have been allowed to deteriorate. Additionally, Argentina's labor code mandates that employer-financed severance be paid to workers dismissed because of economic difficulties or the insolvency of a firm. However, in 2018, only a third of people who reported losing a formal job for these reasons received severance pay, about the same share who received severance in 2009.

The registration, identification, and delivery systems developed by the Argentine government to quickly shift working people and their families from the country's contributory family allowances to the AUH are, for this reason, serving a vital unemployment insurance function that the country's other social protection instruments are no longer able to serve.

*Source*: World Bank 2020.

social registry of the social safety net program, which ranges from almost 100 percent of the population in Argentina and Uruguay to about 5 percent in Bolivia (figure 4.9, panel a). When a greater share of the population is covered by these social registries, governments are better able to expand benefits to the newly poor and newly vulnerable. Another determinant of success is whether these registries have dynamic intake systems that allow programs to quickly expand to include previously nonpoor groups. Countries with initially weaker safety nets were less able to provide robust income protection through this route (figure 4.9, panel b). In general, the LAC region lacks reliable and robust income protection, in addition to sufficient job search support to curb human capital losses (as will be discussed in the following subsection).

How can the LAC region do better for its workers and communities in terms of its social protection and labor responses to crises?

Years of investment in developing information management and benefit delivery systems are making the LAC region's cash transfer programs more responsive. Figure 4.10 illustrates the expansion of cash transfer programs in response to crises in Latin America. At the time of the global financial crisis, countries that had CCTs and other transfer programs expanded these programs "vertically" (by increasing the amount paid by the program to existing recipients) and "horizontally" (by extending coverage to previously uncovered households). Brazil did both by expanding the coverage of *Bolsa Familia* to a total of 12 million families and increasing the benefit amount by 10 percent. Colombia's government expanded the coverage of *Familias en Acción* to new households, and Mexico's *Progresa* (which later became *Opportunidades* and then *Prospera*) increased the amount paid to existing beneficiaries (Grosh, Bussolo, and Freije 2014). With the benefit of greater experience, governments in the region have repeated this

**FIGURE 4.9** **Coverage of social registries and support received through social assistance programs during the COVID-19 (coronavirus) pandemic**

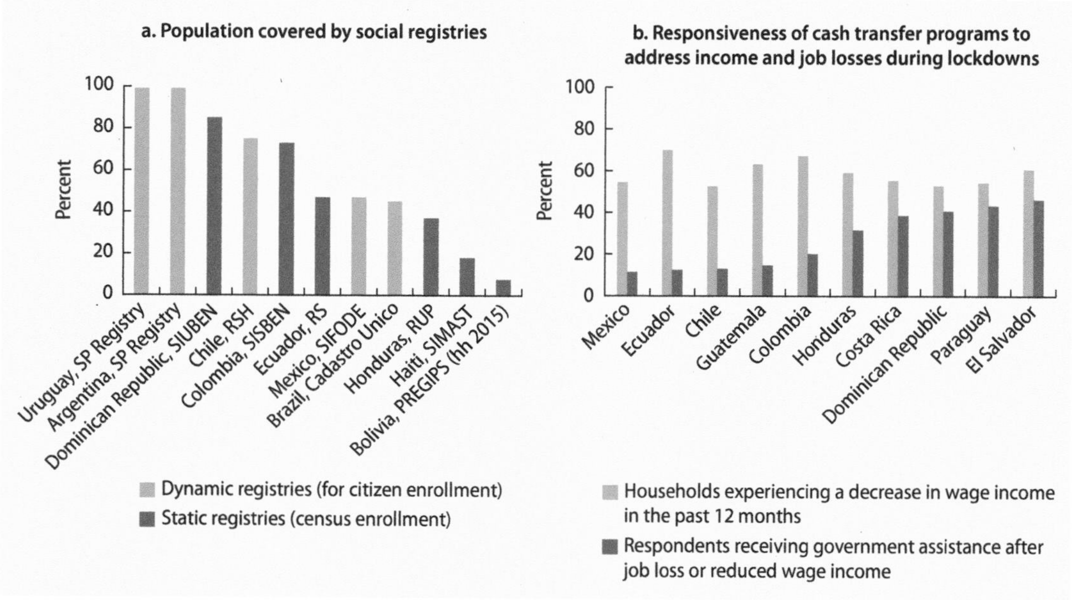

**a. Population covered by social registries**

**b. Responsiveness of cash transfer programs to address income and job losses during lockdowns**

■ Dynamic registries (for citizen enrollment)
■ Static registries (census enrollment)

■ Households experiencing a decrease in wage income in the past 12 months
■ Respondents receiving government assistance after job loss or reduced wage income

*Sources:* Morgandi et al. 2020; World Bank High Frequency Phone Surveys, first and second rounds, Poverty and Equity Global Practice.
*Note:* The medium blue bars in panel a denote dynamic registries that are open to citizen enrollment, enabling rapid expansion; the dark blue bars denote static registries populated by census sweeps. hh = household survey; PREGIPS = Registro Integrado de Programas Sociales del Estado Plurinacional de Bolivia (Bolivia's system for selecting beneficiaries of social programs); RS = Registro Social (Ecuador's system for selecting beneficiaries of social programs); RSH = Registro Social de Hogar (Chile's system for selecting beneficiaries of social programs); RUP = El Registro Único de Participantes (Honduras's system for selecting beneficiaries of social programs); SIFODE = Sistema de Focalización de Desarrollo (Mexico's system for selecting beneficiaries of social programs); SIMAST = Information System of the Ministry of Social Affairs and Labour (Haiti's social registry database); SISBEN = Sistema de Selección de Beneficiarios de Programas Sociales (Colombia's system for selecting beneficiaries of social programs); SIUBEN = Sistema Único de Beneficiarios (Dominican Republic's Colombia's system for selecting beneficiaries of social programs); SP = social protection.

**FIGURE 4.10** **Expansion of cash transfer programs in response to crises**

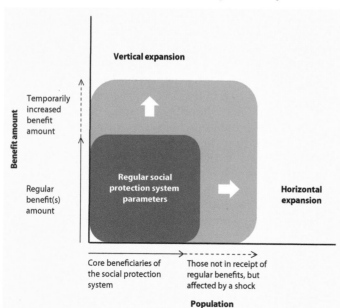

*Sources:* Bowen et al. 2020; Morgandi et al. 2020; Williams and Berger-Gonzalez 2020.

strategy to rapidly provide support to help households through the economic impact of the COVID-19 pandemic (Morgandi et al. 2020). Box 4.2 discusses Brazil's response to the pandemic along these lines.

As argued earlier, although Latin America's national social assistance cash transfer programs fall short of the ideal countercyclical safety net, they still have considerable social and economic value in a crisis. What are the effects of the expansion of these programs? Can such cash transfers perform a "stabilizer" function? On the basis of a rare quasinatural experiment, Gerard, Naritomi, and Silva (2021) show that a social assistance program's expansion has aggregate benefits (for the entire local economy) in addition to individual-level benefits. These positive effects on employment and income work as automatic stabilizers for the economy and counter crisis-induced inequality. Social assistance cash transfer programs

### BOX 4.2   Brazil's social protection response to the COVID-19 (coronavirus) pandemic

Social protection and labor measures were at the center of the fiscal response package to the COVID-19 crisis in Brazil. These measures explicitly targeted several vulnerable groups, including the preexisting poor, families working in the informal economy who became temporarily poor because of the crisis, low-income single mothers, and formal workers at risk of losing their income from dismissal (figure B4.2.1). The measures had two objectives: to make social distancing possible for those economically affected by it and to mitigate the negative impacts of the crisis on welfare and human capital.

The first line of Brazil's policy response expanded the existing flagship social protection and labor programs, including the *Bolsa Familia* conditional cash transfer and unemployment insurance, both horizontally (by adding new beneficiaries) and vertically (by providing greater benefits to existing beneficiaries). These goals were achieved in two ways: (a) by relaxing budget constraints so that already eligible and newly eligible families could gain coverage by *Bolsa Familia* through the automatic absorption of new claims submitted to the unemployment insur-

ance program, and (b) by advancing payments of regular entitlements, including special withdrawals from the FGTS *(Fundo de Garantia do Tempo de Serviço)* employer-sponsored savings accounts.

As a second line of response, Brazil launched two temporary social protection and labor programs to address specific vulnerabilities in the formal and informal labor markets generated by COVID-19 that were not covered by the expansion of existing programs. One program was an emergency cash transfer program for the poor (defined as participants in the *Bolsa Familia* program) as well as those outside formal wage employment but normally ineligible for social assistance, such as nonpoor informal workers and formal freelance self-employed workers. And for formal sector workers, Brazil introduced a temporary wage subsidy for those who were furloughed or had their hours temporarily reduced, under the requirement that their firms maintain the employment relationship for a certain amount of time after the program ends. These measures targeting workers were complemented by subsidies to firms and other measures; altogether, they have amounted to 4.1 percent of Brazil's gross domestic product.

**FIGURE B4.2.1   Brazil's COVID-19 (coronavirus) social protection and labor response strategy for two major vulnerable groups**

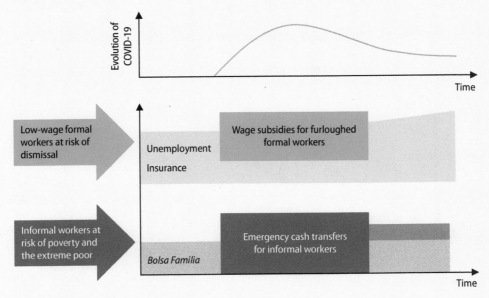

*Source:* World Bank 2020.
*Note:* This figure illustrates Brazil's response to protect two major vulnerable groups from the COVID-19 crisis: low-wage formal employees and low-income families working in the informal economy.

inject funds into local economies, potentially raising the demand for labor, including in the formal sector. The paper links administrative records on the universe of *Bolsa Familia* recipients and formal workers in Brazil to provide evidence of the program's effects on formal labor markets. Using variation across municipalities in the program's expansion in 2009, the paper finds that this expansion increased formal employment. Its evidence is consistent with the large multiplier effect of *Bolsa Familia* benefits, which dominate the negative effects on the formal labor supply at the individual level, as is also documented using variation caused by income eligibility thresholds.

Importantly, Gerard, Naritomi, and Silva (2020) also show that the program expansion had positive aggregate effects beyond its effects on individual beneficiaries through spillovers to nonbeneficiaries. Taking advantage of their linked data on formal employment and the poor and vulnerable, they investigate whether the additional formal employment they observe comes from beneficiaries or nonbeneficiaries. Panel a of figure 4.11 presents their results: the effect of the program's expansion is positive and significant among noneligible families. This

increase in formal employment could occur through either the creation of new jobs or the formalization of jobs that were previously informal (although in the latter case, the program expansion would not be associated with an increase in overall employment). The program's expansion did in fact have positive and significant effects on GDP (figure 4.11, panel b), suggesting that the expansion led to employment creation, not just the conversion of informal jobs to formal jobs. Local gross products increased by 1.5 percent as a consequence of the program expansion. These results highlight the importance of accounting for both the individual and the aggregate effects of social assistance welfare programs in policy debates.

To deliver emergency social transfers in response to crises and to maximize their positive effects, the LAC countries must ensure their cash transfer programs are sufficiently responsive and adaptive to the needs created by systemic shocks, and they must substantially augment their delivery capacity. Key to this change is expanding population registries to cover all the poor and vulnerable—indeed, extending the registries as far up the income distribution as is practicable—and sharing their information among all social

**FIGURE 4.11**   **Positive effects of welfare transfers on local formal employment**

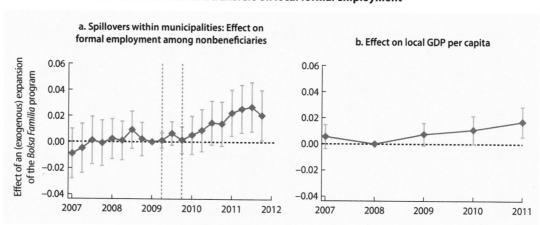

*Source:* Gerard, Naritomi, and Silva 2020.
*Note:* This figure shows the effect of a 2009 expansion of the *Bolsa Familia* program on the number of formal employees among nonbeneficiaries (panel a) and local GDP per capita (panel b). The vertical lines represent 95 percent confidence intervals on the basis of robust standard errors clustered at the municipality level In panel a, the data are from the first quarter of all years shown.

programs rather than keeping registries program-specific. Moreover, because most LAC countries use social assistance transfers as an instrument in crisis response, these countries' governments must better manage the processes of enrollment, registration, and recertification for these transfers and make these processes rapid and effective. The administrators of the region's national cash transfer programs aspire to make more flexible enrollment and exit processes for beneficiaries so that previously nonpoor families can receive benefits when needed and so that those whose incomes grow beyond the programs' eligibility thresholds have every incentive to move into sustainable, productive livelihood activities. However, because CCT programs are designed to address chronic poverty, they typically have lengthy intake processes to identify, enroll, and recertify beneficiaries that are implemented uniformly across all prospective beneficiary households.[11]

Thus, although the LAC countries with national CCT programs and other cash transfer programs have used them to effectively help households adjust to shocks, these programs are not yet a sufficiently nimble policy instrument to address the needs of poor and nonpoor vulnerable groups during transient systemic shocks (such as financial crises or long recessions). Because of the demands they make on administrative capacity, cash transfer systems on their own are not yet effective substitutes for fuller national risk-sharing arrangements.

Crises are very costly for some workers, and for most people, policy responses to these crises have failed to compensate for the costs or to offer effective remedies. One key reason for this failure is that social protection and labor systems in the LAC region are not yet fully in place, so they are certainly not yet able to provide a dynamic safety net that responds robustly to shocks and crises (Packard and Onishi 2020; Williams and Berger-Gonzalez 2020).

### What can be done?

Social assistance cash transfers are an important source of income support during crises in Latin America. In many cases, because of these programs' administrative capacity and broad registries, they are one of the few options to deliver benefits to the population quickly. However, the support they provide in response to crises is insufficient, and many are left behind, because these programs are targeted at the preexisting poor. Going forward, it will be important to improve the capacity of these programs to countercyclically increase their level of benefits and their coverage of vulnerable populations.[12]

There are three main policy priorities to improve the dynamism of social assistance cash transfers. The first is to improve the adaptability of these programs—that is, their capacity to be responsive to households suffering the impacts and repercussions of various shocks, including hurricanes, earthquakes, and tsunamis as well as economic crises. This reform will include establishing comprehensive and dynamic social registries that are usable by all social programs, such as Brazil's *Cadastro Unico* (Lindert et al. 2020). The second priority is to move from budgeted programs and rationed *cupos* to protection guarantees, that is, from merely assisting the chronically poor to building safety nets that can expand to catch all who are vulnerable to impoverishment before they become poor. (Packard et al. 2019). And the third is to prevent the emergence of assistance "ghettos" by structuring benefits to incentivize the return to work (with support from augmented reemployment services).

The COVID-19 global pandemic has spurred governments to quickly enact many parts of this agenda (see box 4.3). Many of the needed changes and additions to the LAC region's social protection and labor systems were already under way prior to the 2020 pandemic, especially in the countries more vulnerable to climate change and other natural disasters (Bowen et al. 2020; Williams and Berger-Gonzalez 2020). Many of the changes that make a social protection system responsive to households suffering the impacts of natural disasters also improve the system's function as part of a country's automatic stabilizers against other systemic

BOX 4.3 **Latin America and the Caribbean's social protection and labor responses to the COVID-19 (coronavirus) contraction of 2020**

Gentilini et al. (2020) have kept a record of the social protection and labor measures taken by Latin American and Caribbean (LAC) countries since the COVID-19 (coronavirus) pandemic was declared in early March 2020. The paper tracks an unprecedented expansion of cash transfers, changes to social insurance plans to ease eligibility requirements and increase benefits, extensive use of employee furlough programs underpinned by public financing, the deployment of grants and "soft" loans to small and micro enterprises, and the launch of employment-intensive public works (although this instrument was used relatively rarely, given the need for social distancing—avoiding congregations of people—and other public health imperatives of the pandemic). In all LAC countries, strict confinements and closures have hit the livelihoods of the informally employed particularly hard and have wiped out many informal businesses. Several Latin American countries have sought to ease the plight of these non-poor but nonetheless vulnerable people—the "missing

middle"—with generous one-off emergency transfers. Among the largest of these transfers are the *Ingreso Familiar de Emergencia* programs launched in Argentina and Chile.

Figure B4.3.1 is a stylized diagram showing how all these social protection and labor measures have been used by the LAC countries to respond to the economic fallout from the pandemic. These countries responded relatively quickly and with a wide array of instruments, having benefited from years of prior investment in making their social protection and labor systems adaptive.

Many of these measures inspired by the crisis are transitory. However, several permanent changes have also been made, especially in how household data are gathered and used and in how benefits are delivered. These changes had long been planned, but they were accelerated in order to help people cope with the economic consequences of vital public health measures.

FIGURE B4.3.1 **Stylized social protection and labor policy responses to the COVID-19 pandemic**

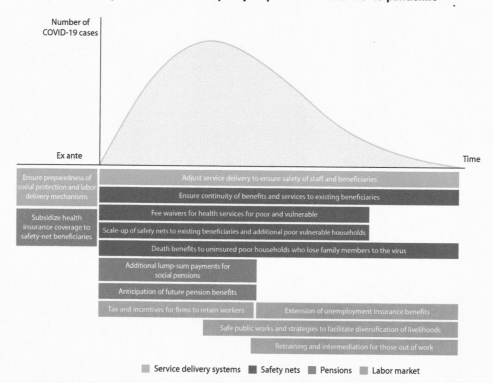

*Sources:* Morgandi et al. 2020; Williams and Berger-Gonzalez 2020.

*Source:* Gentilini et al. 2020.

economic shocks. In advanced economies and in several LAC countries (such as Brazil and Peru), very large fiscal packages have been deployed to deal with the current COVID-19 crisis. LAC countries as a group have acted countercyclically in response to it. The concern now is to not withdraw this support too quickly. Although some countries have renewed their support as the pandemic has continued, others have not, and this renewal (or lack thereof) has fiscal implications.

## Preparing workers for change: (short-term) retention subsidies and (long-term) reemployment and reskilling support

In addition to the short-term impacts of crises on workers, this study highlights that during crises, workers suffer unemployment, loss of durable earnings, and worse career starts that are hard to recover from. These effects are long lived. What can be done to mitigate them? Past research on crises suggests that the persistence of these effects depends on how a crisis is handled and how well, in consequence, workers adjust. Historical evidence shows that the longer a crisis lasts, the more difficult it is for workers to move from declining to expanding sectors. The previous sections of this chapter emphasized the importance of automatic stabilizers and effective income support as policy responses to help workers maintain their level of consumption. This section focuses instead on employment assistance and on reemployment and reskilling schemes. It also discusses job retention programs (furloughs with pay and other short-term schemes that keep workers matched with their jobs, helping to restore employment to previous levels and to prevent the loss of human capital specific to certain sectors and firms), given their prominence in the response to the current crisis in countries like Argentina; Brazil, especially; and Chile.

Increasing the speed and quality of job matches or investments in new skills can mitigate the effects of crises on workers and improve prospects for the affected regions' future growth. The traditional first line of response to crisis-induced threats to employment is intermediation and job search support, for people who have lost their jobs, and the creation of affordable opportunities for upskilling and reskilling.

### Landscape of reemployment and reskilling support in Latin America

Noncash reemployment services provide a vital complement to income support for people who have been displaced by crises and other categories of shocks. Reemployment services include programs that help displaced workers to renew their skills. Such reskilling and reemployment support measures (sometimes collectively known as active labor market programs, or ALMPs) are necessary in two ways. First, along with the combined and coherent use of individual savings and risk pooling for income support, intensively engaging people who have lost jobs with support to help them find new work has been shown to lower the risks of moral hazard and perverse labor supply incentives that arise almost inevitably from offering unemployment insurance (Fietz 2020). And second, these programs help to compensate for people's bounded rationality, behavioral limitations, and less-than-perfect information about new work prospects and the demand for skills. However, the global evidence to date on the effectiveness of ALMPs can be discouraging.

A recent review of the more rigorous evidence from impact evaluations of skill training, wage subsidy, and job search assistance programs by McKenzie (2017) shows that these programs' impacts are modest at best in most circumstances.[13] Public employment services are typically the least resourced branches of national social protection and labor systems. Most governments are unable to offer interventions specifically suited to particular shocks, to the varying needs of different groups of job seekers (such as young people, parents, or the elderly), or to particular industries or places. The track record of traditional ALMPs has also been marred by governments' tendency to deploy them instead of—rather than in support of—necessary structural, institutional, and regulatory reforms. A further limitation on the provision of these services in response to crises is that in countries across the world, public employment services suffer from poor funding and low investment in their implementation capacity, and private programs suffer from limited supply. Even countries in Latin America with long track records of administering public employment assistance programs, such as Argentina, Colombia, and Peru, fail to fund them properly (ILO 2016). This lack of resources leads to low coverage and difficulties in implementing and tailoring programs to the needs of different groups.

A renewed policy emphasis on reemployment support will require four elements rarely associated with traditional ALMPs: (a) specificity to the shocks that caused unemployment or to the particular needs of job seekers; (b) coherence and coordination with other parts of the social protection and labor system (most obviously the unemployment insurance or other income support plan); (c) monitoring of their implementation and evaluation of their impact; and (d) adequate resources from national budgets.

Figure 4.12 conceptually organizes shocks experienced by labor market participants and proposes sets of interventions (other than income support) that are best suited to getting people back to work after each type of shock. Crises such as the 2008–09 global financial crisis, because they affect an entire country, are classified as transient systemic shocks (on the top left). They differ from permanent systemic shocks (on the top right), which consist of disruptions driven by structural transformations (such as climate change, the widespread adoption of new technologies, and changes in trade policy) that destroy certain occupations and create new ones with different skill sets. Shocks also differ from those that are transient but idiosyncratic

**FIGURE 4.12** **Employment and reemployment policies, by the nature of the shock causing displacement**

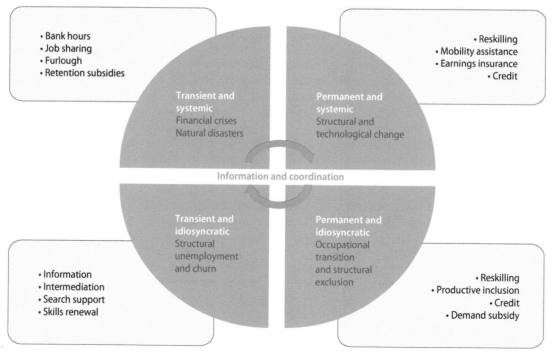

*Source:* Adapted from Packard et al. 2019.

to individuals or households (bottom left), such as increased competition, more flexible dismissal procedures, structural churn, and cyclical fluctuations that lead to more frequent separation and reemployment or to variations in earnings. Finally, permanent idiosyncratic shocks (bottom right) call for policies to facilitate longer-unfolding transitions from lower- to higher-productivity jobs, particularly in lagging areas and regions, or out of long-term unemployment and inactivity (Packard et al. 2019; Robalino, Romero, and Walker 2020). However, as this study shows, crises can leave long-lasting scars, and thus some of their impact is not transitory but long-term (tending toward permanent). Therefore, programs typically associated with permanent systemic shocks, such as reemployment and reskilling support, should be considered in response to crises.

### Mixed record of reemployment assistance services

A recent review by Card, Kluve, and Weber (2017) synthesizes the findings of more than 200 recent studies of active labor market programs. The authors distinguish between three postprogram time horizons and use regression models to determine the programs' estimated effects, for studies that model the probability of employment, and the sign and significance of the estimated effects for all the studies in their sample. They conclude that the average effects of ALMPs are close to zero in the short run but that the effects become more positive two to three years after completion of the programs. The time profile of these impacts varies by the type of program, with larger average gains shown by programs that emphasize human capital accumulation. There is also systematic heterogeneity across groups, with larger impacts for women and for participants coming from long-term unemployment.

The combination and intensity of interventions required to successfully get people back to work could be different for each type of shock. The standard reemployment services (dealing with information and skill constraints) should continue to include counseling, various types of training, job search assistance, intermediation, and various forms of wage subsidies. However, the combination of services required to support those transitioning between similar types of jobs when an individual firm downsizes will be different from those needed to support people displaced by structural changes, such as trade liberalization or the widespread adoption of new technologies, which affect whole industries and places. Probably the most difficult interventions are those needed to facilitate transitions out of very-low-productivity activities (such as subsistence agriculture or own-account work in household enterprises). In these cases, if ensuring access to quality public services and adequate connective infrastructure is not enough, traditional active labor measures may need to be combined with "demand-side" interventions to mobilize investment and create new job opportunities (Robalino, Romero, and Walker 2020). This approach is being followed and evaluated in several countries (box 4.4).

### Beyond short-term income support: Policy actions to get people back to work and reskill them

Employment policies are the traditional response to the challenges of reemployment and reskilling. However, most LAC countries spend very little on active labor measures: about 0.5 percent of GDP. Even those that spend at higher levels have rather poor track records of performance (McKenzie 2017). For instance, among 90 youth employment programs in the LAC region that were rigorously evaluated, only 30 percent had positive effects on employment rates or earnings, and these effects were small (Kluve et al. 2016; Robalino and Romero 2019). Moreover, there were no significant differences in effectiveness between types of programs (for example, training versus job search assistance). Most active labor measures managed by public employment offices have not been evaluated. But their institutional capacity is usually lacking, they face severe constraints in terms of human and financial resources, and their

## BOX 4.4    Permanent, systemic shocks: Responses to job dislocation caused by structural changes

Even the best-performing, modern, generously funded public employment services will struggle to meet the needs of people who have lost jobs in the wake of systemic shocks that bring permanent consequences. Thankfully, there are examples of countries that have responded to help the people who bore the brunt of immediately disruptive but ultimately beneficial structural changes. The interventions used include targeted labor adjustment assistance programs that create appropriate incentives to return to work and can minimize mobility costs and accelerate employment transitions.

The Trade Adjustment Assistance Program in the United States is a federal program that helps workers by providing job search assistance, training, wage subsidies to their prospective new employers, health insurance for the unemployed, and reallocation allowances. The program helps workers who have been displaced because their firm relocated to another country or because of trade liberalization (for workers in the import-competing industry as well as for those employed by downstream or upstream producers). Evaluations of this program show mixed results, including limited effectiveness at helping trade-affected workers obtain reemployment at a suitable wage (Schochet et al. 2012).

Evidence on the targeting of beneficiaries on the basis of their sector of employment, as done in this program, is not encouraging. It shows that (a) regional mobility frictions are higher than sectoral mobility frictions and (b) a crisis that is initially transmitted through one sector quickly spreads to other sectors. (For instance, estimates in the United States and the European Union suggest that

a job in a tradable sector creates between 0.5 and 1.5 extra jobs in nontradable sectors [Ehrlich and Overman 2020]; thus, the loss of a tradable job might lead to additional job destruction in downstream or upstream sectors.) The most affected workers will be difficult to identify, because they are likely to work in sectors not initially affected by the shock.

Critics of the program emphasize that the best reskilling is delivered on the job. They have proposed an alternative of "wage insurance"—time-bound payments made directly to workers in order to reduce the difference between what they earned in the jobs just lost and in their new jobs, up to a ceiling. Wage subsidies instead of classroom training could encourage workers to seek reemployment rapidly and thus improve their access to on-the-job learning (Vijil et al. 2018).

In Austria, the Austrian Steel Foundation has helped displaced workers find new work since the privatization of the country's steel industry. It offers a wide range of services, including vocational orientation programs, small-business start-up assistance, extensive training and retraining programs, formal education, and job search assistance. The foundation is financed by all participants: the trainees themselves, the steel firms, local government (through unemployment benefits), and the remaining workers in the steel industry, who pay a solidarity share of their gross wages to the foundation. The program has increased the probability of participants being employed (Winter-Ebmer 2000).

*Source*: Vijil et al. 2018.

existing staff have weak incentives to respond to the needs of job seekers and employers.

Several lessons from the international experience can be used to guide the reform of active labor measures in the LAC region. First, the evidence shows the importance of moving from solitary interventions to providing an integrated package of services. Even individuals affected by the same type of shock seldom face identical constraints to accessing a new job. Thus, the success of a program

depends on its ability to adapt its services to very different profiles and to the demands of different workers. To do this, reemployment assistance services have to set up registration and statistical profiling systems to help them identify the types of constraints facing individuals. Additionally, modern monitoring and evaluation practices are key to assessing the results of programs and to introducing corrections when they are needed. The fiscal sustainability of larger, more effective programs will also require diverse sources of financing. When governments make risk-pooling structures more widely available to cover shocks with uncertain and catastrophic losses, it is reasonable to expect the resources contributed to these programs by people and firms to meet the needs caused by more foreseeable and less costly shocks. Most active labor measures today are financed from general budget expenditures. Given the nature of shocks and losses and the degree of the market failures involved, this source of funding is appropriate for some but not necessarily all needs. More robust and coordinated employment assistance is needed, with greater focus on these programs' results and unintended consequences.

In terms of reskilling policies, is important to support working people in the face of change. This support involves strengthening technical education and vocational training,

promoting short-cycle higher education programs, expanding access to low-income students, and conditioning these programs' funding on students' employability.

All things considered, a more complete characterization of the possible policy areas of focus to achieve a stronger social protection response to crises in Latin America (second policy dimension) is illustrated in figure 4.13. Evidence from multiple contexts shows that each priority area included in that figure can make a real difference in labor market adjustment.

## Structural: Greater competition and place-based policies

Chapters 2 and 3 of this report document the importance of demand factors and the three structural issues that magnify the impacts of crises on welfare and efficiency in the LAC

**FIGURE 4.13  Addressing crises' impacts and preparing for change: Policy reforms**

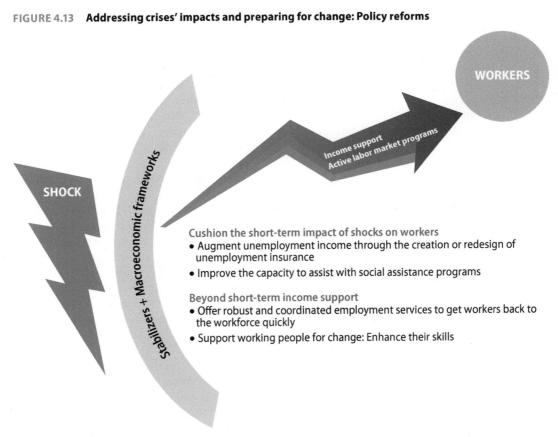

region: labor rigidity, which complicates employment transitions; the dichotomy in the region between protected and unprotected firms (caused by factors such as lack of competition and excessive market power among protected firms); and low levels of mobility among workers. In light of these issues, LAC countries' policy actions may need to go beyond traditional social protection and labor reforms in order to make a difference (third policy dimension) is illustrated in figure 4.1. What does this mean?

The following section discusses the key institutional impediments to employment transitions and the key agenda items to reform them. It then discusses the insider story and some practical examples of how better competition policies can change the status quo and bring needed dynamism to employment recovery after crises. It concludes with a discussion of how to address the spatial dimension of labor market adjustment through a dual-dimension policy response, including both well-designed regional development policies supporting job creation in depressed regions and place-based policies to reduce the costs of mobility between regions or neighborhoods. Helping people to overcome the structural and, especially, spatial constraints they face to employment is a necessary focus of an augmented deployment of active labor market policies.

## Facilitating employment transitions: Labor market regulatory rigidity

Chapter 2 showed that in countries with very different labor market regulations, the natures of the markets' adjustments and their consequences for firms' productivity and survival also differ. This section discusses the key areas in which the LAC region has labor market rigidities and how to address those rigidities for better crisis response. A long and fierce debate among economists on the benefits and costs to employment outcomes of labor market regulations is slowly moving toward a consensus: when policy makers avoid extremes of either too little or too much regulation, reasonable levels of regulation

can improve outcomes with minimal distortions or efficiency costs (World Bank 2012).

Some of the most contentious regulatory instruments are restrictions on firms' contracting and dismissal decisions, known collectively as employment protection legislation (EPL). EPL is part of the institutional framework around the labor market. Other elements of this framework are (the existence of and) rules for unemployment insurance, ALMPs, and governance structures such as tripartite collective bargaining (between trade unions, employers or business associations, and the government as the convener). This institutional framework affects both the functioning of labor markets and firms' productivity (Betcherman 2014). Within this framework, labor regulations determine the types of employment contracts permitted; employers' ability to adjust wages, benefits, and hours; working times and conditions; forbidden employment practices; and the rules governing the hiring and dismissal of workers (Kuddo, Robalino, and Weber 2015). Designed to protect or redistribute income to workers, these regulations are normally intended to address a flaw in the labor market (such as imperfect information, uneven market power between employers and workers, discrimination, or inadequacies of the market to provide insurance for employment-related risks).

In the LAC region, where job displacement income support has limited coverage, some governments took the policy stance to address the risk of job loss and other employment shocks in the formal sector by preventing or slowing adjustments rather than by helping affected workers manage and recover from these shocks. This approach relies heavily on restricting dismissals, mandating employer-provided severance obligations, and limiting the use of flexible employment contracts, such as fixed-term contracts or outsourcing.

Evidence shows that when these regulations are set at overly restrictive levels they can generate undesirable economic and social impacts that exacerbate the labor market imperfections they were originally intended to address

(Betcherman 2014). The LAC region has some examples of regulations set at extreme levels compared with countries in other regions. In Bolivia and the República Bolivariana de Venezuela, for instance, the labor code does not allow contract termination for "economic reasons" (that is, poor performance or market downturns), limiting grounds for dismissal to disciplinary reasons. In Ecuador, the use of fixed-term contracts as well as outsourcing are severely limited. In Suriname, employers must seek approval from the Ministry of Labor to dismiss a worker. Mexico, Panama, and Peru have similarly restrictive procedures for dismissals. As long as there is a requirement to give employees reasonable advance notice of dismissal, firms should be given more flexibility in their human resource decisions. To prevent abuse and discriminatory practices by firms, ministries of labor can implement risk-based, ex post audits and apply severe penalties where infractions are found (Packard and Onishi 2020).

In an environment with critical pockets of overly rigid labor regulation, high costs of job destruction, and slow labor market adjustment, fewer job offers will be made, lengthening unemployment spells.[14] Overly restrictive employment regulations affect employers' decisions on how to adjust to demand shocks, altering how workers are reallocated over the business cycle.[15] In the LAC region, the devil is in the details of this issue—labor markets are rigid only in some countries and only in some key dimensions. The region's regulations vary considerably according to widely used indicators of the extent of labor market regulation, such as the OECD's EPL index (which the Inter-American Development Bank [IADB] expanded to cover many LAC countries). Even in countries where regular employment contracts are restricted similarly to or less than the OECD average (such as Colombia, Panama, Peru, and Uruguay, as shown in figure 4.14), fixed-term (temporary) employment is more restricted and collective dismissals are substantially more difficult. However, enforcement capacity makes all the difference as to whether regulation as written does in fact constrain employment practices and create significant friction in the labor market's adjustment (Kanbur and Ronconi 2018).

**FIGURE 4.14** **Employment protection legislation in OECD member countries and selected Latin American countries, 2014 or most recent data**

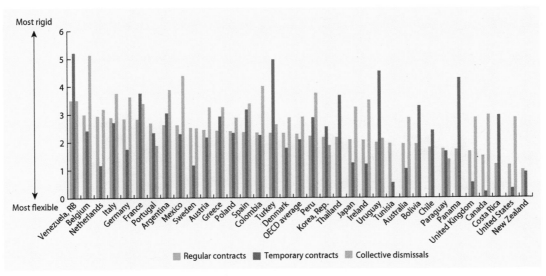

*Sources:* OECD Stat, Employment Protection Legislation (version 3), augmented for Latin America and the Caribbean for the years 2013 and 2014 by the Inter-American Development Bank's Database of Labor Markets and Social Security Information Systems (SIMS).
*Note:* These countries' employment protection regulations are ranked on a scale from 0 to 6, where 0 = most flexible and 6 = most rigid. OECD = Organisation for Economic Co-operation and Development.

Going deeper than these aggregate indices of employment protection legislation, more granular indicators of labor regulation show how specific regulatory instruments are used with differing intensities across the LAC countries. The World Bank's Doing Business project's Employing Workers data set can distinguish among the regulation of hiring practices, working hours, the handling of redundancies, and dismissal costs.[16] In the four panels of figure 4.15, a single composite index of overall labor regulation rigidity constructed on the basis of all of these indicators is plotted against separate subindices that capture (a) restrictions on hiring (i.e., on the use of part-time and temporary workers, the repeated use of fixed-term contracts, and outsourcing), (b) the regulation of work time (that is, what defines the working day and business days), (c) rules for dismissal procedures (such as requirements for third-party notification and even approval for single or collective redundancies), and (d) the actual financial costs of dismissal (severance pay, payouts from accumulated leave, and other financial penalties required of firms). These indices are constructed with principal component analysis (PCA) and normalized on a scale ranging from –3 (least rigid) to 3 (most rigid), with 0 assigned to the LAC region's

**FIGURE 4.15**  **Regulation of employment in the LAC countries, circa 2019**

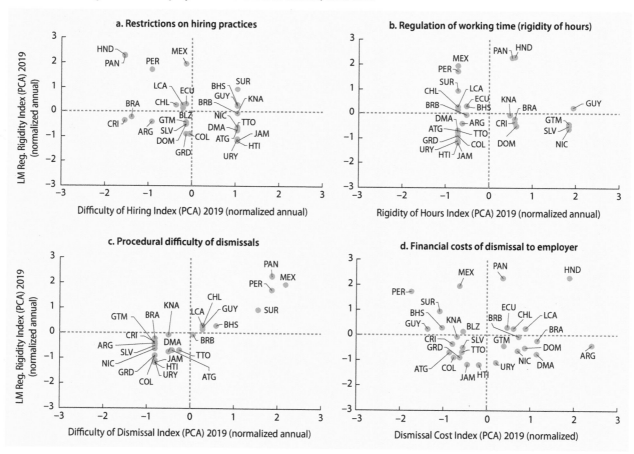

*Sources:* Packard and Onishi 2020; indices constructed by Maratou-Kolias et al. 2020 using Employing Workers data from the Doing Business project, World Bank.
*Note:* Following Packard and Montenegro 2017, five indices of de jure regulations are constructed using principal component analysis (PCA): a composite "overall labor market regulation rigidity" index of all the Doing Business project's Employing Workers labor market regulation indicators (plotted on the vertical axis in each panel) and four indices for different subsets of regulation measures. PCA values have been normalized to the LAC regional mean values (indicated by blue horizontal and vertical lines, respectively) to create a scale ranging from –3 (most flexible) to 3 (most rigid). LAC = Latin America and the Caribbean; LM Reg. = labor market regulations.

mean values. Thus, countries in the top half of each panel have more rigid regulations overall, and countries' placement in the right or left quadrant of the panel (their distance from the mean) indicates what specific aspect of labor regulation explains their rigidity (or lack thereof).

As shown in figure 4.15, overall labor regulation rigidity in the sample of LAC countries for which the Employing Workers indicators are collected is driven mostly by restrictions on hiring practices (panel a) and the procedural difficulty of dismissals (panel c). Consistent with the OECD-IADB EPL index presented earlier, the statutory financial costs of dismissal, such as paid notice periods, severance, and payout of unused leave (panel d) and rigidity of hours (panel b) appear to be lesser contributors to overall regulatory rigidity, although their contribution varies considerably across countries.[17]

Rigid regulation of regular employment contracts and large disparities between the protections extended by these contracts and those offered with nonstandard forms of employment can create an insider-outsider labor market even within formal employment. This effect can add to the formidable obstacles caused by the formal/informal divide: a large set of protections are associated with formal employment, but also a large tax wedge. Betcherman (2014) shows that employment protection legislation has been found to have an equalizing effect among covered, full-time workers of prime working age but that it leaves groups such as youth, women, and the less skilled disproportionately outside its coverage and its benefits (Betcherman 2014; Heckman and Pagés 2004). The attempt to mitigate the impact of overly rigid regulation with special forms of contracts only exacerbates these adverse distributional impacts. Youth and women are disproportionally likely to be hired on temporary contracts, which leave them without access to many benefits and protections against dismissal (Gatti, Goraus, and Morgandi 2014; Kuddo, Robalino, and Weber 2015).

### What can be done?
Reducing the intensity with which countries regulate firms' human resource decisions is likely to affect workers. With broader access to national unemployment insurance programs, more dynamic safety net transfers, and a robust system of reemployment support services, labor market adjustments, including regulatory changes, will be smoother (Andersen 2017; Bekker 2018). Similarly, the principles of protecting working people rather than protecting employment and of decoupling protections from where and how people work in response to the permanent effects of economic transformations might not help with a crisis in the short-run but might be applicable in the medium run.[18] The effects of this change will also depend on whether broader access to national unemployment insurance programs is available and on the employment dynamism of the economy.

Figure 4.16 shows a stylized plot comparing countries in the LAC region with those in other regions according to (a) the flexibility of their labor market regulation (along the horizontal axis, the inverse of the rigidity index in figure 4.15) and (b) the extent to which key protections are available outside the employment relationship (along the vertical axis, an index of public spending on education, health, social assistance, and labor market support programs as a percentage of GDP). In the upper right quadrant of figure 4.16 are Denmark, New Zealand, the United Kingdom, and other countries that have shifted their policy stance to combine greater labor market flexibility with more robust human capital and social protection services to help people navigate transitions between jobs. Although a handful of LAC countries are in that same quadrant (with high flexibility and high protection), many lag behind in at least one of these dimensions.

The current overreliance in some countries on employment protection regulations instead of income support and reemployment services comes at a cost: it damages the job prospects of many people, particularly young people and people of all ages who prefer or need to combine work with study or care

**FIGURE 4.16** Flexibility of labor regulation and spending on human capital and labor programs in selected countries in LAC compared to other regions

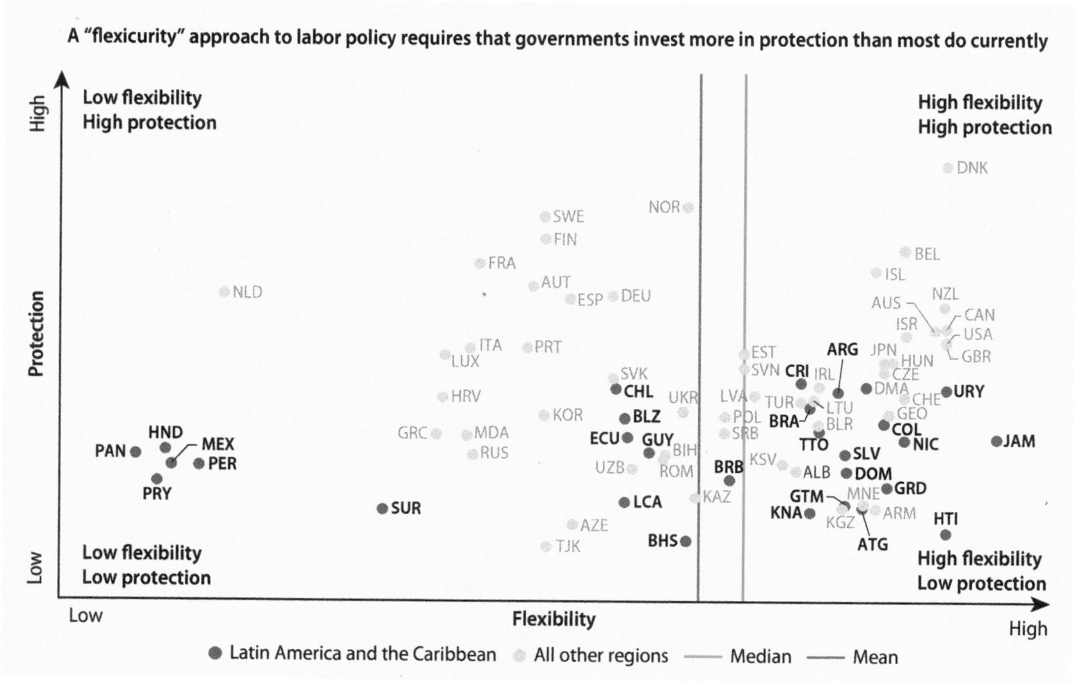

A "flexicurity" approach to labor policy requires that governments invest more in protection than most do currently

*Source:* Onishi and Packard 2020, based on Packard et al. 2019.
*Note:* All other regions = East Asia and Pacific, Europe and Central Asia, Middle East and North Africa, and North America. The horizontal axis shows the inverse of labor market regulation principal component analysis of the composite rigidity index using the Doing Business project's Employing Workers data set; the vertical axis charts the index of "protections" (measured as government spending on health, education, and social protection support) that are accessible outside the employment relationship.

responsibilities. It is also associated with longer average job searches and thus slower labor market adjustments. Exploiting the extensive country coverage of uniform survey microdata in the International Income Distribution Database (I2D2) and the Employing Workers indicators, Packard and Montenegro (2021) analyze the association between the average duration of unemployment and various forms of labor regulations, controlling for economic growth, average educational attainment, and other relevant factors. Figure 4.17 shows statistically significant coefficients for several labor regulation variables (including an enforcement capacity indicator from Kanbur and Ronconi [2018]). The interpretation of the positive, significant association between duration of unemployment and factors like home ownership, educational attainment, and the levels of employers' social insurance contributions is ambiguous (for instance,

people with more physical and human capital working in countries with extensive social insurance systems can take more time after losing jobs to find better matches). However, the significant associations between the duration of job searches and de jure restrictions on hiring practices, working hours, and dismissal procedures are less ambiguous. The size and statistical significance of these associations increases when the country's capacity and efforts to enforce regulations are included in the analysis.

International experience shows that loosening restrictions on firms' hiring and dismissal decisions needs to be accompanied by establishing more effective protections outside the employment contract, including reemployment support such as income and job search assistance (Kuddo, Robalino, and Weber 2015; see also the OECD Jobs Strategy in footnote 18). The goal is not

**FIGURE 4.17   Labor market regulation instruments and the duration of unemployment**

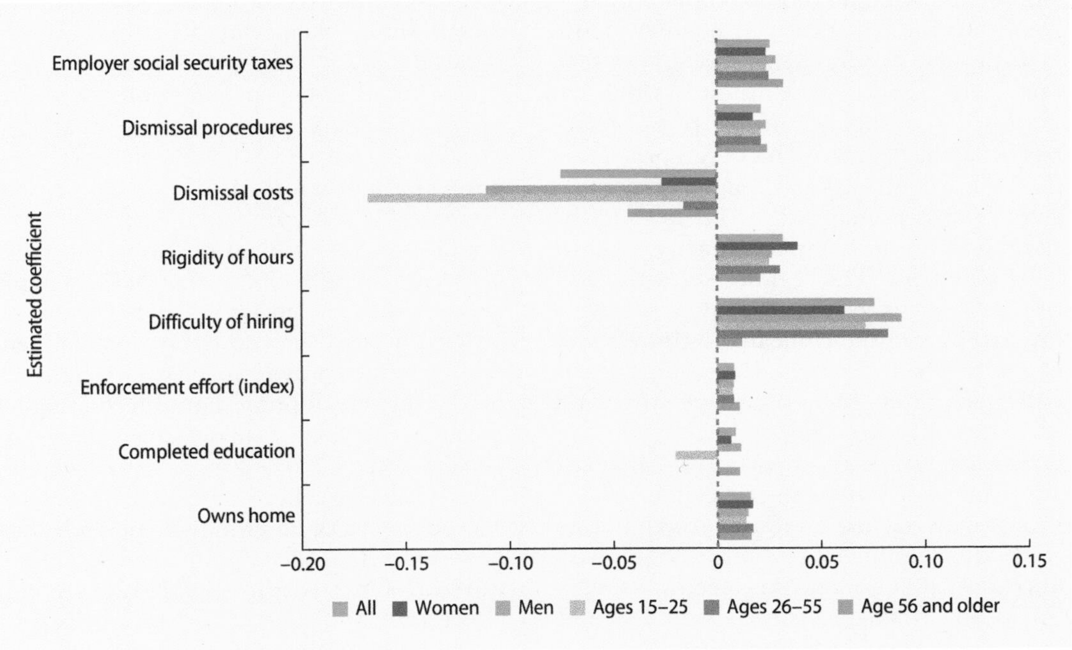

*Sources:* Packard and Montenegro 2021; data are from the International Income Distribution database (I2D2) and the World Bank's *Employing Workers* data set. The "Enforcement effort" index was adopted from Kanbur and Ronconi (2018).
*Note:* Estimated coefficients on the variable that controls for economic growth have been omitted from the figure. "All" indicates estimated coefficients for the whole sample of individuals. For the variables "Employer social security taxes," coefficients are statistically significant at the 1 percent level for all groups; "Dismissal procedures" coefficients are statistically significant at the 1 percent level for all groups. "Dismissal costs" coefficients are not statistically significant. "Rigidity of hours" are significant at the 5 percent level for All, Women, and those aged 26 to 55; at the 10 percent level for men and those aged 15 to 25; and not significant for those 56 and older. "Difficulty of hiring" coefficients are statistically significant at the 1 percent level for All, Men, and those aged 15 to 25 and 26 to 55; at the 10 percent level for Women; and not significant for those 56 and older. "Owns own home" is statistically significant at the 1 percent level for all groups.

deregulation but smarter regulation that reflects the risks and opportunities available in modern, diverse labor markets. As long as firms are required to give employees reasonable advance notice of dismissal, they should be given more flexibility in their human resource decisions. To prevent abuse or discrimination, ministries of labor can implement risk-based, ex post audits and apply severe penalties in such cases. Greater regulatory flexibility for firms must be accompanied by more concerted and robust reemployment support. Without responsive income and employment support in place to help absorb the shock of unemployment and assist with job searches, loosening labor regulations would simply shift the risk burden from firms onto working people and raise the likelihood of segmentation and abusive

employment practices. The frequency of "nonstandard" forms of work in the LAC region (including self-employment) poses additional challenges. In Argentina, Brazil, Chile, and many other LAC countries, formal but nonstandard forms of work appear to be growing at the expense of formal dependent employment. The profile of those in nonstandard employment has also changed dramatically since the mid-1990s: people in formal nonstandard employment today are younger and better educated than before (Apella and Zunino 2018).

How should LAC countries make protection accessible to not only formal workers (regardless of their contract type) but also informal workers? The challenge is to restructure the countries' social protection and labor systems so that support is accessible no matter where or how people work (Packard et al 2019). Many countries—spanning the full range of economic and institutional development—are giving serious, if cautious, consideration to the fiscal viability and social benefits of universal basic income plans to achieve full protection (Gentilini et al. 2020), though such extensive safety nets may still be far beyond the fiscal and administrative capacity of most LAC countries. The region's social protection and labor systems today are greatly improved from the truncated welfare states of the 1980s and 1990s. However, there is still much to be done to achieve efficiency, effectiveness, and sustainability.

A good place to start to improve the adjustment of Latin America's labor markets is with extensive reforms to regulatory restrictions on hiring and dismissals, severance, and other employer-specific benefits (including firm- or sector-specific health insurance). The idea behind Europe's recent labor and social protection policy reforms was to transform unfunded, firm-specific protection to nationally administered plans consisting of portable "backpacks," delinked from specific jobs, that working people could "carry" with them from job to job. Instead of making contributions at levels consistent with previous severance obligations, employers and workers could make contributions into individuals' savings accounts (either stand-alone unemployment savings accounts or accounts combined with retirement savings, per Feldstein and Altman [1998]). These savings would be underpinned by a risk-pooling mechanism that guaranteed benefits proportionate to workers' contribution history but with a guaranteed minimum benefit financed by the broadest-based taxes, much as the LAC region's CCTs and other social assistance transfers are today. The main advantage of this approach is that it opens access to effective and efficiently priced protection to a larger share of working people. Protection would no longer be segmented by type of employment. Also, the present incentives for employers and job seekers to game the system, underdeclare earnings,

evade taxes and statutory contributions, or disguise actual employment relationships as self-employment would be substantially reduced.

The disadvantage to this approach is that organizing social protection and labor support in this way demands much more from governments than the LAC region's present systems. But this is the challenge of economic and institutional development. Governments in the region would have to apply taxation instruments far more effectively and efficiently than they do today and augment their administrative capacity, especially by more quickly adopting digital technologies, to enable information management as well as benefit delivery.

Liberalizing labor contracts initially has a positive effect on employment under the new, more flexible type of contract (Bentolila, Dolado, and Jimeno 2012). But this effect gradually fades as the stock of permanent workers is replaced with workers under flexible contracts. In Latin America, the effect of these regulatory changes has been evaluated in some countries using panel data (household or firm) and time-series models, and the results have been mixed. Although Kugler (2004) in Colombia, Mondino and Montoya (2004) in Argentina, and Saavedra and Torero (2004) in Peru identify a negative effect on employment of new job security rules, De Barros and Corseuil (2004) for Brazil; Downes, Mamingi, and Antoine (2004) for three Caribbean countries; and Petrin and Sivadsadan (2006) for Chile find no significant effect.

## Breaking the insider story: More than just labor market reform

Results in the previous chapter show that effects of crises are lessened for firms with more market share and for those with state ownership. In particular, Fernandes and Silva (2020) show that product market concentration affects the magnitude and distribution of crises' effects on workers. Shocks cause greater losses in employment and wages in sectors with low market concentration (many players). In contrast, in sectors where a few players hold a large share of the market (high market concentration), shocks actually increase employment and wages do not adjust (the reverse of what normal economic mechanisms would bring about). Whether a certain labor market regulation helps or hinders employment outcomes is also determined by the extent of product and service market concentration and the bargaining power of employers relative to that of workers. The aggregate data are directionally consistent with this observation, including the fact that large firms in Latin America (often protected firms in the energy, commodities, and retail sectors) have been more resilient to crises and have recovered faster from them (see chapter 1).

This section discusses (a) the institutional peculiarities in Latin America that are giving rise to this insider-outsider labor market and allowing segmentation to persist and (b) the types of complementary policy responses beyond the labor market that could address concerns about crises' effects on workers.

Market power in product and service markets, defined as the ability to drive prices and returns above competitive levels, is coming under increasing scrutiny for causing adverse socioeconomic outcomes beyond just higher prices for consumers. Increasing concentration in product and service markets in high-income countries often translates into concentration in labor markets and to dominant employers engaging in exploitative practices (Azar et al. 2019). In many Latin American countries, market concentration is linked with close ties between large firms and governments. An extreme example is the prevalence of state-owned enterprises in the region: many of the region's largest firms are partially or totally owned by governments. Familial and social ties between the political and entrepreneurial elite throughout the region are another important factor. Close links between business and political elites result in protectionism and favoritism in domestic markets, favoring incumbents and strangling new entrants (Clarke, Evenett, and Lucenti 2005; De Leon 2001; OECD 2015).

Two main mechanisms may create the relationship between a lack of competition in product markets and the ways crises affect workers. First, protectionism generates rents for employers. Rents can influence the distribution of losses between workers and firms, and in sectors with more market power (particularly in monopolies), firms are able to adjust their prices less in the wake of shocks. This factor affects the distribution of losses across firms and translates into higher prices for consumers, including client firms downstream, which may harm employment dynamics. Market power can also be driven by the structure of the market for a particular good, as well as by the distribution of firm-specific technology. The latter effect may mean that firms' reactions to crises have some stickiness, in the sense that they generate persistent changes that firms cannot revert.

The second channel through which economic rents affect adjustments to crises is by changing the willingness of workers to adjust and to incur adjustment costs. Firms may pass economic rents on to their workers, increasing the workers' reservation wages, which in turn makes it harder for them to find well-enough paying replacement jobs if their current ones are lost. At a time when reallocation is difficult but needed, this effect may increase pressure for additional protectionism and favoritism, a further impediment to efficient resource allocation.

In light of these effects, lowering barriers to competition in product markets could increase job creation and productivity growth. It would shrink the share of firms earning above-normal returns on capital—and, therefore, the share of workers producing and sharing in those above-normal returns. This change, in turn, would lead to higher labor mobility, because the rents these workers earn are discouraging them from leaving their firms. Compensation policies to smooth the adjustments for these workers could also make their transitions less costly.

At the same time, there are too few large firms in Latin America. Not all sources of economic market power in the region should be eliminated. Some degree of product market power is desirable in order to create positive incentives to innovate. However, these incentives could be improved in other ways, such as instituting transparent intellectual property and patent regulations, that do not sacrifice the benefits of market contestability and competition. Regulators' focus should be on the abuse of market power by dominant companies to restrict competition, the formation of cartels (illegal agreements between firms not to compete), and the removal of unnecessary anticompetitive regulations that decrease labor market dynamism without encouraging innovation. A recent study using data for Brazil, Chile, China, Estonia, India, Indonesia, Israel, the Russian Federation, Slovenia, and South Africa, found that reducing barriers to entrepreneurship (such as barriers to entry and antitrust exemptions) to a level consistent with the current best practices among OECD members would lead to 0.35 percent to 0.4 percent higher annual GDP growth per capita (Wölfl et al. 2010). Protectionism and favoritism protect some large firms at the cost of preventing new entrants from effectively competing and themselves growing into large firms.

As economies stabilize after crises, it is essential, in order to improve labor market performance, for policy makers to safeguard against threats to competitive and contestable product and service markets. Structural changes brought by the advent of technology have contributed to growing concentration. The market power of firms is growing in many parts of the world (Diez, Leigh, and Tambunlertchai 2018). Ensuring competitive and contestable markets has long been a challenge in low- and middle-income countries, where governance institutions are weak and can be especially vulnerable to oligopolistic pressures and collusion problems. However, many of the same pressures and dangers of market concentration are increasing in high-income countries as well (Aznar, Marinescu, and Steinbaum 2017). A growing body of research from the United Kingdom, the United States, and other high-income countries shows that as local-level employer concentration grows, wages stagnate and that the negative impact on wages of a given level of concentration is increasing (Benmelech,

Bergman, and Kim 2018). Concentration is often accompanied by restrictive practices, such as the proliferation of local licensing requirements or the extensive use of non-compete clauses, even in industries that hire mostly low-skilled people (Naidu, Posner, and Weyl 2018). These restrictions on competition combine with declining labor mobility to put downward pressure on earnings (Konczal and Steinbaum 2016).

### What kind of reforms?

Breaking the insider story of the LAC region would require policy levers outside the labor market. Possible areas of focus include changes to competition laws, subsidies, procurement, and the level of state participation in various industries. These types of policies could complement other policy responses to address concerns about crises' effects on workers (as discussed in Baker and Salop [2015]). Calls are growing for competition policy regulators to look beyond their traditional toolkit. These regulators have been criticized for keeping too strict of a focus on consumer prices (ignoring, for example, the emergence of monopsonist employment practices). Taking into account a wider range of socioeconomic indicators can reveal contestability and competition problems that do not manifest immediately as higher prices.

## Addressing the spatial dimension of crises' impacts on workers

Results from the previous chapter show that shocks' impacts on workers vary in size and persistence depending on local economic conditions. For example, in Brazil, employment and wage losses in response to shocks are higher for formal workers who live in more informal local labor markers than for those in less informal places. Why do shocks pass through to workers more in some places than in others? The way the places' structural features interact with the shocks is important. Evidence suggests that the relevant features include the place's sectorial composition, the types of firms, and the size of the informal sector. In general, workers in places with fewer alternative job opportunities end up more severely scarred by crises. To the extent that shocks lead to labor scarring and that mobility across regions is limited, shocks can have permanent effects that differ across space.

Is a spatially differentiated approach needed to address scarring in the LAC region as a result of temporary shocks such as crises? Regional policies are generally considered for issues associated with permanent shocks, such as trade liberalization or technological change. However, if jobs are permanently lost, effects are spatially concentrated, and worker mobility is low, workers will be scarred by crises. In these cases, retraining and other ALMP polices will not be enough, nor will private incentives on their own. Instead, these places will need to be revitalized by, for example, increasing public investment in them.

This report shows that even temporary shocks have spatially differentiated long-term consequences. Two aspects of these shocks make regional policies useful to address their long-term consequences. The first is the presumption that the effects of these shocks are localized. The second is that the shocks will have structural and permanent effects. Many spatially differentiated effects can be addressed with nonspatial policies. For example, ALMPs will be cheaper to institute than place-based policies. But some structural issues cannot be addressed except by the latter type of policy, such as a lack of opportunities in a place. The previous chapters show the importance of being proactive to prevent scarring. How can policy makers proactively confront scarring with place-based policies, and why should they?

Two dimensions are relevant to a regional policy response to crises. If welfare losses are linked with a lack of geographic mobility, removing barriers to mobility and enhancing connectedness across regions can be a good solution. Transitioning between locations brings a wide range of costs, including search costs to determine where to go, the cost of moving to the new location, a wide range of psychological

costs (Brand 2015), and transportation costs (Zarate 2020).

Many of the root causes of low labor mobility are imperfections in housing and credit markets (Bergman et al. 2019). Place-based policies can promote regional mobility, for example, by addressing the lack of affordable housing, improving land-use policies, adjusting zoning rules, or developing mortgage finance. But many areas are already congested, the noneconomic costs of moving are difficult to compensate for, and many people do not want to move. Thus, a second policy dimension is also important: well-designed regional development policies to support job creation. Such policies can increase long-run growth and benefit a region's development. They can also help reintegrate displaced workers by creating more jobs where those workers are. And they could address business climate, infrastructure, and profit opportunities locally so that income-generating opportunities are spread throughout the country (to the level that makes sense on the basis of the local resources, population, and such). Finally, they could generate local multiplier effects, stimulating consumption and demand and, through this channel, employment. Regional policies are therefore needed in a broader sense in order to strengthen regions' economic opportunities. As discussed in box 4.5, whether these policies achieve this objective depends on the modality of the policies and on the characteristics of the region.

Evidence regarding the ability of place-based policies to reduce the costs of mobility between regions or neighborhoods is growing but remains limited (box 4.6).

How large are these effects? Artuc, Bastos, and Lee (2020) develop a reduced-form regression and structural model for the effects of changes in external demand on welfare (i.e., a worker's lifetime utility) and for the role of mobility in these effects. The analysis shows that a shock-induced welfare reduction would be lessened if mobility, particularly across regions (within a country), was higher. In other words, the reduction of mobility costs across regions would do more to mitigate a crisis-induced welfare reduction

**BOX 4.5 How well have regional policies performed at strengthening economic opportunities?**

Local job creation efforts often involve (a) investments in infrastructure and in local public goods and services, (b) direct subsidies to firms, or (c) the relocation of public sector employment or large public agencies to depressed areas. Neumark and Simpson (2015) provide an overview of the literature on these types of policies, updated by Ehrlich and Overman (2020) in the context of the European Union (EU). Overall, the evidence suggests that investment in transportation infrastructure and in local public goods and services in a mix of firm subsidies and training, as is done by the EU's cohesion funds, has on average been effective at fostering growth in recipient localities and thus at reducing disparities across places in economic opportunities (Becker, Egger, and Ehrlich 2010; Giua 2017; Mohl and Hagen 2010; Pellegrini et al. 2013).

However, the effects of these programs vary considerably across areas: they are high in regions with high human capital and high-quality local governments but low elsewhere, yielding different trade-offs between spatial inequality and aggregate efficiency (Becker, Egger, and Ehrlich 2013). They also have diminishing returns: the effectiveness of these programs decreases as transfers increase (Becker, Egger, and Ehrlich 2012; Cerqua and Pellegrini 2018). And there is no evidence that their effects last for long (after the region loses eligibility for the program) (Barone, David, and de Blasio 2016; Becker, Egger, and Ehrlich 2018; Di Cataldo 2017). Recent literature has emphasized the importance of thinking about a region's transportation network (Redding and Turner 2015) and incremental changes in road infrastructure (Gibbons et al. 2019), finding positive local effects from these changes on employment, the number of establishments, and, to a smaller extent, the productivity of incumbent firms. These studies show sizable local effects but they do not all identify the aggregate effects from these improvements' impacts on the entire network. In a more recent paper, Zarate (2020) shows that informal workers are more responsive to transportation costs than are their formal counterparts and that therefore the former tend to work closer to their residences. As a result, investment in transportation infrastructure in Mexico City reduced informality by increasing access to formal jobs, which tend to be concentrated

in in the city center and thus are inaccessible to workers who live on the periphery.

Evidence is more mixed on the effectiveness of direct subsidies or discretionary grants from the government to firms in disadvantaged areas. These grants aim to support employment at individual firms or to attract new employers to an area. The two key concerns with these programs are that they finance activities that recipient firms would have undertaken anyway and that the new activity in the targeted areas comes at the cost of activity displaced from nontargeted areas. Some studies suggest that subsidies, if well designed, increase local employment, mainly at small firms. This increase, in turn, can generate positive multipliers (i.e., additional jobs) by increasing productivity (Greenstone, Hornbeck, and Moretti 2010) or demand for local goods and services. Estimates from the United States and the EU suggest that each job in a tradable sector creates between 0.5 and 1.5 extra jobs in nontradable sectors (Ehrlich and Overman 2020). But not all evidence is as encouraging. First, positive local effects may be offset by general equilibrium effects in the form of higher wages and prices. Second, some programs show evidence of substantial deadweight and displacement of existing jobs (Bronzini and de Blasio 2006). This evidence is particularly strong concerning enterprise zones, which some countries have moderated by requiring that supported firms demonstrate that they do not predominantly serve local markets and by requiring a certain percentage of workers in the zones to live locally (see, for example, Mayer, Mayneris, and Py [2017] and Neumark and Simpson [2015]).

Decisions about public sector employment, including the relocation of large public agencies to depressed areas, can also affect the spatial allocation of employment. Evidence suggests that public sector jobs have positive multiplier effects on employment in services and that the relocation of large public agencies has positive effects on overall local employment (Faggio and Overman 2014). However, more recent evidence points to negative effects of such moves on private sector employment in manufacturing (What Works Centre for Local Economic Growth 2019). Note that general national-level policies, such as funding for schools or training or even a nationwide minimum wage, also affect spatial disparities.

## BOX 4.6    Evidence on the effects of place-based policies on mobility and labor market outcomes

Traditional place-based policies include mobility subsidies, rental assistance programs in high-opportunity areas, and informational interventions. Evidence on a mobility subsidy for unemployed job seekers in Germany shows that it extended those job seekers' search radiuses and increased their probability of moving to a more distant region. The program also led to higher job-finding rates and higher wages; the latter was mainly due to an improvement in workers' job matches (Caliendo, Künn, and Mahlstedt 2017a, b). In a related paper on a Romanian program to reimburse unemployed individuals for the expenses of migration, the program was observed to be effective at improving labor market outcomes (Rodríguez-Planas and Benus 2006).

Bergman et al. (2019) use a randomized controlled trial to evaluate the effects of an alternative approach: a US program called Creating Moves to Opportunity offers services to reduce barriers to moving into high-upward-mobility neighborhoods, such as customized home search assistance, landlord engagement, and short-term financial assistance. The intervention increased the share of families who moved into high-upward-mobility areas from 15 percent in the control group to 53 percent in the treatment group.[1] The researchers also evaluate the effects of more traditional programs offering higher voucher payment standards in high-rent postal codes within a metro area (the Small Area Fair Market Rents program). They find that changing payment standards did not increase the rate of moves to high-opportunity areas. In another program that increased payment standards specifically in high-opportunity neighborhoods, only 20 percent of voucher recipients with children moved. In terms of programs providing information to those considering moving, the available evidence is also not very encouraging, although it focuses mostly on the United States. For example, Bergman et al. (2019) find only limited effects from the provision of information to families about the quality of schools associated with various rental units on a website commonly used by voucher holders. Results from Schwartz, Mihaly, and Gala (2017) on light-touch counseling also indicate limited effects. Lagakos, Mobarak, and Waugh (2018) show that subsidizing mobility for rural-to-urban migration in Bangladesh has aggregate welfare impacts similar to unconditional cash transfers. They show that the welfare gains are highest for the poorest households, which had a greater propensity to migrate even before the policy intervention. They also find that the main obstacle to mobility is the disutility of moving rather than a failure or distortion in the housing market, which implies that targeted policies to incentivize mobility would be ineffective.

than the reduction of mobility costs across sectors.

What are the driving mechanisms of this effect? Artuc, Bastos, and Lee (2020) emphasize an important motivation for mobility: the number of job opportunities provided by different sectors and regions. First, if a worker has more job opportunities to choose from, the best of those opportunities will likely deliver greater welfare. Second, even if that worker is hit by a negative labor demand shock in the future, the worker will more likely be able to find another job without having to move to a different region or sector. A negative temporary shock in a region will reduce the number of job opportunities created there and the region's internal churning (that is, job switching within the local labor market), both of which lead to a loss of welfare.

Considering these new channels, Artuc, Bastos, and Lee (2020) explore the role of mobility frictions faced by workers by quantifying the effects of potential policies meant to mitigate these frictions. The paper shows the effects of higher mobility of workers across regions and sectors compared with two alternative scenarios: higher mobility across only sectors and higher mobility across only regions. Mobility frictions 20 percent lower across regions and sectors reduce welfare losses from the same benchmark shock by 16.5 percent, and the welfare-enhancing effect of a policy of the same magnitude is greater when the policy targets regional frictions than when it targets sectoral frictions. In particular, although the reduction in welfare is mitigated by 13.4 percent when regional frictions alone are targeted, it is mitigated by only 2.3 percent when sectoral frictions alone are targeted.

Why is there more pass-through to workers in some places than in others? Vijil et al. (2020), studying Brazil from 1991 to 1999, show that some metropolitan areas were almost bypassed by the trade liberalization shock that occurred during that period because of their low internal market integration. Market structures, influenced, for instance, by the quality or quantity of

transportation infrastructure or by the level of competition in transportation and distribution services, were approximated by location fixed effects and thus were shown to lead to significant differences in tariff pass-through rates between metropolitan regions. Similarly heterogeneous effects across localities of trade liberalization shocks have been observed in China (Han et al. 2016), India (Marchand 2012), and Mexico (Nicita 2009). For instance, after China's entry to the World Trade Organization, the market structure at the city level (as measured by the share of private sector participation in distribution services and in the production of final goods impacted by the shock, as proxies for the level of competition) led to differences in the transmission of tariff prices between cities: prices responded

**FIGURE 4.18  Tackling structural issues that worsen the impacts of crises on workers**

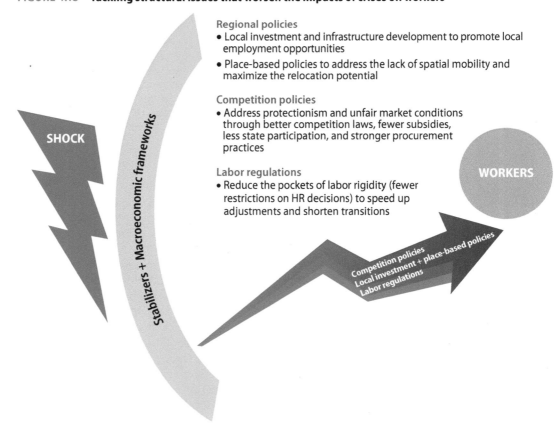

more to the trade shock in cities that benefited from higher competition (Han et al. 2016).

### What can be done?

Chapter 3 shows that the LAC region faces structural issues that affect the magnitude of the impacts of crises on workers. The policy implication of these findings and the related literature is that even if macroeconomic and labor market policies are in pristine order, better outcomes to crises could be achieved for workers by complementing these policies with sectoral and place-based policies to address the structural issues that impede strong recoveries from crises and have long-lasting productivity effects, as described in this report. This change would involve addressing the inefficiencies in labor market adjustment caused by labor market legislation, product market structures, the lack of geographic mobility, and depressed areas. All things considered, a more complete characterization of the possible policy areas of focus to tackle these structural issues (third policy dimension 3) is illustrated in figure 4.18.

## Conclusion

This chapter presented this study's policy implications and the current context in the LAC region. It argued that LAC countries' policy responses to crises need to squarely tackle three key dimensions of adjustment. These dimensions are not inconsistent, and they have different weights in each country or setting. They call for a triple entry of policies.

The first line of response to crises is policies that lead to fewer crises and that smooth out their impacts at the aggregate level. Reducing the number of crises requires creating a more stable macroeconomic environment and establishing adequate automatic stabilizers that provide countercyclical, publicly financed income support for people negatively affected by labor market adjustments. Prudent macroeconomic (fiscal and monetary) policies prevent certain types of crises and ensure the fiscal space needed to provide support and avert system-wide

financial strain if other types of crises occur. Moreover, nationally administered income protection arrangements, such as unemployment insurance, have smoothed consumption and served as automatic stabilizers in most OECD countries. The costs of these programs and the LAC region's smaller tax base might necessitate a different approach for expanding these programs in the region, such as combining individual savings and risk pooling.

Other potential alternative mechanisms include making the job retention schemes currently employed for the COVID-19 crisis permanent features of the LAC countries' respective economies by making them state-contingent and automatically activated when, for example, unemployment reaches a certain rate or a recession worsens. By complementing existing adjustment-assistance mechanisms with countercyclical, publicly financed income support for affected individuals, the LAC region could achieve smoother, better-quality adjustments to crises and faster recoveries from them.

Some crises, however, are unavoidable, and better outcomes from them could be achieved if, in addition, the region transitions into augmented social protection programs that reduce scarring effects. The existence of these effects implies that the region could increase its long-term growth if crisis-induced, worker-level human capital decay were reduced. This change would require income support to cushion the short-term impacts of crises and protect welfare as well as social protection policies aimed at building human capital and promoting faster, better-quality transitions across jobs for displaced workers. Social protection systems provide more than just income support; they also help build human capital. For these reasons, the second line of response includes deep reforms to the LAC region's existing social protection and labor programs.

Traditionally, crises were viewed as transient (as opposed to permanent) systemic (affecting the whole economy) shocks. Although permanent systemic shocks such as trade liberalization and technological change also affect employment and productivity, they do so over long time horizons. Cycle-independent ("secular") forces cause some jobs to become permanently nonviable; these jobs will not rebound in the same firm, sector, or locality. In contrast, effects from exchange rate fluctuations or changes in the terms of trade are more likely to be temporary. Understanding is emerging that crises may have sticky effects on labor markets and productivity that differ from those generated by technology or globalization. However, because crises' effects occur while changes in trends and structural factors and the normal churning of the economy are already happening, distinguishing these effects and better deploying programs to assist workers is difficult.

The standard advice in the presence of adverse permanent systemic shocks is to protect workers, not jobs—to prepare workers for change rather than prevent the change from coming about. Allowing sectoral or spatial restructuring is bound to increase efficiency; in contrast, retention subsidies and temporary employment programs delay (while the support lasts) but do not avoid job destruction. However, this advice does not apply to systemic shocks that are only temporary. In these cases, temporary retention programs may avoid the dissolution of employer-employee matches that took a long time to build but are threatened by a temporary shock, and they may stem productivity losses from the unnecessary destruction of job-specific human capital.[19]

When crises lead to permanent changes in labor demand or supply, however, reskilling initiatives and demand stimulus may be more appropriate responses. In addition, even though crises are systemic shocks, they generate highly heterogeneous effects across initially similar workers, so adaptive programs usually deployed to deal with more individual or idiosyncratic shocks (such as customized intermediation and job search support) may be adequate to address them. Moving from budgeted programs and rationed *cupos* to protection guarantees (i.e., from assisting only the chronically poor to offering benefits to all people in need), preventing the emergence of assistance "ghettos," and structuring

benefits to incentivize the return to work are key steps to ensure that social protection better cushions the short-term impacts of crises. Although it is clear that without job vacancies, placements will not occur, a normal economic rebound from a crisis will include job creation, and active searching is key to placing workers in these new jobs. More robust and coordinated employment services, with a greater focus on results and unintended consequences, are thus needed.

But will macroeconomic stabilizers and reforms to social protection and labor systems be able to spur enough job creation to generate better recoveries? In light of the evidence presented in this report, the LAC region urgently needs to tackle structural issues in order to improve its response to crises. The needed reforms include addressing the sectoral and spatial dimensions behind poor labor market adjustments. Without addressing these fundamental challenges, recoveries in the region will remain characterized by sluggish job creation. In this context, competition policies, regional policies, and labor regulations are a third key dimension of the policy response. This study highlights, for example, the dichotomy between protected and unprotected firms in the LAC region and the impact of low geographic mobility among workers, both of which serve to magnify the welfare effects of crises. It also highlights pockets of labor rigidity that hinder necessary transitions and adjustments in the labor market.

The policy implications of these findings and of the related literature are that even if macroeconomic, social protection, and labor systems are pristine and flawlessly implemented, they are insufficient unless complemented with sectoral and place-based policies that address the underlying structural issues impeding strong recoveries from crises. The existing literature and policy experiences suggest that place-based policies could address the lack of geographic mobility and maximize workers' relocation potential. Reducing pockets of labor rigidity (by loosening restrictions on the human resource decisions of firms and individuals) could speed up adjustments and shorten transitions. Similarly, addressing protectionism and unfair market conditions through better competition laws, lower subsidies, less state participation, and stronger procurement practices could promote stronger recoveries. LAC countries' policy responses need to tackle these issues, which will have different weights depending on the country, the period, and other circumstances.

The COVID-19 pandemic is a convulsive, catastrophic crisis that is exacting a savage toll on labor markets in the LAC region. The region is experiencing an extraordinary rate of destruction of employment, massive negative income shocks, and rising levels of poverty. Between 35 and 45 million people in the region may become newly poor in 2020 as a result of the pandemic, and although the region's middle class has grown significantly since 2000, the crisis could reduce it by 5 percent, pushing out 32 to 40 million people (Diaz-Bonilla, Moreno Herrera, and Sanchez Castro 2020). This shrinking of the middle class and increase in poverty are driven by losses of labor earnings; the crisis is projected to be the most severe labor market recession in some LAC countries' history. Millions of workers in the region have lost their jobs, and millions more have seen significant reductions in their earnings. And these losses are not expected to be evenly spread across the income distribution—rather, the crisis could increase inequality substantially, pushing the region's Gini coefficient from 51.5 to as high as 53.4 (Diaz-Bonilla, Moreno Herrera, and Sanchez Castro 2020).

Although this crisis—which was triggered by the public health imperatives of mitigating a global pandemic—is exceptional in some ways, it is also yet another in a long series of aggregate demand shocks that have hit the LAC countries. On one hand, the crisis has several distinctive factors. First, the lockdown caused by the pandemic was bad for many jobs and worse for those for which home-based work is not an option (or for workers who lack quality access to the internet). Second, the prolonged uncertainty around this crisis, particularly around the form in which employment will rebound, has

delayed investment. Third, some LAC countries have exhibited strong policy responses to the crisis, although the effectiveness of these responses has varied considerably.

On the other hand, this crisis is not so different from others before. A large part of the crisis's effects on the LAC region derive from the global recession, the sharp fall in demand for many months, and the possibility of financial crises in some countries. The region has a notable history of frequent and often severe economic slowdowns. What happens to workers during these slowdowns is largely determined by aggregate demand fluctuations (although some domestic crises have been self-inflicted by economic mismanagement).

This deep crisis arrived just as many governments in the LAC region were grappling with known structural challenges. It has accelerated some long-running structural shifts that have been changing the nature of work, magnifying the crisis's potential to further reduce employment opportunities in what were traditionally considered "good jobs"—the standard, stable, protected employment associated with the formal sector (Beylis et al. 2020).

The employment dynamics already observed in many LAC countries will lead this crisis to cause sizable labor scarring effects. Sector and location characteristics are likely to further magnify these effects for some workers. However, the three-dimensional policy framework presented in this study provides a roadmap that could lead to a more resilient recovery. How public and business policies address the current challenges will shape the progress of the LAC countries' economies and the well-being of their workers and citizens for decades. The challenge is immense, but now is the defining time to take it on.

## Notes

1. Although monetary and fiscal stabilization policies (including the management of a country's capital account, exchange rate policy, fiscal rules, and sovereign welfare funds and

the adjustment of its interest rate) are power-ful tools to respond to crises, they are not the main focus of this study.

2. These safety-net stabilizers work best when supported by monetary and fiscal measures, including exchange rate policies and capital account management; interest rates and other levers of monetary policy; fiscal rules and sovereign precautionary savings funds; and access to global financial and risk-sharing markets and international risk-pooling mechanisms (such as the International Monetary Fund and the World Bank). Each of these examples is supported by a vast academic and policy literature. The discussion of such measures in this report, however, is limited to the measures most directly linked to labor market outcomes.

3. These estimates are based on the World Economic Outlook. Inflation rates are compounded. The values for Argentina for 1981–97 are from the World Development Indicators.

4. Nominal downward wage rigidity is a feature of most economies, and the LAC region is no exception (see Castellanos, García-Verdú, and Kaplan [2004]; Dickens et al. [2007]; Holden and Wulfsberg [2009] and the references therein; and Schmitt-Grohé and Uribe [2016]). Moreover, the evidence suggests that the region's lower inflation in recent decades increased the downward rigidity of nominal wages. Hence, to the extent that the 2011–16 slowdown was marked by low and relatively stable inflation, real wage adjustments are likely to have been lower during that period than during the slowdowns and crises in the 1980s and 1990s, which were characterized by large increases in inflation.

5. However, there have been some episodes of significant inflation spikes and corresponding reductions in real wages in the region since the early 2000s, including the 2004 banking crisis in the Dominican Republic, which resulted in a significant and long-term wage correction.

6. The discussion here focuses on job displacement and other livelihood losses caused by shocks to aggregate demand. However, state-contingent support programs can help households cope with a wide range of shocks.

7. These figures are taken from the International Labour Organization's LABORSTA database.

8. This program's combination of individual savings accounts and risk pooling provides effective financial support while incentivizing job searches and reemployment (Hartley, van Ours, and Vodopivec 2011). Four features of the plan are particularly attractive. First, its "hybrid" insurance model is able to address the needs of workers who change jobs frequently as well as those of the long-term unemployed (although it is debated whether the maximum payout period from the risk-pooling component is adequate, given the observed duration of unemployment spells among the country's lowest-paid workers). Second, the plan provides better levels of compensation and consumption smoothing than Chile's purely noncontributory flat unemployment benefit. Third, the plan's benefits are indexed to protect their value from inflation and to stabilize replacement rates at their starting levels. And fourth, the system has a sound financial basis, underpinned by reserves that serve as an additional channel of fiscal support to weather crises. Since its inception, the plan has included an automatic extension of benefits triggered when the national unemployment rate rises above a certain level. In the current COVID-19 contraction, the plan has also served as the platform for additional protections, such as subsidized furloughs.

9. The "tax wedge" for formally employed workers is the difference between take-home pay and the total amount that the law requires that the employer and employee pay (including income taxes, statutory contributions to social insurance, and other mandated benefits) in order to have the employee (Summers 1989).

10. There are no clear-cut guidelines to set appropriate transfer amounts, and the appropriate level of benefits depends on the program's objective. The transfer values of CCT programs should therefore reflect such programs' twin objectives of reducing current poverty among beneficiaries and providing incentives for human capital accumulation (Grosh et al. 2008). One of the most generous CCT programs in the LAC region is Bolivia's (which combined two CCT programs, the *Bono Juancito Pinto* and the *Bono Juana Azurdy*), which provided 36 percent of prior income, followed by Honduras's *Bono Programa de Asignación Familiar,* later renamed *Bono 10,000* and now *Bono Vida Mejor.*

11. Although the length of time CCT programs take to enroll new beneficiaries varies from country to country, the Jamaican Program for Advancement through Health and Education (PATH) sets its service standard for the enrollment of new beneficiary households to take no longer than four months after the household's application. As of 2017, PATH has been able to meet this service standard about 60 percent of the time. Its lengthy intake processes imply considerable financial and political costs.

12. Although this report focuses on social protection policies and worker-level scarring, scarring also occurs at the firm level. Minimizing this scarring will require policies such as (a) providing financing to firms, (b) enhancing insolvency proceedings (as a key doing-business reform), and (c) improving managerial capabilities for business continuity planning (to help businesses navigate crises), as well as more generally reducing barriers to firm entry and exit. Insolvency reforms aimed at preserving viable enterprises under temporary distress could also support workers and reduce unnecessary frictional unemployment. And improving managerial capabilities would enhance firms' productivity growth, which is likely to lead to firm survival and some employment retention (rather than the alternative of firm exit and consequent job destruction).

13. This review of the evidence concluded that most traditional ALMPs have had at best modest impacts on employment; a typical intervention leads to a 2-percentage-point increase in employment, which is usually not statistically significant (McKenzie 2017).

14. For empirical evidence on the impacts of social protection and labor policies and their possible distortions to labor markets, see Frolich et al. (2014).

15. Furthermore, changes in labor demand and supply factors driven by technological change, regional and global integration, and population aging threaten to render the institutional apparatus of labor regulation increasingly ineffective or counterproductive, as is discussed at length in Packard et al. (2019).

16. These data are available at https://www.doingbusiness.org/en/data/exploretopics/employing-workers/reforms.

17. However, these cross-country measures fail to capture several mandated dismissal payments that are unique to particular countries, such as Ecuador's *deshaucio* and the *jubilacion patronal*, which are described in Gachet, Packard, and Olivieri (2020).

18. One such agenda is the new OECD Jobs Strategy, details about which can be found here: https://www.oecd.org/employment/jobs-strategy.

19. Note that evidence shows that retention subsidies (such as wage subsidies or payroll tax rebates) can be effective at protecting employment in firms going through difficulties, and these subsidies can be used to stimulate the hiring of unemployed young people and informal workers. But they may also lead to higher wages among incumbent workers rather than greater employment, and they can crowd out employment in nonsubsidized firms and sectors. Similarly, temporary employment programs can be effective at keeping people at work. But workers in temporary employment programs tend to have low levels of job satisfaction, and their contracts are most often a palliative rather than a steppingstone to more permanent employment.

## References

Almeida, R. K., and T. G. Packard. 2018. *Skills and Jobs in Brazil: An Agenda for Youth.* Washington, DC: World Bank.

Andersen, T. M. 2017. "The Danish Labor Market, 2000–2016." *IZA World of Labor* 2017: 404.

Antón, A., F. H. Trillo, and S. Levy. 2012. *The End of Informality in México? Fiscal Reform for Universal Social Insurance.* Washington, DC: Inter-American Development Bank.

Apella, I., and G. Zunino. 2018. "Nonstandard Forms of Employment in Developing Countries: A Study for a Set of Selected Countries in Latin America and the Caribbean and Europe and Central Asia." Policy Research Working Paper 8581, World Bank, Washington, DC.

Artuc, E., P. Bastos, and E. Lee. 2020. "Trade Shocks, Labor Mobility, and Welfare: Evidence from Brazil." Background paper written for this report. World Bank, Washington, DC.

Azar, J., H. Hovenkamp, I. Marinescu, E. Posner, M. Steinbaum, and B. Taska. 2019. "Labor Market Concentration and Its Legal

Implications." OECD Seminars, Organisation for Economic Co-operation and Development, Paris. https://www.oecd.org/els/emp/OECD-ELS-Seminars-Marinescu.pdf.

Aznar, J., I. Marinescu, and M. I. Steinbaum. 2017. "Labor Market Concentration." Working Paper 24147, National Bureau of Economic Research, Cambridge, MA.

Baker, J., and S. Salop. 2015. "Antitrust, Competition Policy, and Inequality." *Georgetown Law Faculty Publications and Other Works* 1462. https://scholarship.law.georgetown.edu/facpub/1462/.

Barone, G., F. David, and G. de Blasio. 2016. "Boulevard of Broken Dreams: The End of EU Funding (1997: Abruzzi, Italy)." *Regional Science and Urban Economics* 60: 31–8.

Becker, S. O., P. H. Egger, and M. von Ehrlich. 2010. "Going NUTS: The Effect of EU Structural Funds on Regional Performance." *Journal of Public Economics* 94 (9): 578–90.

Becker, S. O., P. H. Egger, and M. von Ehrlich. 2012. "Too Much of a Good Thing? On the Growth Effects of the EU's Regional Policy." *European Economic Review* 56 (4): 648–68.

Becker, S. O., P. H. Egger, and M. von Ehrlich. 2013. "Absorptive Capacity and the Growth and Investment Effects of Regional Transfers: A Regression Discontinuity Design with Heterogeneous Treatment Effects." *American Economic Journal: Economic Policy* 5 (4): 29–77.

Becker, S. O., P. H. Egger, and M. von Ehrlich. 2018. "Effects of EU Regional Policy: 1989–2013." *Regional Science and Urban Economics* 69: 143–52.

Bekker, S. 2018. "Flexicurity in the European Semester: Still a Relevant Policy Concept?" *Journal of European Policy* 25 (2): 175–92.

Benmelech, E., N. Bergman, and H. Kim. 2018. "Strong Employers and Weak Employees: How Does Employer Concentration Affect Wages?" Working Paper 24307, National Bureau of Economic Research, Cambridge, MA.

Bentolila, S., J. J. Dolado, and J. F. Jimeno. 2012. "Reforming an Insider-Outsider Labor Market: The Spanish Experience." *IZA Journal of European Labor Studies* 1 (4): 1–29.

Bergman, P., R. Chetty, S. DeLuca, N. Hendren, L. F. Katz, and C. Palmer. 2019. "Creating Moves to Opportunity: Experimental Evidence on Barriers to Neighborhood Choice." Working Paper 26164, National Bureau of Economic Research, Cambridge, MA.

Betcherman, G. 2014. "Labor Market Regulations: What Do We Know about Their Impacts in Developing Countries?" Policy Research Working Paper 6819, World Bank, Washington, DC.

Beylis, G., R. F. Jaef, R. Sinha, and M. Morris. 2020. *Going Viral: COVID-19 and the Accelerated Transformation of Jobs in Latin America and the Caribbean.* Washington, DC: World Bank.

Bowen, T., C. del Ninno, C. Andrews, S.Coll-Black, U. Gentilini, K. Johnson, Y. Kawasoe, A. Kryeziu, B. Maher, and A. Williams. 2020. *Adaptive Social Protection: Building Resilience to Shocks.* Washington, DC: World Bank Group.

Brand, J. E. 2015. "The Far-Reaching Impact of Job Loss and Unemployment." *Annual Review of Sociology* 41: 359–75.

Bronzini, R., and G. de Blasio. 2006. "Evaluating the Impact of Investment Incentives: The Case of Italy's Law 488/1992." *Journal of Urban Economics* 60 (2): 327–49.

Caliendo, M., S. Künn, and R. Mahlstedt. 2017a. "The Return to Labor Market Mobility: An Evaluation of Relocation Assistance for the Unemployed." *Journal of Public Economics* 148: 136–51.

Caliendo, M., S. Künn, and R. Mahlstedt. 2017b. "Mobility Assistance Programmes for Unemployed Workers: Job Search Behavior and Labor Market Outcomes." Discussion Paper Series 11169, Institute for the Study of Labor, Bonn, Germany.

Card, D., J. Kluve, and A. Weber. 2017. "What Works? A Meta-Analysis of Recent Active Labor Market Program Evaluations." Working Paper 21431, National Bureau of Economic Research, Cambridge, MA.

Casarín, D., and L. Juárez. 2015. "Downward Wage Rigidities in the Mexican Labor Market 1996–2011." Unpublished manuscript. Bank of Mexico.

Castellanos, S. G., R. García-Verdú, and D. S. Kaplan. 2004. "Nominal Wage Rigidities in Mexico: Evidence from Social Security Records." *Journal of Development Economics* 75 (2): 507–33.

Castro, R., M. Weber, and G. Reyes. 2018. "A Policy for the Size of Individual Unemployment Accounts." *IZA Journal of Labor Policy* 7: 9.

Cerqua, A., and G. Pellegrini. 2018. "Are We Spending Too Much to Grow? The Case of

Structural Funds." *Journal of Regional Science* 58 (3): 535–63.

Céspedes, L. F., R. Chang, and A. Velasco. 2014. "Is Inflation Targeting Still on Target? The Recent Experience of Latin America." *International Finance* 17 (2): 185–208.

Clarke, J., S. Evenett, and K. Lucenti. 2005. "Anti-competitive Practices and Liberalising Markets in Latin America and the Caribbean." *World Economy* 28 (7): 1029–56.

Cruces, G., A. Ham, and M. Viollaz. 2012. "Scarring Effects of Youth Unemployment and Informality: Evidence from Argentina and Brazil." Center for Distributive, Labor and Social Studies (CEDLAS) working paper, Economics Department, Universidad Nacional de la Plata, Argentina.

Da Silva Teixeira, G., G. Balbinotto Neto, and P. H. Soares Leivas. 2020. "Evidence on Rule Manipulation and Moral Hazard in the Brazilian Unemployment Insurance Program." *International Journal of Social Science Studies* 8 (1).

De Barros, R. P., and C. H. Corseuil. 2004. "The Impact of Regulations on Brazilian Labor Market Performance." In *Law and Employment: Lessons from Latin America and the Caribbean*, edited by J. J. Heckman and C. Pagés, 273–350. Chicago: University of Chicago Press.

De Ferranti, D., G. Perry, I. Gill, and L. Serven. 2000. *Securing Our Future in a Global Economy*. Washington, DC: World Bank.

De Leon, I. 2001. *Latin American Competition Law and Policy: A Policy in Search of Identity*. Kluwer Law International: London.

Di Cataldo, M. 2017. "The Impact of EU Objective 1 Funds on Regional Development: Evidence from the U.K. and the Prospect of Brexit." *Journal of Regional Science* 57 (5): 814–39.

Diaz-Bonilla, C., L. Moreno Herrera, and D. Sanchez Castro. 2020. *Projected 2020 Poverty Impacts of the COVID-19 Global Crisis in Latin America and the Caribbean*. Washington, DC: World Bank.

Dickens, W. T., L. Goette, E. L. Groshen, S. Holden, J. Messina, M. E. Schweitzer, J. Turunen, and M. E. Ward. 2007. "How Wages Change: Micro Evidence from the International Wage Flexibility Project." *Journal of Economic Perspectives* 21: 195–214.

Diez, F., D. Leigh, and S. Tambunlertchai. 2018. "Global Market Power and Its Macroeconomic Implications." Working Paper WP/18/137, International Monetary Fund, Washington, DC.

Downes, A., N. Mamingi, and R. M. B. Antoine. 2004. "Labor Market Regulation and Employment in the Caribbean." In *Law and Employment: Lessons from Latin America and the Caribbean*, edited by J. J. Heckman and C. Pagés, 517–52. Chicago: University of Chicago Press.

Ehrlich, M. V., and H. G. Overman. 2020. "Place-Based Policies and Spatial Disparities across European Cities." *Journal of Economic Perspectives* 34 (3): 128–49.

Faggio, G., and H. G. Overman. 2014. "The Effect of Public Sector Employment on Local Labour Markets." *Journal of Urban Economics* 79: 91–107.

Farooq, A., A. D. Kugler, and U. Muratori. 2020. "Do Unemployment Insurance Benefits Improve Match Quality? Evidence from Recent U.S. Recessions." Working Paper 27574, National Bureau of Economic Research, Cambridge, MA.

Feldstein, M., and D. Altman. 1998. "Unemployment Insurance Savings Accounts." Working Paper 6860, National Bureau of Economic Research, Cambridge, MA.

Fernandes, A., and J. Silva. 2020. "Labor Market Adjustment to External Shocks: Evidence for Workers and Firms in Brazil and Ecuador." Background paper written for this report. World Bank, Washington, DC.

Fietz, K. M. 2020. "Unemployment Insurance in Latin America and the Caribbean: A Comparative Review of Current and Leading Practices." Social Protection and Jobs, Human Development Department for Latin America and the Caribbean, World Bank, Washington, DC.

Fiszbein, A., and N. R. Schady. 2009. "Conditional Cash Transfers: Reducing Present and Future Poverty." Policy Research Report, World Bank, Washington, DC.

Frolich, M., D. Kaplan, C. Pagés, J. Rigolini, and D. Robalino, eds. 2014. *Social Insurance, Informality and Labor Markets: How to Protect Workers While Creating Good Jobs*. Oxford: Oxford University Press.

Furman, J., T. Geithner, G. Hubbard, and M. S. Kearney. 2020. "Promoting Economic Recovery after COVID-19." Economic Strategy Group, Aspen Institute, Washington, DC.

Gachet, I., T. Packard, and S. Olivieri. 2020. "Ecuador's Labor Market Regulation: A Case for Reform." Unpublished paper. World Bank, Washington, DC.

Gambetti, L., and J. Messina. 2018. "Evolving Wage Cyclicality in Latin America." *The World Bank Economic Review* 32 (3): 709–26.

Garganta, S., and L. Gasparini. 2015. "The Impact of a Social Program on Labor Informality: The Case of AUH in Argentina." *Journal of Development Economics* 115: 99–110.

Gatti, R. V., K. M. Goraus, M. Morgandi, E. J. Korczyc, and J. J. Rutkowski. 2014. *Balancing Flexibility and Worker Protection: Understanding Labor Market Duality in Poland.* Washington, DC: World Bank.

Gentilini, U., M. Almenfi, P. Dale, G. Demarco, and I. Santos. 2020. "Social Protection and Jobs Responses to COVID-19: A Real-Time Review of Country Measures." Social Protection and Jobs Global Practice, World Bank, Washington, DC.

Gentilini, U., M. Grosh, J. Rigolini, and R. Yemtsov, eds. 2020. *Exploring Universal Basic Income: A Guide to Navigating Concepts, Evidence, and Practices.* Washington, DC: World Bank.

Gerard, F., and J. Naritomi. 2019. "Job Displacement Insurance and (the Lack of) Consumption-Smoothing." Working Paper 25749, National Bureau of Economic Research, Cambridge, MA.

Gerard, F., J. Naritomi, and J. Silva. 2021. "The Effects of Cash Transfers on Formal Labor Markets: Evidence from Brazil." Background paper written for this report. World Bank, Washington, DC.

Gibbons, S., T. Lyytikäinen, H. G. Overman, and R. Sanchis-Guarner. 2019. "New Road Infrastructure: The Effects on Firms." *Journal of Urban Economics* 110: 35–50.

Giua, M. 2017. "Spatial Discontinuity for the Impact Assessment of the EU Regional Policy: The Case of Italian Objective 1 Regions." *Journal of Regional Science* 57 (1): 109–31.

Greenstone, M., R. Hornbeck, and E. Moretti. 2010. "Identifying Agglomeration Spillovers: Evidence from Winners and Losers of Large Plant Openings." *Journal of Political Economy* 118 (3): 536–98.

Grosh, M., M. Bussolo, and S. Freije, eds. 2014. *Understanding the Poverty Impact of the Global Financial Crisis in Latin America and the Caribbean.* Washington, DC: World Bank.

Grosh, M., C. Del Ninno, E. Tesliuc, and A. Ouerghi. 2008. *For Protection and Promotion:*

*The Design and Implementation of Effective Safety Nets.* Washington, DC: World Bank.

Han, J., R. Liu, B. U. Marchand, and J. Zhang. 2016. "Market Structure, Imperfect Tariff Pass-Through, and Household Welfare in Urban China." *Journal of International Economics* 100: 220–32.

Hartley, G. Reys, J. C. van Ours, and M. Vodopivec. 2011. "Incentive Effects of Unemployment Insurance Savings Accounts: Evidence from Chile." *Labor Economics* 18 (6): 798–809.

Heckman, J. J., and C. Pagés. 2004. "Law and Employment: Lessons from Latin America and the Caribbean—An Introduction." In *Law and Employment: Lessons from Latin America and the Caribbean,* edited by J. J. Heckman and C. Pagés, 517–52. Chicago: University of Chicago Press.

Holden, S., and F. Wulfsberg. 2009. "How Strong Is the Macroeconomic Case for Downward Real Wage Rigidity?" *Journal of Monetary Economics* 56 (4): 605–15.

Holzmann, R., Y. Pouget, M. Vodopivec, and M. Weber. 2012. "Severance Pay Programs around the World: History, Rationale, Status, and Reforms." In *Reforming Severance Pay: An International Perspective,* edited by R. Holzmann and M. Vodopivec. Washington, DC: World Bank.

ILO (International Labour Organization). 2016. *What Works: Active Labour Market Policies in Latin America and the Caribbean.* Studies on Growth with Equity. Geneva: International Labour Organization.

ILO (International Labour Organization). 2019. *World Social Protection Report 2017–19: Universal Social Protection to Achieve the Sustainable Development Goals.* Geneva: International Labour Organization.

ILO (International Labour Organization). 2020. "Panorama Laboral 2020 América Latina y el Caribe." Regional Office for Latin America and the Caribbean, International Labour Organization, Geneva.

IMF (International Monetary Fund). 2010. *World Economic Outlook, April 2010: Rebalancing Growth.* Washington, DC: International Monetary Fund.

Jalan, J., and M. Ravallion. 2003. "Estimating the Benefit Incidence of an Antipoverty Program by Propensity-Score Matching." *Journal of Business & Economic Statistics* 21 (1): 19–30.

Kanbur, R., and L. Ronconi. 2018. "Enforcement Matters: The Effective Regulation of Labour." *International Labour Review* 157 (3).

Kluve, J., S. Puerto, D. Robalino, J. R. Romero, F. Rother, J. Stöterau, F. Weidenkaff, and W. Witte. 2016. "Do Youth Employment Programs Improve Labor Market Outcomes? A Systematic Review." Discussion Paper 10263, Institute for the Study of Labor, Bonn, Germany.

Konczal, M., and M. Steinbaum. 2016. "Declining Entrepreneurship, Labor Mobility, and Business Dynamism: A Demand-Side Approach." Working Paper, Roosevelt Institute, New York, NY.

Kuddo, A., D. Robalino, and M. Weber. 2015. *Balancing Regulations to Promote Jobs: From Employment Contract to Unemployment Benefits.* Washington, DC: World Bank.

Kugler, A. D. 2004. "The Effect of Job Security Regulations on Labor Market Flexibility. Evidence from the Colombian Labor Market Reform." In *Law and Employment: Lessons from Latin America and the Caribbean*, edited by J. J. Heckman and C. Pagés, 183–228. Chicago: University of Chicago Press.

Lagakos, D., A. M. Mobarak, and M. E. Waugh. 2018. "The Welfare Effects of Encouraging Rural-Urban Migration." Working Paper 24193, National Bureau of Economic Research, Cambridge, MA.

Lederman, D., W. F. Maloney, and J. Messina. 2011. "The Fall of Wage Flexibility." World Bank, Washington, DC.

Levy, S. 2018. *Under-Rewarded Efforts: The Elusive Quest for Prosperity in Mexico.* Washington, DC: Inter-American Development Bank.

Lindert, K., T. G. Karippacheril, I. Rodriguez Caillava, and K. Nishikawa Chavez. 2020. *Sourcebook on the Foundations of Social Protection Delivery Systems.* Washington, DC: World Bank.

Maratou-Kolias, L., K. M. Fietz, M. Weber, and T. Packard. 2020. "Quantifying and Validating the Cliffs of the Labor Market Regulation 'Plateau': A Global Review of Labor Market Institutions." Jobs Group, Social Protection and Jobs Global Practice, World Bank, Washington, DC.

Marchand, B. U. 2012. "Tariff Pass-Through and the Distributional Effects of Trade Liberalization." *Journal of Development Economics* 99: 265–81.

Mayer, T., F. Mayneris, and L. Py. 2017. "The Impact of Urban Enterprise Zones on Establishment Location Decisions and Labor Market Outcomes: Evidence from France." *Journal of Economic Geography* 17 (4): 709–52.

McKenzie, D. 2017. "How Effective Are Active Labor Market Policies in Developing Countries? A Critical Review of Recent Evidence." *World Bank Research Observer* 32 (2): 127–54.

Messina, J., and A. Sanz-de-Galdeano. 2014. "Wage Rigidity and Disinflation in Emerging Countries." *American Economic Journal: Macroeconomics* 6 (1): 102–33.

Messina, J., and J. Silva. 2020. "Twenty Years of Wage Inequality in Latin America." *World Bank Economic Review* 35 (1): 117–47.

Mohl, P., and T. Hagen. 2010. "Do EU Structural Funds Promote Regional Growth? New Evidence from Various Panel Data Approaches." *Regional Science and Urban Economics* 40 (5): 353–65.

Mondino, G., and S. Montoya. 2004. "The Effects of Labor Market Regulations on Employment Decisions by Firms: Empirical Evidence for Argentina." In *Law and Employment: Lessons from Latin America and the Caribbean*, edited by J. J. Heckman and C. Pagés, 351-400. Chicago: University of Chicago Press.

Morgandi, M., M. Ed, B. Wilson, A. Williams, and T. Packard. 2020. "Potential Responses to COVID-19 in Latin American and Caribbean Countries." Social Protection and Jobs Global Practice, World Bank, Washington, DC.

Naidu, S., E. A. Posner, and E. G. Weyl. 2018. "Antitrust Remedies for Labor Market Power." Research Paper 850, Coase-Sandor Institute for Law & Economics, University of Chicago, Chicago.

Neumark, D., and H. Simpson. 2015. "Place-Based Policies." In *Handbook of Regional and Urban Economics* vol. 5B, edited by G. Duranton, V. Henderson, and W. Strange, 1197–1287. Amsterdam: Elsevier

Nicita, A. 2009. "The Price Effect of Tariff Liberalization: Measuring the Impact on Household Welfare." *Journal of Development Economics* 89: 19–27.

OECD (Organisation for Economic Co-operation and Development). 2013. "The 2012 Labour Market Reform in Spain: A Preliminary Assessment." Organisation for Economic Co-operation and Development, Paris.

OECD (Organisation for Economic Co-operation and Development). 2015. "Competition and Market Studies in Latin America: The Case of Chile, Colombia, Costa Rica, Mexico,

Panama and Peru." Organisation for Economic Co-operation and Development, Paris. http://www.oecd.org/daf/competition/competition-and-market-studies-in-latin-america2015.pdf.

OECD (Organisation for Economic Co-operation and Development). 2017. "Labour Market Reforms in Portugal 2011–2015: A Preliminary Assessment." Organisation for Economic Co-operation and Development, Paris.

OECD (Organisation for Economic Co-operation and Development). 2019. "Special Feature: Government Expenditures by Functions of Social Protection and Health (COFOG)." In *Government at a Glance 2019*. Paris: OECD Publishing.

Packard, T., U. Gentilini, M. Grosh, P. O'Keefe, R. Palacios, D. Robalino, and I. Santos. 2019. *Protecting All: Risk Sharing for a Diverse and Diversifying World of Work*. Washington, DC: World Bank.

Packard, T. G., and C. E. Montenegro. 2017. "Labor Policy and Digital Technology Use: Indicative Evidence from Cross-Country Correlations." Policy Research Working Paper 8221, World Bank, Washington, DC.

Packard, T. G., and C. E. Montenegro. 2021. "Labor Market Regulation and Unemployment Duration: Indicative Evidence from Cross-Country Correlations." Social Protection and Jobs, Human Development Department for Latin America and the Caribbean, Washington, DC.

Packard, T., and J. Onishi. 2020. "Social Insurance and Labor Market Policies in Latin America and the Margins of Adjustment to Shocks." Background paper written for this report. World Bank, Washington, DC.

Packard, T., and M. Weber. 2020. "Managing the Employment Impacts of the COVID-19 Crisis Policy Options for the Short Term." World Bank: Washington DC.

Pellegrini, G., F. Terribile, O. Tarola, T. Muccigrosso, and F. Busillo. 2013. "Measuring the Effects of European Regional Policy on Economic Growth: A Regression Discontinuity Approach." *Papers in Regional Science* 92 (1): 217–33.

Perry, G., W. Maloney, O. Arias, P. Fajnzylber, A. Mason, and J. Saavedra-Chanduvi. 2007. *Informality: Exit and Exclusion*. Washington, DC: World Bank.

Petrin, A., and J. Sivadasan. 2006. "Job Security Does Affect Economic Efficiency:

Theory, a New Statistic, and Evidence from Chile." Working paper 12757, National Bureau of Economic Research, Cambridge, MA.

Pinelli, D., R. Torre, L. Pace, L. Cassio, and A. Arpaia. 2017. "The Recent Reform of the Labour Market in Italy: A Review." European Economy Discussion Paper 072, Directorate General for Economic and Financial Affairs, European Commission, Brussels.

Pinto, R. de Carvalho Cayres. 2015. "Three Essays on Labor Market Institutions and Labor Turnover in Brazil." Departamento de Economia, Pontifícia Universidade Católica do Rio de Janeiro, Rio de Janeiro, Brazil.

Portela Souza, A., G. Ulyssea, R. Paes de Barros, D. Coutinho, L. Finamor, and L. Lima. 2016. "Rede de Proteção ao Trabalhador no Brasil: Avaliação Ex-Ante e Proposta de Redesenho." Center for Learning on Evaluation Results (CLEAR), Fundação Getúlio Vargas Escola de Economia de São Paulo, Sao Paulo, Brazil.

Redding, S. J., and M. A. Turner. 2015. "Transportation Costs and the Spatial Organization of Economic Activity." In *Handbook of Regional and Urban Economics* vol. 5, edited by G. Duranton, J. V. Henderson, and W. C. Strange, 1339–98. Amsterdam: Elsevier.

Robalino, D., and J. Romero. 2019. "A Purchaser Provider Split in Public Employment Services? Lessons from Healthcare Systems." Social Protection and Jobs Global Practice, World Bank, Washington, DC.

Robalino, D. A., J. M. Romero, and I. Walker. 2020. "Allocating Subsidies for Private Investments to Maximize Jobs Impacts." Jobs Working Paper 45, World Bank, Washington, DC.

Robalino, D., and M. Weber. 2014. "Designing and Implementing Unemployment Benefit Systems in Middle- and Low-Income Countries: Key Choices between Insurance and Savings Accounts." Social Protection and Labor Discussion Paper 1303, World Bank, Washington, DC.

Robertson, R. 2020. "The Change in Nature of Labor Market Adjustment in Latin America and the Caribbean." Background paper written for this report. World Bank, Washington, DC.

Rodríguez-Planas, N., and J. Benus. 2006. "Evaluating Active Labor Market Programs in Romania." Working Paper 2464, Institute for the Study of Labor, Bonn, Germany.

Saavedra, J., and M. Torero. 2004. "Labor Market Reforms and Their Impact over Formal Labor Demand and Job Market Turnover: The Case of Peru." In *Law and Employment: Lessons from Latin America and the Caribbean*, edited by J. J. Heckman and C. Pagés, 131–82. Chicago: University of Chicago Press.

Schmieder, J. F., and T. von Wachter. 2016. "The Effects of Unemployment Insurance Benefits: New Evidence and Interpretation." Working Paper 22564, National Bureau of Economic Research, Cambridge, MA.

Schmitt-Grohé, S., and M. Uribe. 2016. "Downward Nominal Wage Rigidity, Currency Pegs, and Involuntary Unemployment." *Journal of Political Economy* 124 (5): 1466–1514.

Schochet, P. Z., R. D'Amico, J. Berk, S. Dolfin, and N. Wozny. 2012. "Estimated Impacts for Participants in the Trade Adjustment Assistance (TAA) Program Under the (2002) Amendments." Office of Policy Development and Research, Employment and Training Administration, US Department of Labor, Washington, DC.

Schwartz, H. L., K. Mihaly, and B. Gala. 2017. "Encouraging Residential Moves to Opportunity Neighborhoods: An Experiment Testing Incentives Offered to Housing Voucher Recipients." *Housing Policy Debate* 27 (2): 230–60.

Subbarao, K., C. del Ninno, C. Andrews, and C. Rodriguez-Alas. 2013. *Public Works as a Safety Net: Design, Evidence, and Implementation.* Washington, DC: World Bank.

Summers, L. H. 1989. "Some Simple Economics of Mandated Benefits." *AEA Papers and Proceedings* 79 (2).

Vegh, C. A., G. Vuletin, D. Riera-Crichton, D. Friedheim, L. Morano, and J. A. Camarena. 2018. *Fiscal Adjustment in Latin America and the Caribbean: Short-Run Pain, Long-Run Gain?* Washington, DC: World Bank.

Vijil, M., V. Amorim, M. Dutz, and P. Olinto. 2018. "Productivity, Competition and Shared Prosperity." In *Jobs and Growth: Brazil's Productivity Agenda,* edited by M. Dutz. Washington, DC: World Bank.

Vijil, M., V. Amorin, M. Dutz, and P. Olinto. 2020. "The Distributional Effects of Trade Policy in Brazil." Background paper written for this report. World Bank, Washington, DC.

What Works Centre for Local Economic Growth. 2019. *Local Multipliers.* London: What Works Centre for Local Economic Growth.

Williams, A., and S. Berger-Gonzalez. 2020. "Towards Adaptive Social Protection Systems in Latin America and the Caribbean: A Synthesis Note on Using Social Protection to Mitigate and Respond to Disaster Risk." World Bank, Washington, DC.

Winter-Ebmer, R. 2000. "Long-Term Consequences of an Innovative Redundancy-Retraining Project: The Austrian Steel Foundation." Working Paper 2000-29, Department of Economics, Johannes Kepler University, Linz, Austria.

Wölfl, A., I. Wanner, O. Roehn, and G. Nicoletti. 2010. "Product Market Regulation: Extending the Analysis Beyond OECD Countries." Economics Department Working Paper 799, Organisation for Economic Co-Operation and Development, Paris.

World Bank. 2012. *World Development Report 2013: Jobs.* Washington, DC: World Bank.

World Bank. 2015. *The State of Social Safety Nets 2015.* Washington, DC: World Bank.

World Bank. 2018. *World Development Report 2019: The Changing Nature of Work.* Washington, DC: World Bank.

World Bank. 2020. "Additional Financing for Argentina Children and Youth Protection Project (P167851)." Project Appraisal Document, World Bank, Washington. DC.

Zarate, R. D. 2020. "Spatial Misallocation, Informality, and Transit Improvements: Evidence from Mexico City." University of California at Berkeley and World Bank, Washington, DC.